The Memoirs of
Arthur Symons

Arthur Symons, 1891. Photograph courtesy Princeton University Library

THE MEMOIRS OF ARTHUR SYMONS

Life and Art in the 1890s

Edited by Karl Beckson

THE PENNSYLVANIA STATE UNIVERSITY PRESS
University Park and London

Library of Congress Cataloging in Publication Data

Symons, Arthur, 1865-1945.
The memoirs of Arthur Symons, edited by Karl Beckson

Includes editor's introduction, bibliographical references and index.
1. Symons, Arthur, 1865-1945—Friends and associates.
2. Authors, English—19th century—Biography.
3. Europe—Intellectual life.
PR5528.A42 1977   821'.8 [B]   76-42229
ISBN 0-271-01244-7

Copyright © 1977 The Pennsylvania State University
All rights reserved
Designed by Gretl Yeager Magadini
Printed in the United States of America

To John M. Munro

Contents

Acknowledgments

For permission to publish Arthur Symons' previously published as well as unpublished material, I am greatly indebted to Mrs. Nona Hill, Symons' niece. I am also indebted to Mr. Alexander Clark, Curator of Rare Books and Manuscripts at Princeton University, for permission to publish those previously unpublished items included in this volume from the Arthur Symons Papers. Likewise, I am indebted to the Beinecke Library at Yale University for permission to publish the previously unpublished essays on André Gide and Édouard Dubus. For permission to quote from the Symons correspondence with his agent Ralph Pinker, I am indebted to the Henry W. and Albert A. Berg Collection of the New York Public Library, Astor, Lenox, and Tilden Foundations.

I am particularly grateful to the following people, who generously responded to my queries or who suggested ways of improving the manuscript: C.L. Cline, Thomas E. Connolly, Ian Fletcher, Peter L. Irvine, James G. Nelson, Philippa Pullar, and Stanley Weintraub.

Finally, I wish to acknowledge, with a special debt of gratitude, the much-valued help of John M. Munro, to whom this volume is dedicated.

Introduction

While visiting Italy in the summer of 1908, Arthur Symons suffered a mental breakdown. For two years, he was kept under close medical supervision, first in Italy and later at mental institutions in England. Regarded, until that time, as one of the foremost literary journalists of his age (indeed, Yeats called him "the best critic of his generation"[1]), Symons had published a continuous stream of books, articles, and reviews, including not only literary criticism but also poetry, fiction, drama, and travel sketches. Many of them admittedly ephemeral, his literary productions include at least one title, *The Symbolist Movement in Literature* (1899), which exerted a major influence on some of the greatest literary figures of the twentieth century.[2]

Symons' literary career brought him into contact with most of the great literary and artistic personalities of his time. As Sir William Rothenstein later noted, Symons was "a veritable amateur of artists," collecting them "with the passion others have for china and pictures, poring over his impressions of their characters like a connoisseur over his treasures."[3] Traveling extensively on the continent, Symons was as well known in the bohemian cafés of the Parisian Left Bank as he was in London. Not surprisingly, then, his writings contain vivid impressions of such widely diverse personalities as Browning, Pater, Verlaine, Rodin, Whistler, Toulouse-Lautrec, Huysmans, Dowson, Frank Harris, Oscar Wilde, George Moore, and Eleonora Duse, as well as revealing accounts of his relationships with music hall dancers, who provided Symons with a release from his strict Wesleyan upbringing.

Reticent, somewhat inhibited in the company of the great and near great, and, one gathers, something less than a witty conversationalist, Symons had difficulty in drawing out the reluctant or taciturn. Yet, as Yeats remarks in his own memoirs, more than any other man he had ever known, Symons had a facility for slipping "as it were into the mind of another," acknowledging that his own "thought gained in richness and clearness from his sympathy."[4] Consequently, though Symons' impressions of his contemporaries may lack the wit and brilliance of, say, Beerbohm's or Yeats', they do contain a perceptive view and understanding rare in critical writing. In addition, a close examination of Symons' writings reveals an aspect little stressed by critics—that Symons is obsessed by the irrational elements in both the artist and his work. Although the product of a repressive religious childhood and an amoral bohemian existence, Symons has a strikingly pre-Freudian awareness of those unconscious forces—perverse and self-destructive—that shape both the artist's personality and his work. He is particularly attracted to those artists whose impulse to creation and self-destruction is most dramatically exposed. Significantly, Symons eventually discovered the impulse in himself.[5] Moreover, his progressive obsession with sin—the ghost, so to speak, of his past—eventually reinstated the drama of his early childhood. In his essay on Hugues Rebell (probably written in the late 1920s), Symons perceived in the French Decadent's life and work a reflection of his own disheartening struggle: Rebell, he wrote, "fought the inevitable battle between the Flesh and the Spirit, which is part of our inevitable Destiny."

After 1910, even though his doctors released him from confinement, Symons never fully recovered from the effects of his disastrous breakdown. Indeed, as late as 1934, the outlook remained bleak. His wife, Rhoda, in a letter to Sylvia Beach, wrote in that year: "He has improved somewhat mentally, but the doctors say he can *never really* recover."[6] Symons, however, managed to complete a prodigious amount of work, though much of it is undistinguished; he habitually reprinted many of his previously published articles in book form or rearranged parts of his published articles that had appeared before his breakdown. Of newly written material, his articles reveal an extraordinary and pathetic incoherence. When, for example, Symons' literary agent, Ralph Pinker, submitted the manuscript of *Confessions: A Study in Pathology* (1930), a brief account of Symons' breakdown, to the publisher William Heinemann, the reader reported: "I do not think I have read anything so pitiable as these *Confessions* of Arthur Symons; for he wrote them when he thought himself sane, but he was mad."[7]

During the late 1920s and early 1930s, Symons assembled previously published essays and wrote new "impressions" for what he called *Memoirs*. But there was difficulty with the manuscript from the beginning, as is evident in Symons' letter to Pinker, dated 7 December 1932, which contains the only description that has survived of the manuscript's contents and arrangement:

> In regard to my *Memoirs,* as I shall soon be 68, I find it impossible to change anything in them. The First Part contains a Record of my Life from my Youth to my Maturity: it contains a Record, and not unlike Casanova's, of my loves and passions and adventures, all of which are personal, and of the people I knew and admired during those years. And it is as far as possible

chronological. The Second Part, which ends the book, has to my mind an equal value. Some of the material is taken from magazines and from books of mine which are out of print: and that is always the case in such *Memoirs*. Like the First Part, they are carefully arranged, and they contain material (which I have kept by me for I know not how many years) and which I value as much as those which were printed before in other books of mine. Again, to return to Casanova, in these pages as in the others, I have brought in the personal touch (which is of immense and intrinsic value). Take, for instance, Browning, Swinburne, Patmore, Yeats, Moore, Bullen, Gemier, Jarry, Dubus, Rebell, Huysmans, Gide, Rodin, de Max, d'Annunzio and Duse. I have dealt with them as they were when I knew them. I refer to their conversations, impressions, their books, and in two cases to their acting; and, in this case as in others, I followed the example of Casanova, who always as I did used notes and memories. All have in them that touch of vivid life which I gave them and which I saw in them. And the book finally ends with Two Confessions. And, as Mrs. Symons certainly knew more of my life, before I had met her and after, you must take it on my word (this is *strictly between us*) that she has seen my *Memoirs* before I took them to you, and that she agreed with me on every point.

So, you would do me a great favour if, as you suggested to me, you would have them sent to Cape: I mean, simply, for his consideration. And that, at least, would give my *Memoirs* a fair chance.[8]

Pinker suggested a different title, probably because the manuscript lacked a continuous narrative and because there was a good deal of literary and art criticism in addition to autobiography. Symons was apparently willing to change it, but no other title is mentioned in his correspondence.

When the manuscript was submitted to Jonathan Cape in late 1932, the reader suggested certain omissions and additions to fill in gaps for the period of the 1890s, Symons' most fruitful and bohemian decade. Agreeing with the reader's suggestions, Symons wrote to Pinker, in an undated letter, that he had "much better material, dating from 1893 to 1896," asking to meet the reader so that "the whole question might be settled." At this point, either Pinker or Cape had apparently suggested that T. Earle Welby, who had published a study titled *Arthur Symons* (1925), examine the manuscript with the possibility of suggesting further editorial revisions. In a letter to Pinker dated 5 February 1933,

Symons responded with no uncertainty: "You must be aware that I have never allowed anyone to interfere with any of my books, and I certainly shall not in this case. The idea of a journalist like Welby being allowed to look on a line of my printed prose!"[9] In the same letter, Symons informs Pinker that he is bringing with him "all the material which must be used in the first part of the book. This instead of the eleven omissions I have made. The second part is all right and can stand as it is, the few omissions being legitimate." Clearly, then, Symons was agreeable to certain omissions, but he was adamant on the subject of extensive editorial changes, particularly as suggested by Welby. Thus, Symons substantially blocked any chance of *Memoirs* being published. In an undated letter to Pinker, written perhaps after Cape had rejected the manuscript, Symons states: "I leave it to you to find a publisher for this book of mine."

When faced with the prospect of an unwanted lengthy manuscript on his hands, Symons may have given thought to publishing individual sections of it. Whatever his plan, the manuscript was apparently broken up; not even a table of contents has survived. Among the Symons Papers at the Princeton University Library are some unpublished essays in typescript (some with accompanying holographs), several of them numbered as though once part of a larger manuscript, clearly the remains of *Memoirs*.

It is not difficult to see why Symons was unable to publish the manuscript. In the post-1910 published and unpublished material, personal reminiscences are often interspersed with extracts from Symons' published works (often introduced without transition or logic) and extracts of the published works of others who had written about him are introduced with equal incoherence. In his unpublished essay on Frank Harris, for example, Symons includes a long section from an article that Harris had published on him, followed by extracts from an article on Harris by the French critic Henry-D. Davray and an obituary from the London *Times* on Harris. This pasting together of miscellaneous material is common in Symons' later work. The finely tuned critical temperament that he had exhibited so brilliantly before 1908 was now hopelessly disintegrated. Only a firm editorial hand could have shaped *Memoirs* for publication. Pinker and the publishers to whom he submitted the manuscript undoubtedly realized that the prospect of bringing order out of such chaos was awesome and the adamancy of Symons' resolve to resist major changes unshakeable.

In preparing *Memoirs* for publication, I have omitted, wherever possible, such incoherence as I have alluded to without sacrificing the intrinsic interest of the whole. These omissions are indicated by asterisks; Symons' own omissions are indicated by ellipses. On several occasions, where the interest of the material warrants it, I have retained sections of essays despite Symons' obvious abandonment of logic. In such instances, I have attempted to adhere to the spirit of Symons' intent. Moreover, I have included certain previously published and unpublished essays which Symons does not specifically mention in his letter to Pinker of 7 December 1932, since the letter does not constitute a complete table of contents. I have therefore added essays on such figures as Walter Pater, John Addington Symonds, Ernest Dowson, Paul Verlaine, and Aubrey Beardsley, who were of major importance in Symons' life. It is likely that he would have included some or all of these essays in *Memoirs,* since they represent much of his best writing (indeed, Yeats called Symons' essay on Beardsley a "masterpiece"[10]). I have also included Symons' "A Prelude to Life," a thinly disguised fictional account of his early years, a portrait of the artist as a young man, which appeared in *Spiritual Adventures* (1905), for in a letter to Pinker (9 January 1933), Symons informs him that he is adding it to *Memoirs.* And from *Confessions,* a striking but incoherent short book not always accessible to readers, I have pieced together a coherent account of Symons' mental collapse. As the final item in *Memoirs,* it has the force of a climax, though not the conclusion, to a brilliant career, one that was abruptly halted at a critical stage of development. The result is, I hope, a reasonably coherent, albeit episodic, account, an authentic record, in Symons' own words, of his "loves, passions, and adventures, all of which are personal, and of the people I knew and admired during those years."

The arrangement of the material is, as Symons wished it, in approximate chronological order, either according to the date of his first meeting with the writer or artist or the period when he and the subject had their most significant relationship. I indicate, in each item, the source of the essay, using "MS" for holographs and "TS" for typescripts. Since Symons' errors in quotations, names, and titles are widespread in the postbreakdown period, I have silently corrected them, except where they are significant. I have also normalized punctuation and adopted new titles of essays (and placed them in square brackets) whenever they are more descriptive and have also expanded the title of the volume to describe its contents more accurately. I have limited identification of persons cited by Symons to those most likely to be unknown to the general reader (normally, birth and death dates are given in the general index); and I have identified sources of only lengthy passages quoted by Symons (usually, he identifies the authors of phrases or single sentences he quotes; I have not gone beyond his own practice except where important to the context). In short, the annotations are not designed to burden the text but to illuminate relatively unknown allusions to persons and events.

K. B.

A Prelude to Life[1]

I

I am afraid I must begin a good way back if I am to explain myself to myself at all satisfactorily. I can see how the queer child I was laid the foundation of the man I became, and yet I remember singularly little of my childhood. My parents were never very long in one place, and I have never known what it was to have a home, as most children know it;[2] a home that has been lived in so long that it has got into the ways, the bodily creases, of its inhabitants, like an old, comfortable garment, warmed through and through by the same flesh. I left the town where I was born when I was one year old, and I have never seen it since. I do not even remember in what part of England my eyes first became conscious of the things about them. I remember the hammering of iron on wood, when a great ship was launched in a harbour; the terrifying sound of cannons, as they burst into smoke on a great plain near an ancient castle, while the soldiers rode in long lines across the grass; the clop-clop of a cripple with a wooden leg; with my intense terror at the toppling wagons of hay, as I passed them in the road. I remember absolutely nothing else out of my very early childhood; I have not even been told many things about it, except that I once wakened my mother, as I lay in a little cot at her side, to listen to the nightingales, and that Victor Hugo once stopped the nurse to smile at me, as she walked with me in her arms at Fermain Bay in Guernsey. If I have been a vagabond, and have never been able to root myself in any one place in the world, it is because I have no early memories of any one sky or soil. It has freed me from many prejudices in giving me its own unresting kind of freedom; but it has cut me off from whatever is stable, of long growth in the world.

I could not read until I was nine years old, and I could not read because I resolutely refused to learn. I declared that it was impossible; that I, at all events, never could do it; and I made the most of a slight weakness in my eyes, saying that it hurt them, and drawing tears out of my eyes at the sight of a book. I liked being read to, and I used to sit on the bed while my sister, who often had to lie down to rest, read out stories to me. I had a theory that a boy must never show any emotion, and the pathetic parts of *Uncle Tom's Cabin* tried me greatly. On one occasion I felt my sobs choking me, and the passion of sorrow, mingled with the certainty that my emotion would betray itself, sent me into a paroxysm of rage, in which I tore the book from my sister's hands, and attacked her with my fists.

I never learned to read properly until I went to school at the age of nine. I had been for a little while to a dame's school, and learned nothing. I could only read easy words, out of large print books, and I was totally ignorant of everything in the world, when I suddenly found I had to go to school. I was taken to see the schoolmaster, whom I hated, because I had been told he had only one lung, and I heard them explaining to him how backward I was, and how carefully I had to be treated. When the day came I left the house as if I were going to the scaffold, walked very slowly until I had nearly reached the door of the school, and then, when I saw the other boys hurrying in with their satchels, and realised that I was to be in their company, to sit on a form side by side with strangers, who knew all the things I did not know, I turned round and walked away much more quickly than I had come. I took some time in getting home, and I had to admit that I had not been to school. In the afternoon I was sent back, not alone. I have no recollection of more than the obscure horror of that first day at school. I went home in the evening with lessons that I knew had to be learned. Life seemed suddenly to have become serious. Up to then I had always fancied that the grave things people said to me had no particular meaning for me; for other people, no doubt, but not for me. I had played with other boys on the terrace facing the sea; I had seen them going off to school, and I had not had to go with them. Now everything had changed. There was no longer any sea; I had to live in a street; I had lessons to learn, and other people were to be conscious how well I learned them.

It was that which taught me to read. What had seemed to me not worth doing when I had only myself to please, for I could never realise that my parents, so to speak, counted, became all at once a necessity, because now there were others to reckon with. It was discovered that in the midst of my unfathomable ignorance I had one natural talent: I could spell, without ever being taught. I saw other boys poring over the columns of their spelling-books, trying in vain to get the order of the letters into their heads. I never even read them through; they came to me by ear, instinctively. Finding myself able to do without trying something that the others could not succeed in doing at all, I felt that I could be hardly less intelligent than they, and I felt the little triumph of outdoing others. I began to learn greedily.

The second day I was at school I found the schoolroom door shut when I came into the playground, and I was told that I could not come in. I climbed the gymnasium ladder and looked through the window. Two

boys were having a furious fight, and the bigger boys of the school were
gravely watching it. I was completely fascinated: it was a new sensation.
That day a boy bigger than myself jeered at me. I struck him. There was
a rapid fight before all the school, and I knocked him down. I never
needed to fight again, nor did I.

When I had once begun to learn, I learned certain things very quickly,
and others not at all. I never understood a single proposition of Euclid; I
never could learn geography, or draw a map. Arithmetic and algebra I
could do moderately, so long as I merely had to follow the rules; the
moment common sense was required I was helpless. History I found
entertaining, and I could even remember the dates, because they had to
do with facts which were like stories. French and Latin I picked up easily,
Greek with more difficulty. German I was never able to master; I had
an instinctive aversion to the mere sound of it, and I could not remember the words; there were no pegs in my memory for them to hang upon,
as there were for the words of all the Romance languages. When a thing
did not interest me, nothing could make me learn it. I was not obstinate,
I was helpless. I have never been able to make out why geography was so
completely beyond my power. I have travelled since then over most of
Europe, and I have learned geography with the sight of my eyes. But
with all my passion for places I have never been able to find my way in
them until I have come to find it instinctively, and I suppose that is why
the names in the book or on the map said nothing to me. At an examination when I was easily taking half the prizes, I have read through my
papers in geography and in Euclid, and taken them up to the head-
master's desk, and handed them back to him, calmly telling him that I
could not answer a single question. I was never able to go in for matricu-
lation, or any sort of general public examination, to the great dissatisfaction of my masters, because, while I could have come out easily at the
top in most of the subjects, there were always one or two in which I
could do nothing.

I was not popular, at any of my schools, either with the boys or with
the masters, but I was not disliked. I neither hated out-of-door games
nor particularly cared for them. I rather liked cricket, but never played
football. I was terribly afraid of making a mistake before other people,
and would never attempt anything unless I was sure that I could do it. I
did not make friends readily, and I was somewhat indifferent to my
friends. I cannot now recollect a single school-friend at all definitely,
except one strange little creature, with the look and the intelligence of a
grown man; and I remember him chiefly because he seemed to care very
much for me, not because I ever cared much for him. He had a mathe-
matical talent which I was told was a kind of genius, but, even then, he

was only just kept alive, and he died in boyhood. He seemed to me different from any one else I knew, more like a girl than a boy; some one to be pitied. I remembered his saying good-bye to me when they took him away to die.

What the masters really thought of me I never quite knew. I looked upon them as a kind of machine, not essentially different from the blackboard on which they wrote figures in chalk. They sometimes made mistakes about things which I knew, and this gave me a general distrust of them. I took their praise coolly, as a thing which was my due, and I was quite indifferent to their anger. I took no pains to conceal my critical attitude towards them, and one classical master in particular was in terror of me. He was not a sound scholar, and he knew that I knew it. Every day he watched me out of the corner of his eye to see if I was going to expose him, and he bribed me by lending me books which I wanted to read. I loathed him, and left him alone. One day he carried his deceit too far; there was an inquiry, and he disappeared. I have no doubt my criticism was often unjust; I had the insolence of the parvenu in learning. It had come to me too late for me to be able to take it lightly. I corrected the dictation, put "Maréchal" for "Marshal" because the word was used in reference to Ney, who I knew was a Frenchman;[3] and was furious when my pedantry lost me a mark.

During all this time I was living in the country, in small country towns in the South of England, places to which Blackmore and Kingsley had given a sort of minor fame.[4] I remember long drives by night over Dartmoor, and the sea at Westward Ho. Dartmoor had always a singular fascination for me, partly because of its rocky loneliness, the abrupt tors on which one could so easily be surprised in the mist, and partly because there was a convict prison there, in a little town which we often had occasion to visit. The most exquisite sensation of pleasure which the drinking of water has ever given me was one hot day on Dartmoor, when I drank the coldest water there ever was in the world out of the hollow of my hand under a little Roman bridge that we had to cross in driving to Princetown. The convict settlement was at Princetown, and as we came near we could see gangs of convicts at work on the road. Warders with loaded muskets walked up and down, and the men, in their drab clothes marked in red with the broad-arrow, shovelled and dug sullenly, like slaves. I thought every one of them had been a murderer, and when one of them lifted his head from his work to look at us as we passed I seemed to see some diabolical intention in his eyes. I still remember one horrible grimace, done, I suppose, to frighten me. I feared them, but I pitied them; I felt certain that some one was plotting how to escape, and that he would suddenly drop his shovel and begin to run, and that I should see the musket pointed at him and hear the shot, and see the man fall. Once there was an alarm that two convicts had escaped, and I expected at every moment to see them jump out from behind a rock as we drove back at night. The warders had been hurrying through the streets, I had seen the bloodhounds in leash; I sickened at the thought of the poor devils who would be captured and brought back between two muskets. Once I saw an escaped convict being led back to prison; his arms were tied with cords, he had a bloody scar on his forehead, his face was swollen with heat and helpless rage.

But I have another association with Princetown besides the convicts. It was in the house of one of the warders that I first saw *Don Quixote*. We had gone in to get some tea, and, as we waited in the parlour, and my father talked with the man, a grave, powerful person dressed in dark-blue clothes, I came upon a book and opened it, and began to read. I thought it the most wonderful book I had ever seen; I could not put it down, I refused to be separated from it, and the warder said he would lend it to me, and I might take it back with me that night. There was a thunderstorm as we drove back over the moor in the black darkness; I remember the terror of the horse, my father's cautious driving, for the road was narrow and there was a ditch on each side; the rain poured, and the flashes of lightning lit up the solid darkness of the moor for an instant, and then left us in the hollow of a deeper darkness. I clutched the book tight under my overcoat; the majesty of the storm mingled in my head with the heroic figure of which I had just caught a glimpse in the book; I sat motionless, inexpressibly happy, and when we reached home I had to waken myself out of a dream.

The dream lasted until I had finished the book, and after. I cannot remember how I felt, I only know that no book had ever meant so much to me. It was *Don Quixote* which wakened in me the passion for reading. From that time I read incessantly, and I read everything. The first verse I read was Scott, and from Scott I turned to Byron, at twelve or thirteen, as to a kind of forbidden fruit, which must be delicious because it is forbidden. I had been told that Byron was a very, very great poet, and a very, very wicked man, an atheist, a writer whom it was dangerous to read. At school I managed to get hold of a Byron, which I read surreptitiously at the same moment that I was reading "The Headless Horseman." I thought "The Headless Horseman" very fine and gory, but I was disappointed in the Byron, because I could not find *Don Juan* in it. I knew, through reading a religious paper which condemned wickedness in great detail, that *Don Juan* was in some way appallingly wicked. I wanted to see for myself, but I never, at that time, succeeded in finding an edition immodest enough to contain it.

II

While all this, and much more that I have forgotten, was building up about me the house of life that I was to live in, I was but imperfectly conscious of more than a very few things in the external world, and but half awake to more than a very few things in the world within me. I lived in the country, or at all events with lanes and fields always about me; I took long walks, and liked walking; but I never was able to distinguish oats from barley, or an oak from a maple; I never cared for flowers, except slightly for their colour, when I saw many of them growing together; I could not distinguish a blackbird from a thrush; I was never conscious in my blood of the difference between spring and autumn. I always loved the winter wind and the sunlight, and to plunge through crisp snow, and to watch the rain through leaves. But I would walk for hours without looking about me, or caring much for what I saw; I was never tired, and the mere physical delight of walking shut my eyes and my ears. I was always thinking, but never to much purpose; I hated to think, because thinking troubled me, and whenever I thought long my thoughts were sure to come round to one of two things: the uncertainty of life, and the uncertainty of what might be life after death. I was terribly afraid of death; I did not know exactly what held me to life, but I wanted it to last for ever. I had always been delicate, but never with any definite sickness; I was uneasy about myself because I saw that others were uneasy about me, and my voracious appetite for life was partly a kind of haste to eat and drink my fill at a feast from which I might at any time be called away. And then I was still more uneasy about hell.

My parents were deeply religious; we all went to church, a Nonconformist church, twice on Sunday; I was not allowed to read any but pious books or play anything but hymns or oratorios on Sunday; I was taught that this life, which seemed so real and so permanent to me, was but an episode in existence, a little finite part of eternity. We had grace before and after meals; we had family prayers night and morning; we seemed to live in continual communication with the other world. And yet, for the most part, the other world meant nothing to me. I believed, but could not interest myself in the matter. I read the Bible with keen admiration, especially Ecclesiastes; the Old Testament seemed to me wholly delightful, but I cared less for the New Testament; there was so much doctrine in it, it was so explicit about duties, about the conduct of life. I was taught to pray to God the Father, in the name of God the Son, for the inspiration of God the Holy Ghost. I said my prayers regularly; I was absolutely sincere in saying them; I begged hard for whatever I wanted, and thought that if I begged hard enough my prayer would be answered. But I found it very difficult to pray. It seemed to me that prayer was useless unless it were uttered with an intimate apprehension of God, unless an effort of will brought one mentally into his presence. I tried hard to hypnotise myself into that condition, but I rarely succeeded. Other thoughts drifted through my mind while my lips were articulating words of supplication. I said, over and over again, "O Lord, for Jesus' sake!" and even while I was saying the words with fervour I seemed to lose hold of their meaning. I was taught that being clever mattered little, but that being good mattered infinitely. I wanted to want to be good, but all I really wanted was to be clever. I felt that this in itself was a wickedness. I could not help it, but I believed that I should be punished for not being able to help it. I was told that if I was very good I should go to heaven, but that if I was wicked I should go to hell. I saw but one alternative.

And so the thought of hell was often in my mind, for the most part very much in the background, but always ready to come forward at any external suggestion. Once or twice it came to me with such vividness that I rolled over on the ground in a paroxysm of agony, trying to pray God that I might not be sent to hell, but unable to fix my mind on the words of the prayer. I felt the eternal flames taking hold on me, and some foretaste of their endlessness seemed to enter into my being. I never once had the least sensation of heaven, or any desire for it. Never at any time did it seem to me probable that I should get there.

I remember once in church, as I was looking earnestly at the face of a child for whom I had a boyish admiration, that the thought suddenly shot across my mind: "Emma will die, Emma will go to heaven, and I shall never see her again." I shivered all through my body, I seemed to see her vanishing away from me, and I turned my eyes aside, so that I could not see her. But the thought gnawed at me so fiercely that a prayer broke out of me, silently, like sweat: "O God, let me be with her! O God, let me be with her!" When I came out into the open air, and felt the cold breeze on my forehead, the thought had begun to relax its hold on me, and I never felt it again, with that certainty; but it was as if a veil had been withdrawn for an instant, the veil which renders life possible, and, for that instant, I had seen.

When my mother talked to me about pious things, I felt that they were extraordinarily real to her, and this impressed me the more because her thirst for this life was even greater than mine, and her hold on external things far stronger. My father was a dryly intellectual, despondent person, whose whole view of life was coloured by the dyspepsia which he was never without, and the sick headaches which laid him up for a whole day, every week or every fortnight. He was quite unimaginative, cautious in his affairs, a great reader of the newspaper; but he never seemed to me to have had the same sense of life as my mother and myself. I respected him, for his ability, his scholarship, and his character; but we had nothing akin, he never interested me. He was severely indulgent to me; I never knew him to be unkind, or even unreasonable. But I took all such things for granted, I felt no gratitude for them, and I was only conscious that my father bored me. I had no dislike for him; an indifference, rather, perhaps a little more than indifference, for if he came into the room, and I did not happen to be absorbed in reading, I usually went out of it. We might sit together for an hour, and it never occurred to either of us to speak. So when he spoke to me of my soul, which he did seriously, sadly, with an undertone of reproach, my whole nature rose up against him. If to be good was to be like him, I did not wish to be good.

With my mother, it was quite different. She had the joy of life, she was sensitive to every aspect of the world; she felt the sunshine before it came, and knew from what quarter the wind was blowing when she awoke in the morning. I think she was never indifferent to any moment that ever passed her by; I think no moment ever passed her by without being seized in all the eagerness of acceptance. I never knew her when she was not delicate, so delicate that she could rarely go out of doors in the winter; but I never heard her complain, she was always happy, with a natural gaiety which had only been strengthened into a kind of vivid peace by the continual presence of a religion at once calm and passionate. She was as sure of God as of my father; heaven was always as real to her as the room in which she laughed and prayed. Sometimes, as she read her Bible, her face quickened to an ecstasy. She was ready at any moment to lay down the book and attend to the meanest household duties; she never saw any gulf between meditation and action; her meditations were all action. When a child, she had lain awake, longing to see a ghost; she had never seen one, but if a ghost had entered the room she would have talked with it as tranquilly as with a living friend. To her the past, the present, and the future were but moments of one existence; life was everything to her, and life was indestructible. Her own personal life was so vivid that it never ceased, even in sleep. She dreamed every night, precise, elaborate dreams, which she would tell us in the morning with the same clearness as if she were telling us of something that had really happened. She was never drowsy, she went to sleep the moment her head was laid on the pillow, she awoke instantly wide awake. There were things that she knew and things that she did not know, but she was never vague. A duty was as clear to her as a fact; infinitely tolerant to others, she expected from herself perfection, the utmost perfection of which her nature was capable. It was because my mother talked to me of the other world that I felt, in spite of myself, that there was another world. Her certainty helped to make me the more afraid.

She did not often talk to me of the other world. She preferred that I should see it reflected in her celestial temper and in a capability as of the angels. She sorrowed at my indifference, but she was content to wait; she was sure of me, she never doubted that, sooner or later, I should be saved. This, too, troubled me. I did not want to be saved. It is true that I did not want to go to hell, but the thought of what my parents meant by salvation had no attraction for me. It seemed to be the giving up of all that I cared for. There was a sort of humiliation in it. Jesus Christ seemed to me a hard master.

Sometimes there were revival services at the church, and I was never quite at my ease until they were over. I was afraid of some appeal to my emotions, which for the moment I should not be able to resist. I knew that it would mean nothing, but I did not want to give in, even for a moment. I felt that I might have to resist, with more than my customary indifference, and I did not like to admit to myself that any active resistance could be necessary. I knelt, as a stormy prayer shook the people about me into tears, rigid, forcing myself to think of something else. I saw the preacher move about the church, speaking to one after another, and I saw one after another get up and walk to the communion rail, in sign of conversion. I wondered that they could do it, whatever they felt; I wondered what they felt; I dreaded lest the preacher should come up to me with some irresistible power, and beckon me up to that rail. If he did come, I knelt motionless, with my face in my hands, not answering his questions, not seeming to take the slightest notice of him; but my heart was trembling, I did not know what was going to happen; I felt nothing but that horrible uneasiness, but I feared it might leave me helpless, at the man's mercy, or at God's perhaps.

As we walked home afterwards, I could see the others looking at me, wondering at my spiritual stubbornness, wondering if at last I had felt something. To them, I knew, I was like a man who shut his eyes and declared that he could not see. "You have only to open your eyes," they said to the man. But the man said, "I prefer being blind." It was inexplicable to them. But they were not less inexplicable to me.

III

From the time when *Don Quixote* first opened my eyes to an imaginative world outside myself, I had read hungrily; but another world was also opened to me when I was about sixteen. I had been taught scales and

exercises on the piano; I had tried to learn music, with very little success, when one day the head-master of the school asked me to go into his
drawing-room and copy out something for him. As I sat there copying,
the music-master, a German, came in and sat down at the piano. He
played something which I had never heard before, something which
seemed to me the most wonderful thing I had ever heard. I tried to go
on copying, but I did not know what I was writing down; I was caught
into an ecstasy, the sound seemed to envelop me like a storm, and then to
trickle through me like rain-drops shaken from wet leaves, and then to
wrap me again in a tempest which was like a tempest of grief. When he
had finished I said, "Will you play that over again?" As he played it
again I began to distinguish it more clearly; I heard a slow, heavy
trampling of feet, marching in order, then what might have been the
firing of cannon over a grave, and the trampling again. When he told
me that it was Chopin's "Funeral March," I understood why it was that
the feet had moved so slowly, and why the cannon had been fired; and I
saw that the melody which had soothed me was the timid, insinuating con-
solation which love or hope sometimes brings to the mourner. I asked
him if he would teach me music and if he would teach me that piece. He
promised to teach me that piece, and I learned it. I learned no more
scales and exercises; I learned few more pieces; but in a little while I
could read at sight; and when I was not reading a book I was reading a
piece of music at the piano. I never acquired the technique to play a
single piece correctly, but I learned to touch the piano as if one were
caressing a living being, and it answered me in an intimate and affectionate voice.

Books and music, then, together with my solitary walks, were the
only means of escape which I was able to find from the tedium of things
as they were. I was passionately in love with life, but the life I lived was
not the life I wanted. I did not know quite what I wanted, but I knew
that what I wanted was something very different from what I endured.
We were poor, and I hated the constraints of poverty. We were surrounded by commonplace, middle-class people, and I hated commonplace
and the middle classes. Sometimes we were too poor even to have a
servant, and I was expected to clean my own boots. I could not endure
getting my hands or my shirt-cuffs dirty; the thought of having to do it
disgusted me every day. Sometimes my mother, without saying anything
to me, had cleaned my boots for me. I was scarcely conscious of the
sacrifices which she and the others were continually making. I made none,
of my own accord, and I felt aggrieved if I had to share the smallest of
their privations.

From as early a time as I can remember, I had no very clear consciousness of anything external to myself; I never realised that others had

the right to expect from me any return for the kindness which they might show me or refuse to me, at their choice. I existed, others also existed; but between us there was an impassable gulf, and I had rarely any desire to cross it. I was very fond of my mother, but I felt no affection towards any one else, nor any desire for the affection of others. To be let alone, and to live my own life for ever, that was what I wanted; and I raged because I could never entirely escape from the contact of people who bored me and things which depressed me. If people called, I went out of the room before they were shown in; if I had not time to get away, I shook hands hurriedly, and slipped out as soon as I could. I remember a cousin who used to come to tea every Sunday for two or three years. My aversion to her was so great that I could hardly answer her if she spoke to me, and I used to think of Shelley, and how he too, like me, would "lie back and languish into hate." The woman was quite inoffensive, but I am still unable to see her or hear her speak without that sickness of aversion which used to make the painfulness of Sunday more painful.

People in general left me no more than indifferent; they could be quietly avoided. They meant no more to me than the chairs on which they sat; I was untouched by their fortunes; I was unconscious of my human relationship to them. To my mother every person in the world became, for the moment of contact, the only person in the world; if she merely talked with any one for five minutes she was absorbed to the exclusion of every other thought; she saw no one else, she heard nothing else. I watched her, with astonishment, with admiration; I felt that she was in the right and I in the wrong; that she gained a pleasure and conferred a benefit, while I only wearied myself and offended others; but I could not help it. I felt nothing, I saw nothing, outside myself.

I always had a room upstairs, which I called my study, where I could sit alone, reading or thinking. No one was allowed to enter the room; only, in winter, as I always let the fire go out, my mother would now and then steal in gently without speaking, and put more coals on the fire. I used to look up from my books furiously, and ask why I could not be left alone; my mother would smile, say nothing, and go out as quietly as she had come in. I was only happy when I was in my study, but, when I had shut the door behind me, I forgot all about the tedious people who were calling downstairs, the covers of the book I was reading seemed to broaden out into an enclosing rampart, and I was alone with myself.

At my last school there was one master, a young man, who wrote for a provincial newspaper, of which he afterwards became the editor, with whom I made friends.[5] He had read a great deal, and he knew a few literary people; he was equally fond of literature and of music. Some school composition of mine had interested him in me, and he began to lend me books, and to encourage me in trying to express myself in writing. I had already run through Scott and Byron, with a very little Shelley, and had come to Browning, whom he detested. When I was laid up with scarlatina he sent me over a packet of books to read; one of them was Swinburne's *Poems and Ballads,* which seemed to give voice to all the fever that I felt just then in my blood. I read *Wuthering Heights* at the same time, and Rabelais a little time afterwards. I read all the bound volumes of the *Cornhill Magazine* from the beginning right through, stories, essays, and poems, and I remember my delight in *Harry Richmond,* at a time when I had never heard the name of George Meredith. I read essays signed "R.L.S.," from which I got my first taste of a sort of gipsy element in literature which was to become a passion when, later on, *Lavengro* fell into my hands.[6] The reading of *Lavengro* did many things for me. It absorbed me from the first page, with a curiously personal appeal, as of some one akin to me, and when I came to the place where Lavengro learns Welsh in a fortnight, I laid down the book with a feeling of fierce emulation. I had often thought of learning Italian: I immediately bought an Italian Bible, and a grammar; I worked all day long, not taking up *Lavengro* again, until, at the end of the fortnight which I had given myself, I could read Italian. Then I finished *Lavengro.*

Lavengro took my thoughts into the open air, and gave me my first conscious desire to wander. I learned a little Romany, and was always on the lookout for gipsies. I realised that there were other people in the world besides the conventional people I knew, who wore prim and shabby clothes, and went to church twice on Sundays, and worked at business and professions, and sat down to the meal of tea at five o'clock in the afternoon. And I realised that there was another escape from these people besides a solitary flight in books; that if a book could be so like a man, there were men and women, after all, who had the interest of a book as well as the warm advantage of being alive. Humanity began to exist for me.

But with this discovery of a possible interest in real people, there came a deeper loathing of the people by whom I was surrounded. I had for the most part been able to ignore them; now I wanted to get away, so that I could live my own life, and choose my own companions. My vague notions of sex became precise, became a torture.

When I first read Rabelais and the *Poems and Ballads,* I was ignorant of my own body; I looked upon the relationship of man and woman as something essentially wicked; my imagination took fire, but I was hardly conscious of any physical reality connected with it. I was inexpressibly timid in the presence of a woman; I hardly ever met young people of my own age; and I had a feeling of the deepest reverence for women, from which I endeavoured to banish the slightest consciousness of sex. I thought it an inexcusable disrespect; and in my feeling towards the one or two much older women who at one time or another had a certain attraction for me, there was nothing, conscious at least, but a purely romantic admiration. At the same time I had a guilty delight in reading books which told me about the sensations of physical love, and I trembled with ecstasy as I read them. Thoughts of them haunted me; I put them out of my head by an effort, I called them back, they ended by never leaving me.

I think it was a little earlier than this that I began to walk in my sleep, and to have nightmares; but it was just then that I suffered most from those obscure terrors of the night. Once, when I was a child, I remember waking up in my nightshirt on the drawing-room sofa, and being wrapped up in a shawl and carried upstairs by my father, and put back into bed. I had come down in my sleep, opened the door, and walked into the room without seeing any one, and laid myself down on the sofa. I did not often dream, but, whenever I dreamed, it was of infinite spirals, up which I had to climb, or of ladders, whose rungs dropped away from me as my feet left them, or of slimy stone stairways into cold pits of darkness, or of the tightening of a snake's coils around me, or of walking with bare feet across a floor curdling with snakes. I awoke, stifling a scream, my hair damp with sweat, out of impossible tasks in which time shrank and swelled in some deadly game with life; something had to be done in a second, and all eternity passed, lingering, while the second poised over me like a drop of water always about to drip: it fell, and I was annihilated into depth under depth of blackness.

Into these dreams of abstract horror there began to come a disturbing element of sex. My books and my thoughts haunted me; I was restless and ignorant, physically innocent, but with a sort of naive corruption of mind. All the interest which I had never been able to find in the soul, I found in what I only vaguely apprehended of the body. To me it was something remote, evil, mainly inexplicable; but nothing I had ever felt had meant so much to me. I never realised that there was an honesty in sex, that nature was after all natural. I reached stealthily after some stealthy delight of the senses, which I valued the more because it was a forbidden thing. Love I never associated with the senses, it was not even passion that I wanted; it was a conscious, subtle, elaborate sensuality, which I knew not how to procure. And there was an infinite curiosity, which I hardly even dared dream of satisfying; a curiosity which was like a fever. I was scarcely conscious of any external temptations. The ideas in which I had been trained, little as they had seemed consciously to affect me, had given me the equivalent of what I may call virtue, in a form of good taste. I was ashamed of my desires, of my sensations, though I made no serious effort to escape them; but I knew that, even if the opportunity were offered, something, some scruple of physical refinement, some timidity, some unattached sense of fitness, would step in to prevent me from carrying them into practice.

IV

Every now and then my father used to talk to me seriously, saying that I should have to choose some profession, and make my own living. I always replied that there was nothing I could possibly do, that I hated every profession, that I would rather starve than soil my hands with business, and that so long as I could just go on living as I was then living, I wanted nothing more. I did not want to be a rich man, I was never able to realise money as a tangible thing, I wanted to have just enough to live on, only not at home; in London. My father did not press the matter; I could see that he dreaded my leaving home, and he knew that, for the time, going to London was out of the question.

One summer I went down to a remote part of England to stay with some of my relations. I had seen none of them since I was a child, I knew nothing about them, except that some were farmers, some business people; there was an astronomer, an old sea-captain, and a mad uncle who lived in a cottage by himself on a moor near the sea, and grew marvellous flowers in a vast garden. I stayed with a maiden aunt, who was like a very old and very gaunt little bird; she was deaf, wrinkled, and bent, but her hair was still yellow, her voice a high piping treble, and she ran about with the tireless vivacity of a young girl. She had been pretty, and had all the little vanities of a coquette; she wore bright, semi-fashionable clothes, and conspicuous hats. She had much of the natural gaiety of my mother, who was her elder sister; and she was infinitely considerate of me, turning out one of her little rooms that I might have it for a study. She liked me to play to her, and would sit by the side of the old piano listening eagerly. The mad uncle was her brother, and he would come in sometimes from his cottage, bringing great bundles of flowers. He was very kind and gentle, and he would sometimes tell me of the letters he had been writing to the Prince of Wales on the subject of sewage, and of how the Prince of Wales had acknowledged his communications. He had many theories about sewage; I have heard that some of them were plausible and ingenious; and he was convinced that his theories would some day be accepted, and that he would become famous. I believe his brain had been turned by an unlucky passion for a beautiful girl; he was only in an asylum for a short time; and for the most part lived happily in his cottage among his flowers, developing theories of sewage, and taking sun-baths naked in the garden.

The people of whom I saw most were some cousins: the father kept a shop, and they all helped in the business. They were very kind, and did all they could for me by feeding me plentifully and taking me for long drives in the country, which was very hilly and wooded, and sometimes to the sea, which was not too far off to reach by driving. We had not an idea in common and I always wondered how it was possible that my aunt, who was my mother's eldest sister, could ever have married my uncle. He was a kind man, and, in his way, intelligent; but he talked incessantly, insistently, and with something unctuous in his voice and manner; he came close to me while he spoke, and tapped my shoulder with his fingers or my leg with his stick. I could not bear him to touch me; sometimes he dropped his h's, and, as I heard them drop, I saw the old man looking fixedly into my face with his large, keen, shifting eyes.

One of the daughters had something inquiring in her mind, a touch of rebellious refinement; she had enough instinct for another kind of life to be at least discontented with her own; with her I could talk. But the others fitted into their environment without a crease or a ruffle. They went to the shop early in the morning, slaved there all day, taught in the Sunday-School on Sundays, said the obvious things to one another all day long, were perfectly content to be where they were, do what they did, think what they thought, and say what they said. Their house reflected them like a mirror. Everything was clean and new, there was plenty of everything; and I used to sit in their drawing-room looking round it in a vain attempt to find a single thing which I could have lived with, in a house of my own.

I went home from the visit gladly, glad to be at home again. We were living then in the Midlands, and I used to spend whole days at Kenilworth, at Warwick, at Coventry; I knew them from Scott's novels, but I had never seen a ruined castle, a city with ancient buildings, and I began to feel that there was something else to be seen in the world besides the things I had dreamed of seeing. I took a boat at Leamington, and rowed up the river as far as the chain underneath Warwick Castle. I do not know why I have always remembered that moment, as if it marked a date to me. It was with a full enjoyment of the contrast that I found them busy preparing for a *fête* when I got back to Leamington; stringing up the Chinese lanterns to the branches of trees, and putting out little tables on the grass. At Coventry I loved going through the narrow streets, looking up at the windows which leaned together under their gabled roofs. I saw Lady Godiva borne through the streets, more clothed than she appears in the pictures, in the midst of a gay and solemn procession, tricked out in old-fashioned frippery. And I spent a long day there, one of the days of the five-day fair, which feasted me with sensations on which I lived for weeks. It was the first time I had ever plunged boldly into what Baudelaire calls "the bath of multitude"; it intoxicated me, and seemed, for the first time in my life, to carry me outside myself. I pushed my way through the crowds in those old and narrow streets, in an ecstacy of delight at all that movement, noise, colour, and confusion. I seemed suddenly to have become free, in contact with life. I had no desire to touch it too closely, no fear of being soiled at its contact; a vivid spirit of life seemed to come to me, in my solitude, releasing me from thought, from daily realities.

Once I went as far as Chester. It was the Cup day, and there was an excursion. I watched the race, feeling a momentary excitement as the horses passed close to me, and the pellets of turf shot from their heels into the air above my head; the crowd was more varied than any crowd I had ever seen, and I discovered a blonde gipsy girl, in charge of a cocoanut-shy, who let me talk a little Romany with her. I thought Chester, with its arcades and its city-walls, the most wonderful old place I had ever seen. As I walked round the wall, a woman leaned out of a window and called to me: I thought of Rahab in the Bible, and went home dreaming romantically about the harlot on the wall.[7]

One day, as I was walking along a country road, I was stopped by a sailor, who asked me how far it was to some distant place. He was carrying a small bundle, and was walking, he told me, until he came to a certain sea-port. He did not beg, but accepted gladly enough what I gave him. He had been on many voyages, and had picked up a good many words of different languages, which he mispronounced in a scarcely intelligible jargon of his own. He had been left behind by his ship in Russia, where he had stayed on account of a woman: she could speak no English, and he but little Russian; but it did not seem to have mattered. It was the first time I had seemed to come so close to the remote parts of the world; and, as he went on his way, he turned back to urge me to go on some voyage which he seemed to remember with more pleasure than any other: to the West Indies, I think. I began to pore over maps, and plan to what parts of the world I would go.

Meanwhile, little by little, I was beginning to live my own life at home; I played the piano on Sundays, to whatever tune I liked; I read whatever I liked on Sundays; and finally, I ceased to go to church. Latterly I had come to put my boredom there to some purpose: I followed the lessons word by word in Bibles and Testaments in many languages, and, while the sermon was going on, I kept my Bible quietly open on my knees, and read on, chapter after chapter, while the preacher preached I knew not what: I never heard a word of it, not even the text. I read, not for the Bible's sake, but to learn the language in which I was reading it.

My parents knew this, but after all it was the Bible, and they could hardly object to my reading the Bible. Sometimes I scribbled down ideas that came into my head; sometimes I merely sat there, with a stony inattention, showing, I fancy, in my face, all the fierce disgust that I felt. During the sermon I always found it quite easy to abstract my attention; during the hymns I amused myself by criticising the bad rhymes and false metaphors; but during prayer-time, though I kept my eyes wide open, and sat as upright as I dared, I could hardly help hearing what was said. What was said, very often, made me ashamed, as if I were unconsciously helping to repeat absurdities to God.

When I told my parents that I could go to church no longer, I had no definite reason to allege, except that the matter did not interest me. I did not doubt the truth of the Christian religion; I neither affirmed nor denied; it was something, to me, beside the question. I could argue about dogma; I defended a liberal interpretation of doctrines; I insisted that there were certain questions which we were bound to leave open. But I was not alienated from Christianity by intellectual difficulties; it had never taken hold of me, and I gave up nothing but a pretence in giving up the sign of outward respect for it. My parents were deeply grieved, but, then as always, they respected my liberty.

The first time I remember going to London, for I had been there when a child, was by an excursion, which brought me back the same night. Of the day, or of what I did then, I can recall nothing; daylight never meant so much to me as the first lighting of the lamps. I found my way back to King's Cross, in some bewilderment, to find that one train had gone, and that the next would leave me an hour or two more in London. I walked among the lights, through hurrying crowds of people, in long, dingy streets, not knowing where I was going, till I found myself outside a great building which seemed to be a kind of music-hall. I went in; it was the Agricultural Hall, and some show was being given there. There were acrobats, gymnasts, equilibrists, performing beasts; there was a vast din, concentrating all the noises of a fair within four walls; people swarmed to and fro over the long floor, paying more heed to one another than to the performance. I scrutinised the show and the people, a little uneasily; it was very new to me, and I was not yet able to feel at home in London. I found my way to the station like one who comes home, half dizzy and half ashamed, after a debauch.

The next time I went to London, I went for a week. I stayed in a lodging-house near the British Museum, a mean, uncomfortable place, where I had to be indoors by midnight. During the day I read in the Museum; the atmosphere weighed upon me, and gave me a headache every day; the same atmosphere weighed upon me in the streets around the Museum; I was dull, depressed, anxious to get through with the task for which I had come to London,[8] anxious to get back again to the country. I went back with a little book-learning, of the kind that I wanted to acquire; I began to have books sent down to me from a library in London; I worked, more and more diligently, at reading and studying books; and I began to think of devoting myself entirely to some sort of literary work. It was not that I had anything to say, or that I felt the need of expressing myself. I wanted to write books for the sake of writing books; it was food for my ambition, and it gave me something to do when I was alone, apart from other people. It helped to raise another barrier between me and other people.

I went up to London again for a longer visit,[9] and I stayed in a lodging-house in one of the streets leading from the Strand to the Embankment, near the stage-door of one of the theatres. A little actress and her mother were staying in the house, and I felt that I was getting an intimate acquaintance with the stage, as I sat up with the little actress, after her mother had gone to bed, and listened timidly to her stories of parts and dresses and the other girls. She was quite young, and still ingenuous enough to look forward to the day when she would have her name on the placards in letters I forget how many inches high. I had been to my first theatre, it was Irving in *King Lear,* and now I was hearing about the stage from one who lived on it. A little actress, afterwards famous for her beauty, and then a child with masses of gold hair about her ears, lived next door, at another lodging-house, which her mother kept. I watched for her to pass the window, or for a chance of meeting her in the street. When I went back again to the country, it was with a fixed resolve to come and live in London, where, it seemed, I could, if I liked, be something more than a spectator of the great, amusing crowd. The intoxication of London had got hold of me; I felt at home in it, and I felt that I had never yet found anywhere to be at home in.

I lived in London for five years,[10] and I do not think there was a day during those five years in which I did not find a conscious delight in the mere fact of being in London. When I found myself alone, and in the midst of a crowd, I began to be astonishingly happy. I needed so little, at the beginning of that time. I have never been able to stay long under a roof without restlessness, and I used to go out into the streets, many times a day, for the pleasure of finding myself in the open air and in the streets. I had never cared greatly for the open air in the country, the real open air, because everything in the country, except the sea, bored me; but here, in the "motley" Strand, among these hurrying people, under the smoky sky, I could walk and yet watch. If there ever was a religion of the eyes, I have devoutly practised that religion. I noted every face that passed me on the pavement; I looked into the omnibuses, the cabs, always with the same eager hope of seeing some beautiful or interesting person, some gracious movement, a delicate expression, which would be gone if I did not catch it as it went. This search without an aim grew to be almost a torture to me; my eyes ached with the effort, but I could not control them. At every moment, I knew, some spectacle awaited them; I grasped at all these sights with the same futile energy as a dog that I once saw standing in an Irish stream, and snapping at the bubbles that ran continually past him on the water. Life ran past me continually, and I tried to make all its bubbles my own.

[Robert Browning]¹

I

In "Memorabilia" Browning wrote:

> Ah, did you once see Shelley plain,
>   And did he stop and speak to you,
> And did you speak to him again!
> How strange it seems and new!
>   *[Men and Women, 1855]*

He wrote these stanzas on the poet and the man whom he admired beyond most other poets; whom he praised in prose, speaking of "this young Titan of genius, murmuring in divine music his human ignorance, through his very thirst for knowledge, and his rebellion, in mere aspiration to law. [. . .] But I prefer to look for his highest attainment, not simply the high,—and seeing it, I hold by it. There is surely enough of the work 'Shelley' to be known enduringly among men, and, I believe, to be accepted of God, as human work may."² So it is I who write these words who had high privilege, denied by Shelley's death to Browning, of meeting Browning once, and once only.

My *Introduction to the Study of Browning* was printed in 1886, when I was living in the country. I sent copies of the book to George Meredith, Robert Browning and Walter Pater. Before then I had written to Meredith, sending him, with the printed proofs, my intended dedication. He answered in this noble and august letter, saying:

> I am honoured by the proposal to dedicate your book to me, and accept with a full sense of the distinction. Permit me, however, to name one reserve. I should be pained by your public statement that I am the "greatest of living novelists." It rings invidiously. As to Browning, my love of him runs beside yours: yet even in his case, whatever you and I may think, the term "greatest" strikes a harsh note in many ears. Your just eulogy sufficiently

establishes that high poetic worth. It seems to me that the measure of greatness belongs to posterity. As regards me, personally, there is, you are aware, a heavy opposition that would not brook the epithet. I may well shrink from superlatives of praise.

I changed the terms of the dedication, which satisfied him. In reply to my sending him my printed book, he wrote:

> I have gone through it with advantage—with some of my old thrills of love for him, when as a boy I chafed at the reviews of *Bells and Pomegranates*. You have done knightly service to a brave leader.

Browning wrote to me from Llangollen, saying:

> How can I manage to thank—much more praise—what, in its generosity and appreciation, makes the poorest recognition "come too near the praising of myself"? It does indeed strike me as wonderful that you should have given such patient attention to all these poems, and (if I dare say farther) so thoroughly entered into—at any rate—the spirit in which they were written, and the purpose they helped to serve.

Pater wrote to me from Brasenose College, saying:

> Accept my sincere thanks for your very interesting and useful volume on Browning, one of my best loved writers.

He gave me his address in London, adding:

> where I should be much pleased to make your acquaintance, should you be able at any time to give me a call.

I called on Pater two years after he had written to me:[3] the result was an intimate acquaintance with him which ended about two years before his death.

James Dykes Campbell had read all my proof-sheets, covering them with a network of criticisms, to the immense advantage of my prose. I must, I think, have made his acquaintance at least a year before that unforgettable Sunday, August 25th, 1889, when he introduced me to Browning. And here I give a few words in regard to the most helpful and judicious friend whom I could possibly have had at my elbow.

To the general public he was scarcely a name, at most a set of initials, "J.D.C."; and it was not until the recent publication of his extraordinarily careful edition of Coleridge's poems, and of the minute and masterly life of Coleridge, that his name was ever seen on the title-page of a book.[4] Yet he was a specialist in a particular branch of literary scholarship, the greatest living authority on Coleridge, Lamb, Wordsworth, and their circle; and his general literary knowledge was probably as extended, and certainly as exact, as that of any contemporary student and critic of letters. Widely read in modern literature, with a strict taste in the appreciation of it, he discovered for himself most of the eminent writers of his time, long before the public had become aware of their existence; but it was no part of his province, as he conceived that province, to proclaim his discoveries. Few men so widely and so profoundly gifted have ever subordinated themselves so completely to the most thankless of literary duties, and to the helpfulness of a disinterested literary conscience. Never professing to be a scholar, he gave his life to the drudgery of a minute, and for the most part unrecognized, literary scholarship. He desired no fame, sought for no rewards, allowed himself no privileges but the passionate satisfaction of an absolute exactitude. People who wrote books on any of the subjects in which he took especial interest came to him with their proof-sheets, and he rewrote their books for them. No name is so frequently referred to with gratitude at the end of prefaces, but few are aware how much is meant by these acknowledgments of help received. He was Quixotic in his disinterestedness; and as truly as it may be said that he devoted his life to an idea of scholarship, so truly may it be said that he devoted his life to an ideal of friendship. He would not allow his friends to do without him. Nor was this helpfulness confined to literature. There are some who look upon him as at once the guide and comrade of their lives: tireless in kindness, constant and unerring in counsel, such a friend as a man may hardly meet twice in a lifetime. And for those even who knew him but slightly he had the charm of a gentle, humorous, and instinctively winning nature, the entertainment of a singularly vivid and varied personality. That personality is scarcely to be realized from his published writings: it can only be truly apprehended from his private letters, which, in their pithiness, wit, and felicity of conversational style, might be taken as models of familiar letter-writing. Here, again, he gave the best of himself to his friends, who alone can estimate at their true value the fineness of a nature, the keenness of an intellect, the charm of a temperament, which were never submitted to the general judgment of the world.

As a matter of fact, in November, 1887, I had sent Dykes Campbell a poem of mine called "The Revenge."[5] I quote from his letter this anecdote:

> I wanted, before writing, to get a chance of showing your *Revenge* to Browning. Opportunities came, but were always interrupted—but this afternoon late I caught the great man alone with his sister and handed him the MS. without a word. Until he turned the leaf I believe he thought the lines were mine. He read them through and said: "That's very good," and he read them again and said, *"very* good, very good *indeed."* The story he knew in Stendhal, "but the ending is original and very fine indeed." I told him how thoroughly I was of that opinion, and asked if I might gratify you by telling you his. And he replied: "Certainly. I hope you will tell Mr. Symons that I think very highly of the poem. I have only one suggestion to make—alter the rhyme at the ends—*then* and *vain.* That's a trifle, easily managed."

Of course I took his suggestion and changed the wrong rhyme into the right one. The lines run now as follows:—

and lo,
She rose, she caught it, all her face one glow,
And clasped it to her bosom, and smiled again,
And died.
    So my revenge had been in vain.

On the 22nd of August, 1889, I wrote to Campbell proposing that I might, if it were convenient to him, run up to London the next day. I received a wire: "Please come, delighted to take you to see Browning. Campbell." I arrived at Victoria Road early on Sunday morning: the arrangement was that we were to go to 29 De Vere Gardens, where Browning lived. On the way Campbell said to me that he had just looked in to see if Browning would be willing to see me, and that Browning had said: "I am *always* glad to see anyone that you bring to me, but I shall be *particularly* glad to see Mr. Symons."

As soon as Campbell had introduced me, Browning shook my hand, saying how delighted he was to see me; and he drew me right across the long room, holding me by the hand; then he thrust me, in a way peculiar to him, into an armchair by his side. There sat beside me the great

Poet whom I had adored to the point of idolatry: the man in the Poet visibly there; for in the greatest of poets the genius is seen in the man.

I still recall Browning's violence of voice; it had the whole gamut of music, it vibrated, it thrilled me, by certain touches of rare magic in it. His gestures were sudden, spontaneous, wrenched out of him by the need of adding gesticulation to words, after the fashion of foreigners. And foreign enough he seemed to me then!

While we were talking of Poe's prose, I referred to "The Raven," and to his curious analysis of that strange poem's creation. * * *

Now it was Browning himself who told me and Dykes Campbell that a certain Buchanan Read[6] had said to him that Poe had described to him the whole process of the composition of his poem, and declared that the suggestion of it lay wholly in a line from "Lady Geraldine's Courtship":

With a murmurous stir uncertain, in the air the purple curtain;
[Elizabeth Barrett Browning, *Poems,* 1844]

a line he compared with his:

And the silken, sad, uncertain rustling of each purple curtain.

" 'And every word a lie,' said old Read," said Browning to me.

Browning talked of his grandfather—so original a man—and of Tennyson, whom he praised generously. Then began a discussion between the three of us concerning the question of long and short poems. I audaciously contended that poems ought to be short; evidently remembering the saying of Poe "that a long poem does not exist." Browning declared that he saw merit in magnitude, with picturesque comparisons. One comparison that greatly struck me was that between "a nut and a mountain." I saw then that he was thinking of *The Ring and the Book*; and I imagined that, always, the entire throng of his creations were moving in the hollow of his mind.

Then he spoke of a letter he had just had from Tennyson: "it was something *sacred,* he would not on any account that it got into the newspapers; even the fact that he had it; he could not show it to us, it was too sacred."[7] All this he said in a voice of genuine emotion. By hazard I spoke of Olive Schreiner's *Story of an African Farm*. "Have we read it, Sis?" he asked Miss Browning, who had joined the group. No, she had not.

All this while Campbell had been conversing with Sarianna, to give me the chance of having my whole talk out with Browning. Nor did any of us imagine for an instant that we should never again see Browning. For, as we left, he shook my hand very warmly, expressing the hope of seeing me again when he had returned from Venice to London.

So it was with a great shock that I heard from the lips of my mother that Browning was dead.

II

In their later work all great poets use foreshortening. They get greater subtlety by what they omit, and suggest to the imagination. Browning, in his later period, suggests to the intellect, and to that only. Hence his difficulty, which is not a poetic difficulty; not a cunning simplification of method like Shakespeare's, who gives us no long speeches of undiluted, undramatic poetry, but poetry everywhere like life blood.

Browning's whole life was divided equally between two things: love and art. He subtracted nothing from the one by which to increase the other; between them they occupied his whole nature, in each he was equally supreme. *Men and Women* and the love-letters are the double swing of the same pendulum; at the center sits the soul, impelled and impelling. Outside those two forms of his greatness Browning had none, and one he concealed from the world. It satisfied him to exist as he did, knowing what he was, and showing no more of himself to those about him than the outside of a courteous gentleman. Nothing in him blazed through, in the uncontrollable manner of those who are most easily recognized as great men. His secret was his own, and still, to many, remains so.

Browning's letters have been condemned by those who are ashamed of the nakedness of truth. It was out of human charity that Browning allowed the revelation of this gospel of love. It leaves all other love letters in an outer sanctuary. And they are almost all written as asides. As Mrs. Browning noted in *Sordello,* his mind worked forward in circles, illustrating and developing every idea with a kind of tenacious imaginative ingenuity. He cannot state a fact simply, or express an idea without lingering over all its corollaries. In his desire to be minutely explicit, he uses what are never found in his poetry, italics for emphasis, further complicated by a multitude of dashes, with notes of interrogation meant to give a subtle new turn to a statement nearly completed. He labors to say more than words can say; and is now dragged back by them, now sets them gloriously alight. Some of his finest flashes of poetry, his rarest images, his most intricate intuitions, almost terrifying in their certainty, are to be found in these letters, annihilating a crammed pedantic discourse. Under all this flowing and tossing to and fro there is visible a steady current, which no obstacle can keep back from its course to the sea. This mind, which whirls, never hesitates. Whatever is, to Browning, is from eternity. No man was ever more sure of himself, so certain of right and wrong, so confident in God, so content with life. He knows love at sight, and then has only one height to climb after another, one glory after another to put on. A sober and unbending ecstasy runs from end to end of the letters, like continuous lightning. They are the stammering of the divine child Love.

Coventry Patmore[1]

There are two portraits of Coventry Patmore by Mr. Sargent. One, in the National Portrait Gallery, gives us the man as he ordinarily was: the straggling hair, the drooping eyelid, the large, loose-lipped mouth, the long, thin, furrowed throat, the whole air of gentlemanly ferocity. But the other, a sketch of the head in profile, gives us more than that; gives us, in the lean, strong, aquiline head, startlingly, all that was abrupt, fiery, and essential in the genius of a rare and misunderstood poet. There never was a man less like the popular idea of him than the writer of *The Angel in the House.* Certainly an autocrat in the home, impatient, intolerant, full of bracing intellectual scorn, not always just, but always just in intention, a disdainful recluse, judging all human and divine affairs from a standpoint of imperturbable omniscience, Coventry Patmore charmed one by his whimsical energy, his intense sincerity, and, indeed, by the child-like egoism of an absolutely self-centered intelligence. Speaking of Patmore as he was in 1879, Mr. Gosse says, in his admirable memoir:

> Three things were in those days particularly noticeable in the head of Coventry Patmore: the vast convex brows, arched with vision; the bright, shrewd, bluish-grey eyes, the outer fold of one eyelid permanently and humorously drooping; and the wilful, sensuous mouth. These three seemed ever at war among themselves; they spoke three different tongues; they proclaimed a man of dreams, a canny man of business, a man of vehement determination. It was the harmony of these in apparently discordant contrast which made the face so fascinating; the dwellers under this strange mask were three, and the problem was how they contrived the common life.[2]

That is a portrait which is also an interpretation, and many of the pages on this "angular, vivid, discordant, and yet exquisitely fascinating person," are full of a similar insight. They contain many of those anecdotes which indicate crises, a thing very different from the merely decorative anecdotes of the ordinary biographer. The book, written by one who has been a good friend to many poets, and to none a more valuable friend than to Patmore, gives us a more vivid sense of what Patmore was as a man than anything except Mr. Sargent's two portraits, and a remarkable article by Mr. Frederick Greenwood, published after the book, as a sort of appendix, which it completes on the spiritual side.[3]

To these portraits of Patmore I have nothing of importance to add; and I have given my own estimate of Patmore as a poet in an essay published in 1897, in *Studies in Two Literatures*. But I should like to supplement these various studies by a few supplementary notes, and the discussion of a few points, chiefly technical, connected with his art as a poet. I knew Patmore only during the last ten years of his life, and never with any real intimacy; but as I have been turning over a little bundle of his letters, written with a quill on greyish-blue paper, in the fine, careless handwriting which had something of the distinction of the writer, it seems to me that there are things in them characteristic enough to be worth preserving.

The first letter in my bundle is not addressed to me, but to the friend through whom I was afterwards to meet him, the kindest and most helpful friend whom I or any man ever had, James Dykes Campbell. Two years before, when I was twenty-one, I had written an *Introduction to the Study of Browning*. Campbell had been at my elbow all the time, encouraging and checking me; he would send back my proof-sheets in a network of criticisms and suggestions, with my most eloquent passages rigorously shorn, my pet eccentricities of phrase severely straightened. At the beginning of 1888 Campbell sent the book to Patmore. His opinion, when it came, seemed to me, at that time, crushing; it enraged me, I know, not on my account, but on Browning's. I read it now with a clearer understanding of what he meant, and it is interesting, certainly, as a more outspoken and detailed opinion on Browning than Patmore ever printed.

MY DEAR MR. CAMPBELL,—I have read enough of Mr. Arthur Symons' clever book on Browning to entitle me to judge of it as well as if I had read the whole. He does not seem to me to be quite qualified, as yet, for this kind of criticism. He does not seem to have attained to the point of view from which all great critics have judged poetry and art in general. He does not see that, in art, the style in which a thing is said or done is of more importance than the thing said or done. Indeed, he does not appear to know what style means. Browning has an immense deal of mannerism—which in art is always bad;—he has, in his few best passages, manner, which as far as it goes is good; but of style—that indescribable reposeful "breath of a pure and unique individuality"—I recognise no trace, though I find it distinctly

enough in almost every other English poet who has obtained so distinguished a place as Browning has done in the estimation of the better class of readers. I do not pretend to say absolutely that style does not exist in Browning's work; but, if so, its "still small voice" is utterly overwhelmed, for me, by the din of the other elements. I think I can see, in Browning's poetry, all that Mr. Symons sees, though not perhaps all that he fancies he sees. But I also discern a want of which he appears to feel nothing; and those defects of manner which he acknowledges, but thinks little of, are to me most distressing, and fatal to all enjoyment of the many brilliant qualities they are mixed up with.—
Yours very truly,

COVENTRY PATMORE.

Campbell, I suppose, protested in his vigorous fashion against the criticism of Browning, and the answer to that letter, dated May 7; is printed on p. 264 of the second volume of Mr. Basil Champney's *Life of Patmore*.[4] It is a reiteration, with further explanations, such as that

> When I said that manner was more important than matter in poetry, I really meant that the true matter of poetry could only be expressed by the manner. [. . .] I find the brilliant thinking and the deep feeling in Browning, but not true individuality—though of course his manner is marked enough.

Another letter in the same year, to Campbell, after reading the proofs of my first book of verse, *Days and Nights,* contained a criticism which I thought, at the time, not less discouraging than the criticism of my *Browning*. It seems to me now to contain the truth, the whole truth, and nothing but the truth, about that particular book, and to allow for whatever I may have done in verse since then. The first letter addressed to me is a polite note, dated March 16, 1889, thanking me for a copy of my book, and saying "I send herewith a little volume of my own, which I hope may please you in some of your idle moments." The book was a copy of *Florilegium Amantis,* a selection of his own poems, edited by Dr. Garnett.[5] Up to that time I had read nothing of Patmore except fragments of *The Angel in the House,* which I had not had the patience to read through. I dipped into these pages, and as I read for the first time some of the odes of *The Unknown Eros,* I seemed to have made a great discovery: here was a whole glittering and peaceful tract of poetry which was like a new world to me. I wrote to him full of my enthusiasm; and, though I heard nothing then in reply, I find among my books a copy of *The Unknown Eros* with this inscription: "Arthur Symons, from Coventry Patmore, July 23, 1890."

The date is the date of his sixty-seventh birthday, and the book was given to me after a birthday-dinner at his house at Hastings, when, I remember, a wreath of laurel had been woven in honour of the occasion, and he had laughingly, but with a quite naive gratification, worn it for a while at the end of dinner. He was one of the very few poets I have seen who could wear a laurel wreath and not look ridiculous.

In the summer of that year I undertook to look after the *Academy* for a few weeks (a wholly new task to me) while Mr. [J.S.] Cotton, the editor, went for a holiday. The death of Cardinal Newman occurred just then, and I wrote to Patmore, asking him if he would do an obituary notice for me. He replied, in a letter dated August 13, 1890:

> I should have been very glad to have complied with your request, had I felt myself at all able to do the work effectively; but my acquaintance with Dr. Newman was very slight, and I have no sources of knowledge about his life, but such as are open to all. I have never taken much interest in contemporary Catholic history and politics. There are a hundred people who could do what you want better than I could, and I can never stir my lazy soul to take up the pen, unless I fancy that I have something to say which makes it a matter of conscience that I should say it.

Failing Patmore, I asked Dr. Greenhill, who was then living at Hastings, and Patmore wrote on August 16:

> Dr. Greenhill will do your work far better than I could have done it.[6] What an intellect we have lost in Newman—so delicately capable of adjustment that it could crush a Hume or crack a Kingsley! And what an example both in literature and in life. But that we have not lost.

Patmore's memory was retentive of good phrases which had once come up under his pen, as that witty phrase about crushing and cracking had come up in the course of a brief note scribbled on a half-sheet of paper. The phrase reappears five years afterwards, elaborated into an impressive sentence, in the preface to *The Rod, the Root, and the Flower,* dated Lymington, May 1895:

The steam-hammer of that intellect which could be so delicately adjusted to its task as to be capable of either crushing a Hume or cracking a Kingsley is no longer at work, that tongue which had the weight of a hatchet and the edge of a razor is silent; but its mighty task of so representing truth as to make it credible to the modern mind, when not interested in unbelief, has been done.

In the same preface will be found a phrase which Mr. Gosse quotes from a letter of June 17, 1888, in which Patmore says that the reviewers of his forthcoming book, *Principle in Art,* "will say, or at least feel, 'Ugh, Ugh! the horrid thing! It's alive!' and think it their duty to set their heels on it accordingly." By 1895 the reviewers were replaced by "readers, zealously Christian," and the readers, instead of setting their heels on it, merely "put aside this little volume with a cry."

I find no more letters, beyond mere notes and invitations, until the end of 1893, but it was during these years that I saw Patmore most often, generally when I was staying with Dykes Campbell at St. Leonards. When one is five-and-twenty, and writing verse, among young men of one's own age, also writing verse, the occasional companionship of an older poet, who stands aside, in a dignified seclusion, acknowledged, respected, not greatly loved or, in his best work at least, widely popular, can hardly fail to be an incentive and an invigoration. It was with a full sense of my privilege that I walked to and fro with Coventry Patmore on that high terrace in his garden at Hastings, or sat in the house watching him smoke cigarette after cigarette, or drove with him into the country, or rowed with him around the moat of Bodiam Castle, with Dykes Campbell in the stern of the boat; always attentive to his words, learning from him all I could, as he talked of the things I most cared for, and of some things for which I cared nothing. Yes, even when he talked of politics, I listened with full enjoyment of his bitter humour, his ferocious gaiety of onslaught; though I was glad when he changed from Gladstone to St. Thomas Aquinas, and gladder still when he spoke of that other religion, poetry. I think I never heard him speak long without some reference to St. Thomas Aquinas, of whom he has written so often and with so great an enthusiasm. It was he who first talked to me of St. John of the Cross, and when, eight years later, at Seville, I came upon a copy of the first edition of the *Obras Espirituales* on a stall of old books in the Sierpes, and began to read, and to try to render in English, that extraordinary verse which remains, with that of St. Teresa, the finest lyrical verse which Spain has produced, I understood how much the mystic of the prose and the poet of *The Unknown Eros* owed to the *Noche Escura* and the *Llama de Amor Viva.* He spoke ·of the Catholic mystics like an explorer who has returned from the perils of far countries, with a remembering delight which he can share with few.

If Mr. Gosse is anywhere in his book unjust to Patmore it is in speaking of the later books of prose, the *Religio Poetae* and *The Rod, the Root, and the Flower,* some parts of which seem to him "not very important except as extending our knowledge of" Patmore's "mind, and as giving us a curious collection of the raw material of his poetry." To this I can only reply in some words which I used in writing of the *Religio Poetae,* and affirm with an emphasis which I only wish to strengthen, that, here and everywhere, and never more than in the exquisite passage which Mr. Gosse only quotes to depreciate, the prose of Patmore is the prose of a poet; not prose "incompletely executed," and aspiring after the "nobler order" of poetry, but adequate and achieved prose, of a very rare kind. Thought, in him, is of the very substance of poetry, and is sustained throughout at almost the lyrical pitch. There is, in these essays, a rarefied air as of the mountain-tops of meditation; and the spirit of their sometimes remote contemplation is always in one sense, as Pater has justly said of Wordsworth, impassioned. Only in the finest of his poems has he surpassed these pages of chill and ecstatic prose.

But if Patmore spoke, as he wrote, of these difficult things as a traveller speaks of the countries from which he has returned, when he spoke of poetry it was like one who speaks of his native country. At first I found it a little difficult to accustom myself to his permanent mental attitude there, with his own implied or stated pre-eminence (Tennyson and Barnes[7] on the lower slopes, Browning vaguely in sight, the rest of his contemporaries nowhere), but, after all, there was an undisguised simplicity in it, which was better, because franker, than the more customary "pride that apes humility," or the still baser affectation of indifference. A man of genius, whose genius, like Patmore's, is of an intense and narrow kind, cannot possibly do justice to the work which has every merit but his own. Nor can he, when he is conscious of its equality in technical skill, be expected to discriminate between what is more or less valuable in his own work; between, that is, his own greater or less degree of inspiration. And here I may quote a letter which Patmore wrote to me, dated Lymington, December 31, 1893, about a review of mine in which I had greeted him as "a poet, one of the most essential poets of our time," but had ventured to say, perhaps petulantly, what I felt about a certain part of his work.[8]

I thank you for the copy of the *Athenæum,* containing your generous and well-written notice of "Religio Poetae." There is much in it that must needs be gratifying to me, and nothing that I feel

> disposed to complain of but your allusion to the "dinner-table domesticities of the 'Angel in the House.' " I think that you have been a little misled—as almost everybody has been—by the differing characters of the metres of the "Angel" and "Eros." The meats and wines of the two are, in very great part, almost identical in character; but, in one case, they are served on the deal table of the octo-syllabic quatrain, and, in the other, they are spread on the fine, irregular rock of the free tetrameter.

In his own work he could see no flaw; he knew, better than any one, how nearly it answered almost everywhere to his own intention; and of his own intentions he could be no critic. It was from this standpoint of absolute satisfaction with what he had himself done that he viewed other men's work; necessarily, in the case of one so certain of himself, with a measure of dissatisfaction. He has said in print fundamentally foolish things about writers living and dead; and yet remains, if not a great critic, at least a great thinker on the first principles of art. And, in those days when I used to listen to him while he talked to me of the basis of poetry, and of metres and cadences, and of poetical methods, what meant more to me than anything he said, though not a word was without its value, was the profound religious gravity with which he treated the art of poetry, the sense he conveyed to one of his own reasoned conception of its immense importance, its divinity.

It was partly, no doubt, from this reverence for his art that Patmore wrote so rarely, and only under an impulse which could not be withstood. Even his prose was written with the same ardour and reluctance, and a letter which he wrote to me from Lymington, dated August 7, 1894, in answer to a suggestion that he should join some other writers in a contemplated memorial to Walter Pater, is literally exact in its statement of his own way of work, not only during his later life:

> I should have liked to make one of the honourable company of commentators upon Pater, were it not that the faculty of writing, or, what amounts to the same thing, interest in writing, has quite deserted me. Some accidental motive wind comes over me, once in a year or so, and I find myself able to write half a dozen pages in an hour or two; but all the rest of my time is hopelessly sterile.

To what was this curious difficulty or timidity in composition due? In the case of the poetry, Mr. Gosse attributes it largely to the fact of a poet of lyrical genius attempting to write only philosophical or narrative poetry; and there is much truth in the suggestion. Nothing in Patmore, except his genius, is so conspicuous as his limitations. Herrick, we may remember from his essay on Mrs. Meynell,[9] seemed to him but "a splendid insect"; Keats, we learn from Mr. Champneys' life, seemed to him "to be greatly deficient in first-rate imaginative power"; Shelley "is all unsubstantial splendour, like the transformation scene of a pantomime, or the silvered globes hung up in a gin-palace"; Blake is "nearly all utter rubbish, with here and there not so much a gleam as a trick of genius." All this, when he said it, had a queer kind of delightfulness, and, to those able to understand him, never seemed, as it might have seemed in any one else, mere arrogant bad taste, but a necessary part of a very narrow and very intense nature. Although Patmore was quite ready to give his opinion on any subject, whether on "Wagner, the musical impostor," or on "the grinning woman, in every canvas of Leonardo," he was singularly lacking in the critical faculty, even in regard to his own art; and this was because, in his own art, he was a poet of one idea and of one metre. He did marvellous things with that one idea and that one metre, but he saw nothing beyond them; all thought must be brought into relation with nuptial love, or it was of no interest to him, and the iambic metre must do everything that poetry need concern itself about doing.

In a memorandum for prayer made in 1861, we read this petition:

> That I may be enabled to write my poetry from immediate perception of the truth and delight of love at once divine and human, and that all events may so happen as shall best advance this my chief work and probable means of working out my own salvation.[10]

In his earlier work, it is with human love only that he deals; in his later, and inconceivably finer work, it is not with human love only, but with "the relation of the soul to Christ as his betrothed wife": "the burning heart of the universe," as he realises it. This conception of love, which we see developing from so tamely domestic a level to so incalculable a height of mystic rapture, possessed the whole man, throughout the whole of his life, shutting him into a "solitude for two" which has never perhaps been apprehended with so complete a satisfaction. He was a married monk, whose monastery was the world; he came and went in the world, imagining he saw it more clearly than any one else; and, indeed, he saw things about him clearly enough, when they were remote enough from his household prejudices. But all he really ever did was to cultivate a little corner of a garden, where he brought to perfection a rare kind of flower, which some thought too pretty to be fine, and some too colourless to be beautiful, but in which he saw the seven celestial colours, faultlessly mingled, and which he took to be the image of the flower most loved by the Virgin in heaven.

Patmore was a poet profoundly learned in the technique of his art, and the "Prefatory Study on English Metrical Law," which fills the first eighty-five pages of the *Amelia* volume of 1878, is among the subtlest and most valuable of such studies which we have in English. In this essay he praises the simplest metres for various just reasons, but yet is careful to define the "rhyme royal," or stanza of seven ten-syllable lines, as the most heroic of measures; and to admit that blank verse, which he never used, "is, of all recognised English metres, the most difficult to write well in." But, in his expressed aversion for trochaic and dactylic measures, is he not merely recording his own inability to handle them? And, in setting more and more rigorous limits to himself in his own dealing with iambic measures, is he not accepting, and making the best of, a lack of metrical flexibility? It is nothing less than extraordinary to note that, until the publication of the nine *Odes* in 1868, not merely was he wholly tied to the iambic measure, but even within those limits he was rarely quite so good in the four-line stanza of eights and sixes as in the four-line stanza of eights; that he was usually less good in the six-line than in the four-line stanza of eights and sixes; and that he was invariably least good in the stanza of three long lines which, to most practical intents and purposes, corresponds with this six-line stanza. The extremely slight licence which this rearrangement into longer lines affords was sufficient to disturb the balance of his cadences, and nowhere else was he capable of writing quite such lines as:

> One friend was left, a falcon, famed for beauty, skill
> 　　and size,
> Kept from his fortune's ruin, for the sake of its
> 　　great eyes.

All sense, not merely of the delicacy, but of the correctness of rhythm, seems to have left him suddenly, without warning.

And then, the straightening and tightening of the bonds of metre having had its due effect, an unprecedented thing occurred. In the *Odes* of 1868, absorbed finally into *The Unknown Eros* of 1877, the iambic metre is still used; but with what a new freedom, and at the summons of how liberating an inspiration! At the same time Patmore's substance is purged and his speech loosened, and, in throwing off that burden or prose stuff which had tied down the very wings of his imagination, he finds himself rising on a different movement. Never was a development in metre so spiritually significant.

In spite of Patmore's insistence to the contrary, as in the letter which I have already quoted, there is no doubt that the difference between *The Angel in the House* and *The Unknown Eros* is the difference between what is sometimes poetry in spite of itself, and what is poetry alike in accident and essence. In all his work before the *Odes* of 1868, Patmore had been writing down to his conception of what poetry ought to be; when, through I know not what suffering, or contemplation, or actual inner illumination, his whole soul had been possessed by this new conception of what poetry could be, he began to write as finely, and not only as neatly, as he was able. The poetry which came, came fully clothed, in a form of irregular but not lawless verse, which Mr. Gosse states was introduced into English by the *Pindarique Odes* of Cowley, but which may be more justly derived, as Patmore himself, in one of his prefaces, intimates, from an older and more genuine poet, Drummond of Hawthornden.[11]

Mr. Gosse is cruel enough to say that Patmore had "considerable affinities" with Cowley, and that "when Patmore is languid and Cowley is unusually felicitous, it is difficult to see much difference in the form of their odes." But Patmore, in his essay on metre, has said,

> If there is not sufficient motive power of passionate thought, no typographical aids will make anything of this sort of verse but metrical nonsense—which it nearly always is—even in Cowley, whose brilliant wit and ingenuity are strangely out of harmony with most of his measures;

and it seems to me that he is wholly right in saying so. The difference between the two is an essential one. In Patmore the cadence follows the contours of the thought or emotion, like a transparent garment; in Cowley the form is a misshapen burden, carried unsteadily. It need not surprise us that to the ears of Cowley (it is he who tells us) the verse of Pindar should have sounded "little better than prose." The fault of his own "Pindarique" verse is that it is so much worse than prose. The pauses in Patmore, left as they are to be a kind of breathing, or pause for breath, may not seem to be everywhere faultless to all ears; but they *are* the pauses in breathing, while in Cowley the structure of his verse, when it is irregular, remains as external, as mechanical, as the couplets of the *Davideis.*[12]

> Whether Patmore ever acknowledged it or no, or indeed whether
> [says Mr. Gosse] the fact has ever been observed, I know not,
> but the true analogy of the *Odes* is with the Italian lyric of the
> early Renaissance. It is in the writings of Petrarch and Dante, and
> especially in the *Canzoniere* of the former, that we must look for
> examples of the source of Patmore's later poetic form.[13]

Here again, while there may be a closer "analogy," at least in spirit, there
is another, and even clearer difference in form. The canzoni of Petrarch
are composed in stanzas of varying, but in each case uniform, length, and
every stanza corresponds precisely in metrical arrangement with every
other stanza in the same canzone. In English the *Epithalamion* and the
Prothalamion of Spenser (except for their refrain) do exactly what
Petrarch had done in Italian; and whatever further analogy there may
be between the spirit of Patmore's writing and that of Spenser in these
two poems, the form is essentially different. The resemblance with
Lycidas is closer, and closer still with the poems of Leopardi, though Patmore has not followed the Italian habit of mingling rhymed and non-
rhymed verse, nor did he ever experiment, like Goethe, Heine, Matthew
Arnold, and Henley,[14] in wholly unrhymed irregular lyrical verse.

Patmore's endeavour, in *The Unknown Eros,* is certainly towards a
form of *vers libre,* but it is directed only towards the variation of the
normal pause in the normal English metre, the iambic "common time,"
and is therefore as strictly tied by law as a metre can possibly be when
it ceases to be wholly regular. Verse literally "free," as it is being attempted in the present day in France, every measure being mingled, and
the disentangling of them left wholly to the ear of the reader, has indeed
been attempted by great metrists in many ages, but for the most part
only very rarely and with extreme caution. The warning, so far, of all
these failures, or momentary half-successes, is to be seen in the most
monstrous and magnificent failure of the nineteenth century, the *Leaves
of Grass* of Walt Whitman. Patmore realised that without law there can
be no order, and thus no life; for life is the result of a harmony between
opposites. For him, cramped as he had been by a voluntary respect for
far more than the letter of the law, the discovery of a freer mode of
speech was of incalculable advantage. It removed from him all temptation
to that "cleverness" which Mr. Gosse rightly finds in the handling of
"the accidents of civilised life," the unfortunate part of his subject-matter
in *The Angel in the House;* it allowed him to abandon himself to the
poetic ecstasy, which in him was almost of the same nature as philosophy,
without translating it downward into the terms of popular apprehension;
it gave him a choice, formal, yet flexible means of expression for his
uninterrupted contemplation of divine things.

Edmund Gosse[1]

Apart from my implacable memory, there are many things I ought to have remembered that I have forgotten: such as the uncertainty, not as to the year, but as to the place, where I first met Yeats and Dowson. In 1887 I wrote a long Introduction to a selection I had made of the prose of Leigh Hunt[2] in which I was helped by Dykes Campbell. To my surprise I received a letter from Edmund Gosse, sending me some card of invitation: and this surprise letter was the beginning of our friendship that lasted for perhaps twenty years. He had a biting wit, very different from that of Patmore—which was ferocious; even when [Patmore] jested, he jested with fury, always accentuated by his crackling laugh: and by the vehemence with which he seized his cigarettes. At the same time [Patmore] was almost totally lacking in the quality of a critic. Himself, always, as it were, on the very pinnacle of Parnassus, from whose height he looked down, with a kind of half friendly and half scornful contempt, on Browning, Tennyson, Swinburne and Rossetti. To have called Wagner "the musical imposter," showed his utter ignorance of music; to have said that Shelley "is all unsubstantial splendour, like the transformation scene of a pantomime, or the silvered globes hung up in a gin-palace," showed that he was probably better acquainted with them than with the genius of Shelley. On the contrary Gosse, for all his fundamental errors, never, I believe, managed to make these stupendous mistakes. Patmore was not the kind of man who cared to come into contact with men of genius; Gosse, being by nature much more fortunate, possessed an almost absolute genius which made his coming in contact with them something surprising, thrilling, exciting. I need but refer to such men as Browning, Swinburne, Pater, Hardy, Yeats, Stevenson; and, also, to some of the illustrious dead, such as Henry James, the exquisite, complex, perverse, unpassionate, subtle, cruel novelist, a continental American who was in love with England—in every way so unlike George Moore, who will always remain the Irishman in love with France. Then there was the astonishingly brilliant J. K. Stephen,[3] who shone like a glow-worm and like a glow-worm was extinguished. There was also the amazingly fantastic Theophile Marzials,[4] who as he drugged his wine assiduously, could astonish and bewilder as by his paradoxes and flights of imagination. I met him several times in Paris; we met on certain nights at a queer kind of music-hall that used to be the Aquarium,[5] where, more than once, we fell into conversation with an exotic girl who had a collection of venomous snakes: on the stage they used to coil round her with that evil fascination they alone possess. We imagined her a modern Salammbô:[6] only, she had no black python.

Gosse holds a middle station between the older and the younger schools of criticism. He is neither a respectable and accomplished fossil, nor a wild and whirling catherine-wheel. He lacks, indeed, the positive manner and the enthusiasm which respectively characterize the two schools. His habitual moderation makes him, certainly, something of an outsider. With all his respect for the past and his curiosity as to the future, he keeps just far enough away from the literary arena of the present not to be soiled by its dust. He seems to lean from the window while the battle of the books is being fought out in the streets. He gently encourages both sides; but the younger men feel that he would like them to win. In this book,[7] *Questions at Issue,* he has come nearer than in any previous book to what is actual and debatable in the literature of the day; and for that very reason it is in some respects the most interesting work of a writer who is, at all events, seldom uninteresting. It seems to us that Gosse is at his best when he adopts—as he does here—"the sauntering step, the conversational tone, the absence of all pedagogic assertion," which he rightly thinks to be "indispensable in the treatment of contemporary themes." It is a tendency of his style to be sometimes not quite simple, not quite free of ornament for ornament's sake; a little prone to licence in metaphor and excess in similitude. In the "conversational" manner of writing there is less temptation to get entangled in the flowers, or brambles, of speech; and these essays on "The Tyranny of the Novel," "The Limits of Realism in Fiction," "Making a Name in Literature," etc., are, perhaps, really better written than anything Gosse has done before. Clear, moderate, persuasive in argument, pleasantly urbane, and touched with a somewhat malicious humour, they are equally agreeable to read and profitable to think over. Keenly sensitive to literary folly or absurdity, to the indecency of public caprice and of private pretentiousness, he never loses his temper over these things, never answers a fool according to his folly, but smiles ironically, and with a phrase of polite deprecation passes on.

The book is full of cautions and counsels, and it is full of passages that we should like to quote—a passage on Browning and the democratic spirit, for instance; a passage on the symbolism of Mallarmé—; and a passage, which must really be quoted, on the probable future of poetry:—

Poetry, if it exist at all, will deal, and probably to a greater degree than ever before, with those more frail and ephemeral shades of emotion which prose scarcely ventures to describe. The existence of a delicately organized human being is diversified by divisions and revulsions of sensation, ill-defined desires, gleams of intuition, and the whole gamut of spiritual notes descending from exultation to despair, none of which have ever been adequately treated except in the hieratic language of poetry. The most realistic novel, the closest psychological analysis in prose, does no more than skim the surface of the soul; verse has the privilege of descending into its depths. In the future lyrical poetry will probably grow less trivial and less conventional, at the risk of being less popular. It will interpret what prose dares not suggest. It will penetrate further into the complexity of human sensation, and, untroubled by the necessity of formulating a creed, a theory, or a story, will describe with delicate accuracy, and under a veil of artistic beauty, the amazing, the unfamiliar, and even the portentous phenomena which it encounters.

This is almost the conclusion of an essay entitled "Is Verse in Danger?"—an ingenious discussion of a somewhat unnecessary question. A question which really is worth discussing—the actual influence upon the public in general of even the most widely popular poet—is handled with much acuteness in "Tennyson—and After." Yet another question in regard to poetry, "Has America produced a Poet?" is handled with the gentlest and keenest discretion; and not merely discretion, but a fine intuition, is shown in a brief consideration of the Symbolist movement in France, as it defines itself in the work of Stéphane Mallarmé. But nothing in the volume is more interesting than those essays which are concerned with prose literature, "The Tyranny of the Novel," "The Limits of Realism in Fiction," "The Influence of Democracy on Literature." In the first of these essays there are two or three pages on the art of Zola, which are, perhaps, the most intelligent, temperate, and justly appreciative pages that have been written on that difficult subject in English. With very much of what Gosse has to say on the subject of the novel we are altogether in agreement; and we are at one with him in his plea for wider human interests in English fiction, now so much given over to the young person and to the love affairs of the young person. "Has the struggle for existence," he asks, "a charm only in its reproductive aspects?" And he demands: "Have the stress and turmoil of a successful political career no charm? Why, if novels of the shop and the counting-house are considered sordid, can our novelists not describe the life of a sailor, of a gamekeeper, of a railway-porter, of a civil engineer?" The demand is a plausible one, but at the same time it is to be hoped that the novelists of the future will not come to think that "the study of Dorsetshire dairy-farms," "the details of apple-culture in the same county," and "just the vivid information we want about the Newlyn pilchard-fishery," have any essential connexion with a good novel. Zola needs all his immense talent to save "Les Rougon-Macquart"[8] from being buried under the weight of second-hand technical information. It is as a picture of humanity that the novel has its reason for existence; and a novel will be good or bad, not because it is or it is not written about a railway-porter, not because it does or does not tell us how the railway-porter's back was affected by carrying heavy luggage, but by its truth or falsehood to what is elemental alike in railway porters and in gentlemen. Let us have this, the one thing needful; and then let that "vivid information about the Newlyn pilchard-fishery" come or go; pleasant, agreeable, valuable in its way, if it be kept in its proper place, as a mere background, but dangerous, tedious, intolerable, if once it be suffered to obtrude itself into the first plane of the composition.

We have only been able to touch, in passing, on a few of the many "questions at issue" which are raised in this suggestive, instructive, interesting book. The most entertaining paper contained in it is called "An Election at the English Academy"—a paper which we would commend, not only for its sprightliness and ingenious wit, to the would-be makers and members of literary academies. It enforces a moral, which might be taken to be the main moral of these pages as a whole: the moral that literature, and nothing else, is the end and aim of literature, and that the popular mind will never realize this primary fact. Gosse militant is still the urbane Gosse; and it would be hard to over-estimate the value of so polite a combatant in the defence of art against the Philistines.

Walter Pater[1]

Writing about Botticelli, in that essay which first interpreted Botticelli[2] to the modern world, Pater said, after naming the supreme artists, Michelangelo or Leonardo:

> But, besides these great men, there is a certain number of artists who have a distinct faculty of their own by which they convey to us a peculiar quality of pleasure which we cannot get elsewhere; and these, too, have their place in general culture, and must be interpreted to it by those who have felt their charm strongly, and are often the objects of a special diligence and a consideration wholly affectionate, just because there is not about them the stress of a great name and authority.

It is among these rare artists, so much more interesting, to many, than the very greatest, that Pater belongs; and he can only be properly understood, loved, or even measured by those to whom it is "the delicacies of fine literature" that chiefly appeal. There have been greater prose-writers in our language, even in our time; but he was, as Mallarmé called him, "le prosateur ouvragé par excellence de ce temps." For strangeness and subtlety of temperament, for rarity and delicacy of form, for something incredibly attractive to those who felt his attraction, he was as unique in our age as Botticelli in the great age of Raphael. And he, too, above all to those who knew him, can scarcely fail to become, not only "the object of a special diligence," but also of "a consideration wholly affectionate," not lessened by the slowly increasing "stress of authority" which is coming to be laid, almost by the world in general, on his name.

In the work of Pater, thought moves to music, and does all its hard work as if in play. And Pater seems to listen for his thought, and to overhear it, as the poet overhears his song in the air. It is like music, and has something of the character of poetry, yet, above all, it is precise, individual, thought filtered through a temperament; and it comes to us as it does because the style which clothes and fits it is a style in which, to use some of his own words, "the writer succeeds in saying what he *wills*."

The style of Pater has been praised and blamed for its particular qualities of colour, harmony, weaving; but it has not always, or often, been
realised that what is most wonderful in the style is precisely its adaptabil-
ity to every shade of meaning or intention, its extraordinary closeness in
following the turns of thought, the waves of sensation, in the man himself. Everything in Pater was in harmony, when you got accustomed to
its particular forms of expression: the heavy frame, so slow and deliberate in movement, so settled in repose; the timid and yet scrutinising
eyes; the mannered, yet so personal, voice; the precise, pausing speech,
with its urbanity, its almost painful conscientiousness of utterance; the
whole outer mask, in short, worn for protection and out of courtesy, yet
moulded upon the inner truth of nature like a mask moulded upon the
features which it covers. And the books are the man, literally the man in
many accents, turns of phrase; and, far more than that, the man himself,
whom one felt through his few, friendly, intimate, serious words: the
inner life of his soul coming close to us, in a slow and gradual revelation.

He has said, in the first essay of his which we have:

> The artist and he who has treated life in the spirit of art desires
> only to be shown to the world as he really is; as he comes nearer
> and nearer to perfection, the veil of an outer life, not simply
> expressive of the inward, becomes thinner and thinner.[3]

And Pater seemed to draw up into himself every form of earthly beauty,
or of the beauty made by men, and many forms of knowledge and
wisdom, and a sense of human things which was neither that of the lover
nor of the priest, but partly of both; and his work was the giving out of
all this again, with a certain labour to give it wholly. It is all, the criticism, and the stories, and the writing about pictures and places, a confession, the *vraie vérité* (as he was fond of saying) about the world in
which he lived. That world he thought was open to all; he was sure that
it was the real blue and green earth, and that he caught the tangible
moments as they passed. It was a world into which we can only look,
not enter, for none of us have his secret. But part of his secret was in the
gift and cultivation of a passionate temperance, an unrelaxing attentiveness to whatever was rarest and most delightful in passing things.

In Pater, logic is of the nature of ecstasy, and ecstasy never soars
wholly beyond the reach of logic. Pater is keen in pointing out the liberal
and spendthrift weakness of Coleridge in his thirst for the absolute, his
"hunger for eternity," and for his part he is content to set all his happi-

ness, and all his mental energies, on a relative basis, on a valuation of the things of eternity under the form of time. He asks for no "larger flowers" than the best growth of the earth; but he would choose them flower by flower, and for himself. He finds life worth just living, a thing satisfying in itself, if you are careful to extract its essence, moment by moment, not in any calculated "hedonism," even of the mind, but in a quiet, discriminating acceptance of whatever is beautiful, active, or illuminating in every moment. As he grew older he added something more like a Stoic sense of "duty" to the old, properly and severely Epicurean doctrine of "pleasure." Pleasure was never, for Pater, less than the essence of all knowledge, all experience, and not merely all that is rarest in sensation; it was religious from the first, and had always to be served with a strict ritual. "Only be sure it is passion," he said of that spirit of divine motion to which he appealed for the quickening of our sense of life, our sense of ourselves; be sure, he said, "that it does yield you this fruit of a quickened, multiplied consciousness." What he cared most for at all times was that which could give "the highest quality to our moments as they pass";[4] he differed only, to a certain extent, in his estimation of what that was. "The herb, the wine, the gem" of the preface to the *Renaissance* tended more and more to become, under less outward symbols of perfection, "the discovery, the new faculty, the privileged apprehension" by which "the imaginative regeneration of the world" should be brought about, or even, at times, a brooding over "what the soul passes, and must pass, through, *aux abois* with nothingness, or with those offended mysterious powers that may really occupy it."

When I first met Pater he was nearly fifty. I did not meet him for about two years after he had been writing to me, and his first letter reached me when I was just over twenty-one.[5] I had been writing verse all my life, and what Browning was to me in verse Pater, from about the age of seventeen, had been to me in prose. Meredith made the third; but his form of art was not, I knew never could be, mine. Verse, I suppose, requires no teaching, but it was from reading Pater's *Studies in the History of the Renaissance,* in its first edition on ribbed paper (I have the feel of it still in my fingers), that I realised that prose also could be a fine art. That book opened a new world to me, or, rather, gave me the key or secret of the world in which I was living. It taught me that there was a beauty besides the beauty of what one calls inspiration, and comes and goes, and cannot be caught or followed; that life (which had seemed to me of so little moment) could be itself a work of art; from that book I realised for the first time that there was anything interesting or vital in the world besides poetry and music. I caught from it an unlimited curiosity, or, at least, the direction of curiosity into definite channels.

The knowledge that there was such a person as Pater in the world, an occasional letter from him, an occasional meeting, and, gradually, the definite encouragement of my work in which, for some years, he was unfailingly generous and attentive, meant more to me, at that time, than I can well indicate, or even realise, now. It was through him that my first volume of verse was published;[6] and it was through his influence and counsels that I trained myself to be infinitely careful in all matters of literature. Influence and counsel were always in the direction of sanity, restraint, precision.

I remember a beautiful phrase which he once made up, in his delaying way, with "wells" and "no doubts" in it, to describe, and to describe supremely, a person whom I had seemed to him to be disparaging. "He does," he said meditatively, "remind me of, well, of a steam-engine stuck in the mud. But he is so enthusiastic!" Pater liked people to be enthusiastic, but, with him, enthusiasm was an ardent quietude, guarded by the wary humour that protects the sensitive. He looked upon undue earnestness, even in outward manner, in a world through which the artist is bound to go on a wholly "secret errand," as bad form, which shocked him as much in persons as bad style did in books. He hated every form of extravagance, noise, mental or physical, with a temperamental hatred: he suffered from it, in his nerves and in his mind. And he had no less dislike of whatever seemed to him either morbid or sordid, two words which he often used to express his distaste for things and people. He never would have appreciated writers like Verlaine, because of what seemed to him perhaps unnecessarily "sordid" in their lives. It pained him, as it pains some people, perhaps only because they are more acutely sensitive than others, to walk through mean streets, where people are poor, miserable, and hopeless.

And since I have mentioned Verlaine, I may say that what Pater most liked in poetry was the very opposite of such work as that of Verlaine, which he might have been supposed likely to like. I do not think it was actually one of Verlaine's poems, but something done after his manner in English, that some reviewer once quoted, saying: "That, to our mind, would be Mr. Pater's ideal of poetry." Pater said to me, with a sad wonder, "I simply don't know what he meant." What he liked in poetry was something even more definite than can be got in prose; and he valued poets like Dante and like Rossetti for their "delight in concrete definition," not even quite seeing the ultimate magic of such things as "Kubla Khan," which he omitted in a brief selection from the poetry of Coleridge.[7] In the most interesting letter which I ever had from him, the only letter which went to six pages, he says:

MY DEAR MR. SYMONS,—I feel much flattered at your choosing
me as an arbiter in the matter of your literary work, and thank
you for the pleasure I have had in reading carefully the two
poems you have sent me.[8] I don't use the word "arbiter" loosely
for "critic"; but suppose a real controversy, on the question
whether you shall spend your best energies in writing verse, between your poetic aspirations on the one side, and prudence
(calculating results) on the other. Well! judging by these two
pieces, I should say that you have a poetic talent remarkable,
especially at the present day, for precise and intellectual grasp on
the matter it deals with. Rossetti, I believe, said that the value of
every artistic product was in direct proportion to the amount of
purely intellectual force that went to the initial conception of it:
and it is just this intellectual conception which seems to me to be
so conspicuously wanting in what, in some ways, is the most
characteristic verse of our time, especially that of our secondary
poets. In your own pieces, particularly in your MS. "A Revenge," I
find Rossetti's requirement fulfilled, and should anticipate great
things from one who has the talent of conceiving his motive with
so much firmness and tangibility—with that close logic, if I may
say so, which is an element in any genuinely imaginative process. It
is clear to me that you aim at this, and it is what gives your verses,
to my mind, great interest. Otherwise, I think the two pieces of
unequal excellence, greatly preferring "A Revenge" to "Bell in
Camp." Reserving some doubt whether the watch, as the lover's
gift, is not a little bourgeois, I think this piece worthy of any
poet. It has that aim of concentration and organic unity which I
value greatly both in prose and verse. "Bell in Camp" pleases
me less, for the same reason which makes me put Rossetti's
"Jenny," and some of Browning's pathetic-satiric pieces, below
the rank which many assign them. In no one of the poems I am
thinking of, is the inherent sordidness of everything in the persons supposed, except the one poetic trait then under treatment,
quite forgotten. Otherwise, I feel the pathos, the humour, of the
piece (in the full sense of the word humour) and the skill with
which you have worked out your motive therein. I think the present age an unfavourable one to poets, at least in England. The
young poet comes into a generation which has produced a large
amount of first-rate poetry, and an enormous amount of good
secondary poetry. You know I give a high place to the literature

of prose as a fine art, and therefore hope you won't think me brutal in saying that the admirable qualities of your verse are those also of imaginative prose; as I think is the case also with much of Browning's finest verse. I should say, make prose your principal *métier,* as a man of letters, and publish your verse as a more intimate gift for those who already value you for your pedestrian work in literature. I should think you ought to find no difficulty in finding a publisher for poems such as those you have sent to me.

I am more than ever anxious to meet you. Letters are such poor means of communication. Don't come to London without making an appointment to come and see me here.—Very sincerely yours,

WALTER PATER.[9]

"Browning, one of my best-loved writers," is a phrase I find in his first letter to me, in December 1886, thanking me for a little book on Browning which I had just published. There is, I think, no mention of any other writer except Shakespeare (besides the reference to Rossetti which I have just quoted) in any of the fifty or sixty letters which I have from him. Everything that is said about books is a direct matter of business: work which he was doing, of which he tells me, or which I was doing, about which he advises and encourages me.

In practical things Pater was wholly vague, troubled by their persistence when they pressed upon him. To wrap up a book to send by post was an almost intolerable effort, and he had another reason for hesitating. "I take your copy of Shakespeare's sonnets with me," he writes in June 1889, "hoping to be able to restore it to you there lest it should get bruised by transit through the post." He wrote letters with distaste, never really well, and almost always with excuses or regrets in them: "Am so over-burdened (my time, I mean) just now with pupils, lectures, and the making thereof"; or, with hopes for a meeting: "Letters are such poor means of communication: when are we to meet?" or, as a sort of hasty makeshift: "I send this prompt answer, for I know by experience that when I delay my delays are apt to be lengthy." A review took him sometimes a year to get through, and remained in the end, like his letters, a little cramped, never finished to the point of ease, like his published writings. To lecture was a great trial to him. Two of the three lectures which I have heard in my life were given by Pater, one on Mérimée, at the London Institution, in November 1890, and the other on Raphael, at Toynbee Hall, in 1892. I never saw a man suffer a severer humiliation. The act of reading his written lecture was an agony which communicated itself to the main part of the audience. Before going into the hall at

Whitechapel he had gone into a church to compose his mind a little, between the discomfort of the underground railway and the distress of the lecture-hall.

In a room, if he was not among very intimate friends, Pater was rarely quite at his ease, but he liked being among people, and he made the greater satisfaction overcome the lesser reluctance. He was particularly fond of cats, and I remember one evening, when I had been dining with him in London, the quaint, solemn, and perfectly natural way in which he took up the great black Persian, kissed it, and set it down carefully again on his way upstairs. Once at Oxford he told me that M. Bourget had sent him the first volume of his *Essais de Psychologie Contemporaine*,[10] and that the cat had got hold of the book and torn up the part containing the essay on Baudelaire, "and as Baudelaire was such a lover of cats I thought she might have spared him!"

We were talking once about fairs, and I had been saying how fond I was of them. He said: "I am fond of them, too. I always go to fairs. I am getting to find they are very similar." Then he began to tell me about the fairs in France, and I remember, as if it were an unpublished fragment in one of his stories, the minute, coloured impression of the booths, the little white horses of the "roundabouts," and the little wild beast shows, in which what had most struck him was the interest of the French peasant in the wolf, a creature he might have seen in his own woods. "An English clown would not have looked at a wolf if he could have seen a tiger."

I once asked Pater if his family was really connected with that of the painter, Jean-Baptiste Pater. He said: "I think so, I believe so, I always say so." The relationship has never been verified, but one would like to believe it; to find something lineally Dutch in the English writer. It was, no doubt, through this kind of family interest that he came to work upon Goncourt's essay and the contemporary *Life of Watteau* by the Count de Caylus, printed in the first series of *L'Art du XVIIIᵉ Siècle*, out of which he has made certainly the most living of his *Imaginary Portraits*, that "Prince of Court Painters" which is supposed to be the journal of a sister of Jean-Baptiste Pater, whom we see in one of Watteau's portraits in the Louvre. As far back as 1889 Pater was working towards a second volume of *Imaginary Portraits*, of which "Hippolytus Veiled" was to have been one. He had another subject in Moroni's *Portrait of a Tailor* in the National Gallery,[11] whom he was going to make a Burgomaster; and another was to have been a study of life in the time of the Albigensian persecution. There was also to be a modern study: could this have been "Emerald Uthwart"? No doubt "Apollo in Picardy," published in 1893, would have gone into the volume. "The Child in the House," which was printed as an *Imaginary Portrait*, in *Macmillan's Magazine* in

1878, was really meant to be the first chapter of a romance which was to show "the poetry of modern life," something, he said, as "Aurora Leigh" does. There is much personal detail in it, the red hawthorn, for instance, and he used to talk to me of the old house at Tunbridge, where his great-aunt lived, and where he spent much of his time when a child. He remembered the gipsies there, and their caravans, when they came down for the hop-picking; and the old lady in her large cap going out on the lawn to do battle with the surveyors who had come to mark out a railway across it; and his terror of the train, and of "the red flag, which meant *blood*." It was because he always dreamed of going on with it that he did not reprint this imaginary portrait in the book of *Imaginary Portraits;* but he did not go on with it because, having begun the long labour of *Marius,* it was out of his mind for many years, and when, in 1889, he still spoke of finishing it, he was conscious that he could never continue it in the same style, and that it would not be satisfactory to rewrite it in his severer, later manner. It remains, perhaps fortunately, a fragment, to which no continuation could ever add a more essential completeness.

Style, in Pater, varied more than is generally supposed, in the course of his development, and, though never thought of as a thing apart from what it expresses, was with him a constant preoccupation. Let writers, he said, "make time to write English more as a learned language." It has been said that Ruskin, De Quincey, and Flaubert were among the chief "origins" of Pater's style; it is curiously significant that matter, in Pater, was developed before style, and that in the bare and angular outlines of the earliest fragment, "Diaphanéité," there is already the substance which is to be clothed upon by beautiful and appropriate flesh in the *Studies in the Renaissance.* Ruskin, I never heard him mention, but I do not doubt that there, to the young man beginning to concern himself with beauty in art and literature, was at least a quickening influence. Of De Quincey he spoke with an admiration which I had difficulty in sharing, and I remember his showing me with pride a set of his works bound in half-parchment, with pale gold lettering on the white backs, and with the cinnamon edges which he was so fond of. Of Flaubert we rarely met without speaking. He thought *Julien l'Hospitalier* as perfect as anything he had done. *L'Education Sentimentale* was one of the books which he advised me to read; that, and *Le Rouge et le Noir* of Stendhal; and he spoke with particular admiration of two episodes in the former, the sickness and the death of the child. Of the Goncourts he spoke with admiration tempered by dislike. Their books often repelled him, yet their way of doing things seemed to him just the way things should be done; and done before almost any one else. He often read *Madame Gervaisais,* and he spoke of *Chérie* (for all its "immodesty") as an admirable thing, and a model for all such studies.

Once, as we were walking in Oxford, he pointed to a window and said, with a slow smile: "That is where I get my Zolas." He was always a little on his guard in respect of books; and, just as he read Flaubert and Goncourt because they were intellectual neighbours, so he could read Zola for mere pastime, knowing that there would be nothing there to distract him. I remember telling him about *The Story of an African Farm*, and of the wonderful human quality in it. He said, repeating his favourite formula: "No doubt you are quite right; but I do not suppose I shall ever read it." And he explained to me that he was always writing something, and that while he was writing he did not allow himself to read anything which might possibly affect him too strongly, by bringing a new current of emotion to bear upon him. He was quite content that his mind should "keep as a solitary prisoner its own dream of a world"; it was that prisoner's dream of a world that it was his whole business as a writer to remember, to perpetuate.

[George Moore]¹

I

I met George Moore, during a feverish winter I spent in Paris in 1890, at the house of Doctor John Chapman, 46 Avenue Kleber; who at one time, before he settled there, had been the Proprietor and then Editor of *The Westminster Review*. In his review appeared in 1886 Pater's wonderful and fascinating essay on Coleridge; in 1887 his penetrating and revealing essay on Wincklemann.² "He is the last fruit of the Renaissance, and explains in a striking way its motives and tendencies."

At that time I had heard a good deal of Moore; I had read very few of his novels; these I had found to be entertaining, realistic, and decadent; and certainly founded on modern French fiction. He made little or no impression on me on that occasion; he was Irish and amusing. Our conversation was probably on Paris and France and French prose. He gave me his address, King's Bench Walk, Inner Temple, and asked me to call on him after my return to London.

I was born, "like a fiend hid in a cloud,"³ cruel, nervous, excitable, passionate, restless, never quite human, never quite normal and, from the fact that I have never known what it was to have a home, as most children know it, my life has been in many ways a wonderful, in certain ways a tragic one: an existence, indeed, so inexplicable even to myself, that I can not fathom it. If I have been a vagabond, and have never been able to root myself in any one place in the world, it is because I have no early memories of any one sky or soil. It has freed me from many prejudices in giving me its own unresting kind of freedom; but it has cut me off from whatever is stable, of long growth in the world.

When I came up to London, in 1889, I was fortunate enough to take one room in a narrow street, named Fountain Court. In 1821 Blake left South Molton Street for Fountain Court, where he remained for the rest of his life. The side window looked down through an opening between the houses, showing the river and the hills beyond; Blake worked at a table facing the window. At that time I had only seen the Temple; so that when I entered it for the first time in my life, to call on Moore, I was seized by a sudden fascination which never left me. I questioned him as to the chances I might have of finding rooms there; he wisely advised me to look at the outside of the window of the barber's shop, where notices of vacant flats were put up. Finally I saw: "Fountain Court: rooms to let." I immediately made all the necessary inquiries; and found myself in March, 1871,[4] entire possessor of the top flat, which had a stone balcony from which I looked down on a wide open court, with a stone fountain in the middle. I lived there for ten years. My most intimate friends were, first and foremost, Yeats, then Moore: all three of us being of Celtic origin.

My intercourse with Moore was mostly at night; that is, when I was not wandering in foreign countries or absorbed in much more animal and passionate affairs. I dedicated to him *Studies in Two Literatures* 1897; the dedication was written in Rome, which begins: "My dear Moore, Do you remember, at the time when we were both living in the Temple, and our talks used to begin with midnight, and go on until the first glimmerings of dawn shivered among the trees, yours and mine; do you remember how often we have discussed, well, I suppose, everything which I speak of in these studies in the two literatures which we both chiefly care about."[5] It ends: "I think of our conversations now in Rome, where, as in those old times in the Temple, I still look out of my window on a fountain in a square; only, here, I have the Pantheon to look at, on the other side of my fountain." * * *

No critic could for one instant apply to any of George Moore's novels the phrase of "grand spiritual realism." A realist he always has been; a realist, who, having founded himself on French novelists, has really, in certain senses, brought something utterly new into English fiction. Luckily, he is Irish; luckily, he lived the best years of his youth in Paris. His prose shows the intense labor with which he produced every chapter of every novel; in fact, there is too much of the laborious mind in all his books. He was right in saying in *Avowals:* "Real literature is concerned with description of life and thoughts of life rather than with acts. He must write about the whole of life and not about parts of life, and he must write truth and not lies." The first sentence expresses the writer's sense of his own prose in his novels: and yet there is always a lot of vivid action in them. * * *

Now, let us return to the modern writer's Confessions. Whether Moore has read the whole of Casanova or not, there are curiously similar touches in both these writers; as, for instance, in the word "alcoves, streets, ballrooms." Instead of the modern "barrooms" use the word *cafés.* One essential difference is that Casanova had a passion for books: the more essential one is, that Casanova was born to be a vagabond and a Wanderer over almost the whole of Europe, that he had tasted all the forbidden fruits of the earth, and that he had sinned with all his body— leaving, naturally, the soul out of the question.

Every great artist has tasted the sweet poison of the Forbidden Fruit. The Serpent, the most "subtile" of all the Beasts, gave an apple he had gathered from the Tree of the Knowledge of Good and Evil to Eve; she having eaten it and having given one to Adam, both saw they were naked, and, with nakedness, Sin entered into the World. Now, what was stolen from the Garden of God has, ever since, been the one temptation which it is almost impossible to resist. For instance Shakespeare stole from Marlowe, Milton stole from Shakespeare, Keats stole from Virgil, Swinburne stole from Baudelaire and Crashaw, Browning stole from Donne; as for Wagner, having stolen a motet from Vittorio[6] which he used, almost note for note in *Parsifal,* also from Palestrina and his school, and from Berlioz and from Liszt, it is impossible to say what he did not steal. Oscar Wilde stripped, as far as he could, all the fruit he could gather from the orchards of half a dozen French novelists; besides those of Poe and of Pater. Gabrielle d'Annunzio has stolen as thoroughly as Wilde; in fact, the whole contents of certain short stories. As for George Moore, he has been guilty of as many thefts as these; only he has concealed his thefts with more stealth. Henry James said to some one of my acquaintance: "Moore has an absolute genius for picking other men's brains." That saying is as final as it is fundamental. * * *

* * * Hawthorne had a magical imagination, a passion for "handling sin" purely; he was haunted by what is obscure and abnormal in that illusive region which exists on the confines of evil and good; his opinion of woman was that she "was plucked out of a mystery, and had its roots still clinging to her." Sin and the Soul, those are the problems he has always before him; Sin, as our punishment; the Soul, in its essence, mistlike and intangible. He uses his belief in witchcraft with admirable effect, the dim mystery which clings about haunted houses, the fantastic gambols of the soul itself, under what seems like the devil's own promptings.

In the whole of Moore's prose there is no such magic, no such mystery, no such diabolism; he is not so lacking in imagination as in style. He has always been, with impressive inaccuracy, described as the English Zola; at the outset of his career he gained a certain notoriety not unlike Zola's; his novels are not based on theories, as some of Zola's are. Moore always knew how to make a cunning plot, to make some of his compositions masterly, and how to construct his characters—which, to a certain extent, are living people, really existent, as their surroundings. As I say further on: "Compare with any of Zola's novels the amazingly clever novel of Moore, *A Mummer's Wife,* which goes with several other novels which are—well—*manqués,* in spite of their ability, their independence, their unquestionable merits of various kinds." The style always drags more than the action. Vivid, sensual, not sensuous, often perverse, never passionate; written with a curious sense of wickedness, of immorality, of vice; extraordinary at times in some of the scenes he evokes in one of several chapters; always with the French element; his prose exotic, morbid, cruel, as cruel as this casuist of the passions, has in it a certain scorn and contempt of mediocrities, which can be delivered with the force of a sledge-hammer that strikes an anvil and shoots forth sparks.

II

George Moore has been described, with impressive inaccuracy, as the English Zola. At what was practically the outset of his career he gained a certain notoriety; which did him good, by calling public attetntion to an unknown name; it did him harm, by attaching to that name a certain stigma. In a certainly remote year, but a year we all of us remember, there were strange signs in the literary Zodiac. There had been a distinctly new growth in the short story, and along with the short story ("poisonous honey stolen from France")[7] came a new license in dealing imaginatively with life, almost permitting the Englishman to contend with the writers of other nations on their own ground; permitting him, that is to say, to represent life as it really is. Foreign influences, certainly, had begun to have more and more effect upon the making of such literature as is produced in England nowadays; we had a certain acceptance of Ibsen, a popular personal welcome of Zola, and literary homage paid to Verlaine. What do these facts really mean? It is certain that they mean something. * * *

Compare with any of Zola's novels the amazingly clever novel of Moore, *A Mummer's Wife,* which goes with several other novels which are—well—*manqués,* in spite of their ability, their independence, their unquestionable merits of various kinds. *A Mummer's Wife* is admirably put together, admirably planned and shaped; the whole composition of the book is masterly. The style may drag, but not the action; the construction of a sentence may be uncertain, but not the construction of a character. The actor and his wife are really living people; we see them in their surroundings, and we see every detail of those surroundings. * * *

George Moore's *Modern Painting* is full of injustices, brutality and ignorances; but it is full also of the most generous justice, the most discriminating sympathy, and the genuine knowledge of the painter. It is hastily thought out, hastily written; but here, in these vivid, direct, unscrupulously logical pages, you will find some of the secrets of the art of painting, let out, so to speak, by an intelligence all sensation, which has soaked them up without knowing it. Yet, having begun by trying to paint, and having failed in painting, and so set himself to the arduous task of being a prose-writer, he is often, in spite of his painter's accuracy as to "values" and "technique" and so on, unreliable.

For, being neither creative as a novelist nor as a critic, he has nothing, as a matter of course, of two among many essential qualities: vision and divination. Take, for instance, a few pages anywhere in *L'Art Romantique* of Baudelaire, or from his prose on Delacroix, on Constantine Guys, on Wagner, on Daumier, on Whistler, on Flaubert, and on Balzac—where he is always supreme and consummate, "fiery and final"—and place these beside any chosen pages of Moore's prose on either Balzac or on Whistler, and you will see all the difference in the world: as I have said above, between the creative and the uncreative criticism.

Had Walter Pater devoted himself exclusively to art criticism, there is no doubt that, in a sense, he would have been a great art critic. There are essays scattered throughout his work, as in the Botticelli where he first introduces Botticelli to the modern world, as in the Leonardo da Vinci—in which the simplest words take color from each other by the cunning accident of their placing in the sentences, the subtle spiritual fire kindling from word to word creates a masterpiece, a miracle in which all is inspiration, all is certainty, all is evocation, and which, in the famous page on *La Gioconda,* rises to the height of actually lyrical prose—in which the essential principles of the art of painting are divined and interpreted with extraordinary subtlety.[8] In the same sense all that Whistler has written about painting deserves to be taken seriously, and read with understanding. Written in French, and signed by Baudelaire, his truths, and paradoxes reflecting truths, would have been realized for what they are. He fought for himself, and spared no form of stupidity: for, in Whistler, apart from his malice, his poisonous angers, taste was carried to the point of genius, and became creative.

George Moore's literary career has been singularly interesting; his character as a writer is very curious. A man who respects his art, who is devoted to literature, who has a French eye for form, he seems condemned to produce work which is always spotted with imperfection. All his life he has been seeking a style, and he has not yet found one. At times he drops into style as if by accident, and then he drops style as if by design. He has a passionate delight in the beauty of good prose; he has an ear for the magic of phrases; his words catch at times a troubled expressive charm; yet he has never attained ease in writing, and he is capable of astounding incorrectness—the incorrectness of a man who knows better, who is not careless and yet who can not help himself. Yet the author of *A Mummer's Wife,* of *The Confessions of a Young Man,* of *Impressions and Opinions,* has more narrowly escaped being a great writer than even he himself, perhaps, is aware.

Paul Verlaine[1]

It was on the 29th of April, 1890, that I first met Verlaine. I remember the hot night, the café on the Boulevard Saint-Michel where Havelock Ellis and I had been dining with Charles Morice[2] and a young painter, a friend of his, whose name I forget. Morice was then the titular apostle of Verlaine; he had written a book about him which still remains better than anything which has been written since; and in his other, not less admirable book, *La Littérature de Tout à l'Heure,* he had planned out, almost prophetically, the course that literature was to take just then in France. Morice had promised to introduce me to Verlaine, and when dinner was over he turned to me in his gentle and urbane way, bending his great blond head a little, and proposed that we should go on to the Café François, where Verlaine was generally to be found. Morice went on talking, as we strolled in the slow French way up the boulevard, through all the noisy, hasty gaiety of the hour; he talked as he always did, in his fluent, ecstatic, rather mad way, full of charm and surprise. I remember nothing that he said; I don't think I knew at the time. I was awaiting, with delight and almost terror, my first sight of the extraordinary creature whom I vaguely expected to find somewhat in the likeness of his caricature in the *Hommes d'Aujourd'hui*—cloven-footed and ending in a green tail.[3] We passed café after café, every *terrasse* and the whole pavement filled with students and women. Higher up the crowd dwindled, and at last we came to the corner of the Rue Gay-Lussac. I saw the name, Morice pushed open the door, we followed.

And there, in the midst of a noisy, laughing company of young men, all drinking, I saw Verlaine, like Pan, I thought, among reveling worshipers. He was smiling benevolently; a large gray hat pushed back on his head, a white scarf around his neck, no collar, the shabbiest of clothes. And my first thought, after a moment's disgust at the company in which he sat, was, What a gentleman! I never saw simpler or more beautiful manners. He got up as Morice introduced us, and sat at our table, and began to talk. The face, with its spiritual forehead, animal jaw, and shifting faun's eye, was unlike that of any portrait I had seen: no wise criminal, but genial, manly, with dignity under a really startling movement of the features. The eyes, eyelids, and eyebrows were in constant oblique gesture: there is no other word for it. But the whole body was gesture, and of a sudden, violent, overwhelming kind, not French gesture at all. The whole body, genial and ferocious, seemed to translate every thought or sensation, with that animal-prompt sincerity which is one of the qualities of his work. There was no pose, no deliberate extravagance; the extravagance, when it came, was momentary and on the spur of the moment—the type of every action of his life.

I saw in that first sight of Verlaine, when he sat there in the café and talked to me about himself, about England, and about English poetry, only a part, no doubt, of what I came to distinguish or interpret afterward. If I think now, I see the great sleepy and gray head as he lies back in his corner at that café, with his eyes half shut; he drags on my arm as we go up the boulevard together; he shows me his Bible in the little room up the back stairs; he climbs the many steps painfully in Fountain Court;[4] he nods his nightcap over a greasy picture-book as he sits up in bed at the hospital. But almost everything that I ever saw in that face has been concentrated into the portrait which Carrière did at Morice's instigation, some years after I first met him. A rough rendering of it is within every one's reach in the *Choix de Poésies*.[5] Morice has told the story of one of the most marvelous portraits of our time, in which, as he justly says, Carrière

a vu et fixé pour toujours la douleur de ce grand sacrifié, de ce crucifié. Le poète, malade, était à l'hôpital, à l'autre extrémité de la ville. Tout avait été preparé, Carrière l'attendait. Mais la traversée ne s'accomplit point sans peine, malgré plusieurs voitures et à cause de l'exaltation du congé d'un jour.—Pas un instant Verlaine ne posa. Durant toute cette unique séance de quelques heures il ne cessa d'arpenter l'atelier, en parlant haut, avec cette effervescente verve, la sienne, folle et belle, qui roulait les pensées, les anecdotes, les images, les poèmes, se reposait en riant et rebondissait dans un sanglot; le capricieux monologue, insoucieux des écoutants, les supposait informés du thème—la vie du poète—et tout au plus les initiait, par des suggestions rapides, aux points essentiels, pour aussitôt s'échapper en divagations d'ironie douloureuse. Je lui donnais parfois la réplique afin de l'arrêter dans un geste en lumière ou d'attirer son regard et son visage vers le chevalet. Pas un instant Carrière ne cessa de travailler. Verlaine partit, je crois bien, sans l'avoir aperçu.[6]

And as I read over this narrative, by the man who first took me to see Verlaine, the scenes come back to me, in Paris and London, and I see Verlaine again. That is just how he talked, "regardless of listeners," or accepting a listener as necessarily a friend and a diviner. I remember how he would sit on my sofa in Fountain Court, and for hours together never cease talking, in a kind of feverish and broken monologue, with pauses, interruptions, outbursts of gaiety, and clamors of rage at something remembered and lived over again; sometimes with half-shut eyes and in an indistinct murmur; sometimes in shouts and with eager gestures; sometimes dropping into English, with some point of humorous emphasis. His face was a tragic mask, grotesque and flexible, through which he seemed to speak as if always in action; something never at rest peered out of the wild crannies of the eyes and out of the weak, exorbitant mouth and out of the bare and rock-like head. I have seen all the deadly sins march in order over his face, and leave it washed and empty for the virtues. When he talked he lived with the same subtle and uneasy vitality with which he lived when he wrote, but without concentration, for it was only in his verse that he could command himself. It was all a confession, and it remembered and repeated everything, with infinite self-pity, yet not without a consciousness of the justice of things. He forgot none of his own sins, nor of the sins of others against him; and he told them over as if only these intimate things mattered. A gross gaiety would come in at times and set him chuckling ignobly; and then an old enthusiasm would possess him, or an old pity lull him into gravity. He would talk of Rimbaud, of his wife, of his son; of the women, neither young nor comely, for whom he wrote the *Odes en son Honneur* and the *Chansons pour Elle,* in which we seem to hear Villon. He lamented with fierce lamentations his poverty and his bodily sickness; he could never forget them nor accustom himself to them: "*Doucement farouche, émergeant de l'ombre d'un invisible et réel Calvaire.*" Morice sees his head in Carrière's great picture; and so I saw it in my little room in the Temple, and in cafés and garrets and hospitals in Paris, and can see it now whenever I think of it.

Daily I come to think him greater: a greater poet, a more wonderful man. I see now how what seemed trivial in him, or uncouth, or ignoble, was a part of that simple and sincere nature to which choice among moods, or conviction after experience, were equally impossible. All that was gentle and brutal in him had its place in the one poet of our day who has given equally exact expression to flesh and spirit, to what we gratuitously call the worse and better side of ourselves. He had vices, because he included everything that sensation can become, vice as well as virtue. He was abnormal, but that was because he included what was abnormal as well as what was normal. He was human "without prejudice," and set no bounds to any passion, not even to love. And out of disorder, disturbance, a life that seemed to be jangled hopelessly out of tune, it was not only in his poetry that he made a final harmony, but even in his sleepy and savage face, in which none of the lines had beauty. * * * Only a few people ever saw (Carrière saw it) that almost divine serenity in the face of Verlaine.

I remember little of what Verlaine said on the night I first met him in the café. He realized at once that I wanted to know exactly what he was, and in the interval of general talk about books and poets (in which Moréas,[7] who was there, asked me what was the longest verse in English: "I have written verses of twenty syllables! Verlaine has stopped at—" I forget the number) Verlaine would tell over the incidents in his life to me, as if he were repeating curious things which had happened to other people and which might interest one. He told me about Rimbaud, about his quarrel with him, and his imprisonment, in a kind of good-humored and impersonal way. He was eager to show his knowledge of England, and told me of when he had been in London, in Bournemouth, in Leamington, in Stickney, where he had taught English, he said, to small boys. He said, jovially, *"Je suis un Roman Catholique,"* but praised the London Sunday and the services of the English Church. The French Sunday, he said, was *"assommant,"* but the English, though *"triste,"* was so religious, and he seemed to pull an imaginary bell-rope. Sometimes he would use English words, words of gross slang, which he chuckled to have remembered.

He asked me to come and see him the next night, and he wrote his name and address very carefully in pencil on the back of one of my cards: "Paul Verlaine, Hôtel des Mines, 125, Bd. St.-Michel, Chambre No. 4." He named an hour, and when I got there, not too long after it, and asked the concierge if No. 4 was at home, she looked at me grimly, jerked her head away, and said, *"Non, Monsieur, il n'est pas ici."* I turned and walked slowly down the boulevard, and had not got far before I saw him coming slowly up, leaning on the arm of an honest-looking, little, shabby man who seemed to be always looking after him. I lifted my hat. He bowed, and began to talk to me quite at random, not remembering who I was or what I wanted. He would say the same thing over and over again with increasing emphasis, an emphasis that became terrible when he had been drinking too long. Suddenly he remembered, and asked me to come in. The little man got the key and candle and led the way. We crossed a court and began to climb a narrow staircase. Verlaine mounted step by step, haltingly; and he would stop on the stairs to apologize for keeping us so long on the way. The room was small and mean, but quite decent; the few things in it were in disorder. There were a few books on the chest of drawers—a Bible and a few of his own books—and on the wall over it were several pencil and chalk sketches of himself. The little man lit two more candles, and Verlaine confided to me, in a deep whisper, that he had just been getting some money. "I have got money. I will have pleasure, pleasure, pleasure," he repeated, slowly, in his difficult, accentuated English, every word a hoarse jerk. He took out his purse and opened it; there was very little in it. There was a knock at the door, and a young man came in, incredibly tall and thin and youthful, with a tired gray look in his eyes; he was an artist, Fernand Langlois, whom I had seen at the café. He sat down on the bed. The little man perched himself on the chest of drawers. Verlaine gave me a chair and began to walk up and down the room. He said he must have some rum: he thought it was an English drink and that I should like it, and he counted out some of the money in his purse to the little man, who came back presently with a bottle of rum and some glasses. Langlois curled himself upon the bed, and said that he must have his rum neat, as he had the toothache. Verlaine grumbled, but at last gave in. At last he sat down and began to talk, while we all sipped rum and smoked cigarettes. He drank very slowly, often raising the glass half-way to his lips and holding it there until he had finished a sentence or a string of them, and sometimes he forgot to drink it and put it down untasted. I suppose he drank somewhat consecutively: I never saw him drink very much at one sitting. His talk dropped every now and then into English, and I can recall the droll accent with which he quoted "To be or not to be." He spoke, as he had the night before, of his admiration of Tennyson, and he showed me his Bible (the only Bible I ever saw in Paris) with a sort of maudlin admiration, patting it, turning it over, pointing out the name of the translator, assuring me that it was an excellent book, and that he was himself a religious man. *"Je suis Catholique,"* he repeated over and over again; *"mais—Catholique du moyen-âge."*

His talk all through the evening was argumentative and explosive; he was restless, vague, and his face worked frantically. At last there was another knock at the door, and more young men came in. Then Verlaine said he must go out—he had some business; he was going to see a debtor, he said. I said good-by; there were all manner of compliments on both sides, and the little man lighted me down the dark stairs with a candle.

From that time I used to see Verlaine at intervals year by year in streets, cafés, and hospitals, and finally in London; and the better I knew him the easier it was for me to think of him apart from all the sordid trouble of his daily life, as he was in a heart and soul that were as rare and honest as the heart and soul of any great man of our time. His last years were spent in a vagabondage not altogether that of his own choice: he had other instincts than those of the vagabond, but the circumstances of his life, acting on the weakness of a will at the mercy of every circumstance, left him no choice. I did not like many of the people in whose company I met him, but to see them about him was to realize all the difference between him and them. And, among many who were worthless, were there not others who were the enthusiasts of ideas, and did not their follies bubble up out of a drunkenness at least as much spiritual as material?

Few of the idealists I have known have been virtuous—that is to say, they have chosen their virtues after a somewhat haphazard plan of their own; some of them have loved absinthe, others dirt, all idleness; but why expect everything at once? Have we, who lack ideas and ideals, enough of the solid virtues to put into the balance against these weighty abstractions? I only ask the question; but I persist in thinking that we have still a great deal to learn from Paris, and especially on matters of the higher morality.

[Remy de Gourmont and Joris-Karl Huysmans][1]

Remy de Gourmont (born in 1858, who died in his rooms, Rue des Saintes-Pères, Paris, on September twenty-fifth)[2] possessed one of those attractive personalities which leave a kind of savor behind them. He had the courtesy of the aristocrat; yet with none of the splendor of Edmond de Goncourt, who was, I thought, the most distinguished man of letters I had ever seen; for he had at once the distinction of race, of fine breeding, and of that delicate, artistic genius which, with him, was so intimately a part of things beautiful and distinguished. Gourmont, an excellent Latin scholar, had a passion for French literature; he had originality. He had also many instinctive qualities; perfect taste, discrimination, force of analysis, a strange satiric gift. His prose had that solidity, that weight of thought, that penetration into ideas, which made him remarkable. "His realm," wrote Pierre Loüys, "is the realm of ideas."[3] "There ended," wrote Rachilde, "one of the rarest spirits of our time."[4]

He had an unrestrained intellectual curiosity; which, with a Pagan spirit, gave him most of his fame. His versatility was amazing; he did more things, of more varied kinds than, I think, any of his contemporaries. Morbid, perverse: in a sense a decadent; not unimaginative; unpassionate, cynical, refined, capable of genuine friendships; a man not unsympathetic, not easily led away, not argumentative; he had a sensitiveness of his own that had its fascination. Gourmont's finest prose is contained in the two admirable volumes: *Le Livre des Masques*. For these pages have in them a subtle sense of values, in prose and verse; they have the merit of being essentially brief; they are living documents; they are touched with fine irony; in a word, they are a revelation of living personalities; they give sensations rather than judgments.

In Paris he gave me his *Sixtine: Roman de la Vie Cléricale* (1890), which shows the bizarre side of his talent for this kind of work. His novels are novels; they are studies in sex, with much that is technical, abstruse; with at times a tragic simplicity. In these curious pages there are mixtures of adulteries with uncloistered passions; women's aberrations, their evasions, their vices; men's brutalities and, at times, abominable animality; these "open the plot." And, with these fevers of the flesh, one finds the writer, who, in his own words, is *"un extraordinaire fondeur de phrases et tailleur d'images."*

It was Gourmont who introduced me to Huysmans, whom I met in a certain house, 9, rue de Varenne, where lived Madame Courrière, the Madame Chantelouve of his *Là-Bas.* The face is gray, wearily alert, with a look of benevolent malice. At first sight it is commonplace, the features are ordinary, one seems to have seen it at the Bourse or the Stock Exchange. But gradually, that strange, unvarying expression, that look of benevolent malice, grows upon you as the influence of the man makes itself felt. I have seen Huysmans in his office—he is an employé in the Ministry of Foreign Affairs, and a model employé. I have seen him in a café, in various houses; but I always see him in memory as I used to see him at the house of the bizarre Madame X. He leans back on the sofa, rolling a cigarette between his thin, expressive fingers, looking at no one, and at nothing, while Madame X moves about with solid vivacity in the midst of her extraordinary menagerie of *bric-a-brac.* The spoils of all the world are there, in that incredibly tiny *salon;* they lie underfoot, they climb up walls, they cling to screens, brackets and tables; one of your elbows menaces a Japanese toy, the other a Dresden china shepherdess; all the colors of the rainbow clash in a barbaric discord of notes. And in a corner of this fantastic room, Huysmans lies back indifferently on the sofa, with the air of one perfectly resigned to the boredom of life. Something is said by my learned friend who is to write for the new periodical, or perhaps it is the young editor of the new periodical who speaks, or (if that were not impossible) the taciturn Englishman who accompanies me;[5] and Huysmans, without looking up, and without taking the trouble to speak very distinctly picks up the phrase, transforms it, more likely transpierces it, in a perfectly turned sentence, a phrase of impromptu elaboration. Perhaps it is only a stupid book that some one has mentioned, or a stupid woman; as he speaks, the book looms up before one, becomes monstrous in its dullness, a masterpiece and miracle of imbecility; the unimportant little woman grows into a slow horror before your eyes. It is always the unpleasant aspect of things that he seizes, but the intensity of his revolt from that unpleasantness brings a touch of the sublime into the very expression of his disgust. Every sentence is an epigram, and every epigram slaughters a reputation or an idea. He speaks with an accent as of pained surprise, an amused look of contempt, so profound that it becomes almost pity for human imbecility.

Always, if I can conceive myself under this image, I have lived as a solitary soul lives in the midst of the world. I have believed more than I doubted; I have conceived more things than I have executed. I have never reasoned deeply on deep questions. I have generally hated logic. And I have imagined more than I have thought. I mean to say that imagination—the life of my senses; my sensations—have meant more to me than most things in one's life. I have never loved nature as I have loved the sea, fire, the voice of the wind, the moon and the sun, the beauty of night, the glory of the light, the scent of heather, the luxury of the flesh. I have the spirit of revenge and of revolt, not of negation, nor, on the whole, of disbelief.

I have little sense of pity, but an innate sense of cruelty. I have been cruel to many women, who have clung to me, implored my forgiveness; and I have shut my door against them. That is, of course, because one is wicked. If men hate you, why hate them back? They have their reason, and I have mine. Indeed, I have never known what it is to be virtuous. * * *

[Bohemian Years in London]¹

When I first settled in London I was far from what one calls virginal, and, certainly, far from being what one names innocent. I began by throwing myself into literary society of a certain minor kind, which pleased me as new things and people always do. Certainly all that was novel. I fell casually in love with woman after woman; who, as a matter of fact, had little attraction to my senses.

Born under the influence of passionate and perverse stars, my life has been utterly unlike that of any man I have ever known. Whether alone, or with others, I was always myself: as lonely a Dreamer as ever existed. I have woven a *Loom of Dreams*.² I am a strange mixture of cruelty and hatred! There is an intolerable sense of aversion and of repulsion; together with a calculated malice, an ambiguous aloofness; with an unlucky way of annoying people who exasperate me—a quality I am proud to share with Baudelaire.

It soon became a question of *Loves Amores;*³ and I dare not conjecture how many of those girls (whatever their reputations may have been) after having given me pleasure for a certain length of time—time never mattered much to me then—tried to meet me again, knocked at my door times out of number and were not admitted. Sometimes I saw them again. More often they tortured me with letters I rarely answered. In either case, they had ceased to exist for me; they were non-existent. I had taken up with others.

All that time—and before then—I was desiring the City's corruptions, which began by revolting me; which feeling before long passed away. One begins by taking a purely spectacular interest in vice and disorder; with things evil, with things forbidden, with things unforbidden. One hears of them, longs for them, reads of them, succumbs to them; they have the fearful attraction of a gulf over the void, into which one never plunges. One is checked by scruples which are in one's blood; by all that in one is virtuous. Then one amuses oneself by amusing and by utterly offending people by proclaiming one's immorality. And take this for certain—one who speaks of immorality is himself immoral.

To take one instance out of many, there was a woman called Kate who was married and had two children by a man she had loved and had come to hate. She married him, she told me, from the fact of her living in an evil family. So had her sister, whom I saw oftener than Kate. A question of clashings of temperament.

As Kate had taken a fancy to me and I to her I sometimes went to her house against my will—but more often dined her in town, when I took her to music-halls; more often she came to me alone in Fountain Court. She had some almost unique charm which captivated one; almost a kind of loveliness in her face; a touch of wildness in her nature. She had a nice voice and sometimes sang songs for me on airs of music I had to write about. She had a caressing manner with me that showed that she had begun to love me. Often she sobbed in my arms and lamented her evil fate.

I never treated her badly, never, that would not have done. But as I had other affairs on hand just then, we drifted asunder; again, after much sobbing on her part. It appeared that she finally eloped with another man for I know not what reason. But—as for the bitterness that had arisen between us—that was a thing, certainly, to terrify my nerves. I was not the cause of it; and, not being then pitiless, I felt some pity for her.

I never could explain to myself why she attracted me to such an extent, and yet she was a woman curiously different from the other women I had known. She always seemed so helpless, so lovely, so uncertain of herself, and at the same time so yielding to one's caresses, so passionately desiring to be passionately loved. I had no passion for her in the sense she required it; I had no love for her in the sense in which she required it. And yet I doubt if she ever really doubted what she supposed to be my love and my passion for her. * * *

* * * Walter Sickert wanted to paint Minnie Cunningham who danced at the Tivoli;[4] so on a certain Sunday I took him with me to where Minnie lived with her mother somewhere I think in Islington; she had made up, on account of Sickert; and there I heard what I have always hated the dreary sound of the toll of the church bells. "April Midnight"[5] was the result of one of our night adventures—the dancer's and the dreamer's and, besides these, in *London Nights,* verses named "The Primrose Dance: Tivoli." "Morbidezza,"[6] which I have a curious liking for, was written—on an impulse—on Yeats' sister, Elizabeth Corbet Yeats. "On the Heath" was inspired by the two beautiful daughters of George du Maurier.[7] "Emmy," of course, by the amazingly lovely and fascinating Polish girl I met in a villainous dancing-hall in Berlin; "Emmy at the Eldorado" was the result of my disappointment when I met her in Paris—she regretting as much as I did "those old days of love on hire"—in spite of the fact that she was with a man, evidently one of her many lovers, who looked at me askance in a surly and aggressive manner after she had come up to me where I sat in one of the stalls

and during our conversation. Out of some morbid curiosity, I imagine, I followed her and her man furtively along several boulevards until I saw them enter the door of a *hôtel garni;* whose evil reputation everyone knows who has lived in Paris and who has frequented them.

I remember vividly when the idea of "In the Haymarket"—the jolliest poem I have ever written—came to me. I had sauntered one night into one of those bars where one had drinks and has something to eat, where one as a rule hoists oneself on to a high stool where one commands the counter. This one, which has vanished, was on the left side of the Haymarket. Who the devil the girl was, and where the devil she was then living, remains a most puzzling fact. I must have known all that at the time; for such bars and such girls as these—girls whom I often met at their own houses—were part and parcel of my existence. * * *

I drifted absolutely away from the virtuous people (who had added to my certainty of never having been virtuous) because they had become to me insupportable. Decorous and half indecorous, they had an appalling ignorance—a kind of stupidity—in regard to what life really is. Heavens, to have heard the word Platonic uttered! It may have been an invention of Plato's; but Plato's works never meant much to me. I had begun to feel an utter lack in any woman who had not something artificial, at least apparently, who was not fragile; who had, in a word, no touch on me.

From that time, without many hesitations on the way, I lived my own life after my own will. I had always been unconventional; I became reckless, a spendthrift; cared for no one's opinion of me, either good or bad. I was careless, a vagabond, a Wanderer, a Bohemian.

Yet—like all artists—I had my exasperating failures with certain women, that leave, as it were, the serpent's trail behind them. I had my absurd timidities, my unspeakable follies, my extravagances, my debts, my evasions, my lies. And above all, I became perverse; not by any means deliberately, but because Perversity was a quality always in me.

I am not inclined to say that there are traces of perversity in all men of genius. There are not. But in how many cases there are more than distinct traces of this saving quality! Shakespeare in his abnormal years, when he wrote *King Lear* and *Troilus and Cressida;* Marlowe in several of his Tragedies; Webster, Ford, Cyril Tourneur; Blake, in certain definite senses; Coleridge, Rossetti, Swinburne, Meredith. Need I add more to my list than Villon, the shameless son of unshamed Fire?

In any case—I am no exception—my aesthetic instincts became perverted. I relished nothing that was not vicious, morbid, fantastic, abnormal. When I was in the company of men and women, of thieves and of prostitutes, I made no excuses—no excuses were ever needed.

During all these years I had an evil reputation—not unlike the evil reputation of Paul Verlaine. I was always aware of it and rather proud of it. In poets' lives and works a man's life is assumed to be evil; a man's works are assumed to be more evil than his life. Nor are modern instances lacking: such as Byron, Swinburne, Rossetti. The whole unleashed pack of the blood-hounds of the Press yelped in exultation over *Don Juan*, *Poems and Ballads*, Rossetti's *Poems* of 1870, and my *London Nights* of 1895. * * *

I either fascinated or was fascinated by a strange, beautiful and exotic Eastern girl,[8] who, alone, as our nerves often quivered in unison, in those tenebrous years of my life, between 1895 and 1896, shared what I can hardly call less than agonies of sensation, with me; in whom they were one burning rage and one consuming fire. Then there was the ravishing and wildly exotic Hungarian girl, who vibrated to every emotion. I was suddenly aware of having fascinated her and of being fascinated by her. She had so much passion and fire; and she and I knew that she was to be given in marriage to a man of a certain age who was certainly not the husband she ought to have chosen. I never saw him and I refused to go to their marriage. The Inevitable occurred, I forget how many years later, when lovers began to throng about her. We had before then one wonderful night. She had never been to the Empire nor had she seen any Ballet. So I, who lived in that frivolous atmosphere, secured tickets for several of us; I dined them out; she sat next to me—in one whirl of enchanted excitement, turning her lovely face to me times out of number, asking questions. I was an enviable man that night: at least for this reason that the eyes of the ballet girls who knew me looked up at us the instant the dances brought them in sight of us. My imagination is vivid enough to recall not only every detail of that night but every detail of the incessant chatter of those girls to me the next night in the wings. One—one only—was furiously jealous.

It would be an interminable thing to have to relate such events and adventures and misadventures, one after another, perhaps on the last one's heels; with that awful rapidity that occurs only in those years when one is young: at least, in that particular sense I have indicated. These things and in fact most of the essential things in my life that had to be kept out of others' listening ears, forced me to be lonely, in a crowd; to be lonely when I was alone with myself; to be able to look with utter indifference on those lives that meant nothing to me; to assume in my utmost solitude certain masks. I had then, and have had since, much of the fever and turmoil—but none of the unattained dreams—of a life like Dowson's, which had in itself so much of the suicidal, swift and disastrous impetus of genius. An existence such as mine must remain forever inexplicable.

Balzac's existence—was that entirely explicable? That I have every reason for doubting: and for two reasons; one, that he put such a tremendous amount of himself into his novels; two, that he left most people in the dark in regard to his adventures with women; in fact, in regard to all his adventures. He left no list of his mistresses, as Baudelaire did in his secret and surreptitious fashion. One of the things I cannot resist in admiring in Baudelaire is not only his intense sense that he is Impeccable, Infallible; but that, to be surreptitious, to mystify men's and women's minds, is to assume some pact with the Devil, to become Diabolical: to have the serpent's sting. I have always wondered whether Baudelaire was even to his inner sense Inexplicable. There is something in his genius that is as inexplicable as it is inevitable; there is something in his face that fascinates me as few faces ever did: the unimaginable depths of those tragic eyes that have seen Hell and Heaven, that have in them the malice of the Prince of the Powers of Evil; those ironical lips that have the cold cruelty of an inviolable reptile. Yet, in all this morbid depravity, how God-like an aspect!

[An Actress in Whitechapel]¹

One night I left Fountain Court and took the train to Whitechapel, as I had heard that a Yiddish troop of actors were performing plays of Shakespeare in their own language at a certain music hall I had often frequented. It was in July 1890 and I had read *The Picture of Dorian Gray* by Oscar Wilde. And what happened to Dorian happened to me. He says: "About half past nine I passed by an absurd little theatre, with great flaring gas-jets and gaudy playbills. A hideous Jew, in the most amazing waistcoat I ever beheld in my life, was standing at the entrance, smoking a vile cigar. He had greasy ringlets, and an enormous diamond blazed in the centre of a soiled shirt. 'Have a box, my Lord?' he said, when he saw me, and he took off his hat with an air of gorgeous servility. There was something about him, Harry, that amused me. He was such a monster. [. . .] I really went in and paid a whole guinea for the stage-box. [. . .] I found myself seated in a horrible little private box, with a vulgar drop-scene staring me in the face. [. . .] The gallery and pit were fairly full, but the two rows of dingy stalls were quite empty. [. . . The play] was *Romeo and Juliet*."²

Now, that is almost literally what occurred to me on the night I have referred to; the same vile Jew with his vile eyes, who actually in the servile fashion lifted his hat and said to me: "Have a box, my Lord?" I was mightily amused by the title he had conferred on me, and I paid half a crown for a private box that looked on the same glaring drop scene. I had come to see how the Jewish actress would represent Juliet; and I was prepared for a disappointment, it is in *Antony and Cleopatra* that Shakespeare expresses the whole Art of Love. There is another garden besides Juliet's in which Sakuntala walked:³ and Isolde, in Wagner's music, has added a cry to "the desire of the woman for the desire of the man." He gives us two lovers, who, besides loving, just remember how to live. They live for their own sakes: they die in all the beauty and passion of their youth, for love's sake. The moment the young Jewish actress came upon the stage, she fascinated me—in spite of the fact that I could not understand anything she said. She was lovely; she was almost pathetic in her loveliness; she had that voice which thrills one's pulses. She expressed the supreme ecstacy of her passion, both in voice and face; in the death scene she expresses the supreme certainty of her innocence and the same intensity and the same beauty. She was the veritable ghost in flesh and blood of her rarer self. Something in the Jewish girl's passion excited in me an abstract passion; she evidently noticed my excitement.

Every nerve in her body lived with a separate life; even when she hardly seemed to be acting, a magnetic current seemed to have been set in motion between her and her audience. The curtain went down on a great actress. When it rose for the third time, as I was leaning forward out of the box which gave on the stage she glanced up at me rapidly and bowed to me after her last Exit.

At that instant the villainous Jew entered my box and said, in a more servile fashion: "My Lord, the leading Actress, Miss Rachel Kahn, wants you to come and see her in her dressing-room."[4] When I went in she was seated before her mirror, staring at herself to see how well her make-up suited her after the performance was over. She just turned, smiled, held out her left hand, and said in English with a delicious foreign accent: "Won't you sit down?" That was the exact instant I had waited for, when I could gaze on her dazzling beauty and pour out—in homage to this "Juliet of a night"[5]—words of passionate praise. She said: "I adore the part of Juliet more than any other. She is so eager to be loved, knowing, as Romeo knows, that there is no other earthly flame which can give a little light and heat on this side of the grave. There's a divine madness in her love—a sacred madness, only when death is before these two lovers and behind them, I invariably shudder—almost as if a snake had stung me when looking down on Romeo in the garden, I cry

> O God, I have an ill-divining soul!
> Methinks I see thee now, thou art so low,
> As one dead in the bottom of a tomb.
> [III.v.54–56]

Then the wonderful girl began to tremble: she fixed her fiery eyes on mine: and was on the point of saying something that I *felt* must be wonderful, when, to our mutual horror, the door was violently flung open, and in reeled her rather drunken mother. The blood went to the girl's face, she blushed crimson under her paint: and, utterly disregarding her mother, stood up, took my hand warmly in both of hers and then went with me into the passage and said: "It may shame you that you have witnessed this lifelong shame of mine, my shameless mother. Write down for me your address and your name. Yes, on that card of yours: let me see: Fountain Court, The Temple. Indeed I ought to know that—What have you written? 'Come and see me next Friday at 3.30.' I shall be there without fault." She shoved my card into her bodice, turned on her heels and slammed the door with much violence behind her. I imagined the scene, her storm of rage, and with heaven knows, what result.

East and West End Silhouettes[1]

I

Those dark, curious cornered, evil-smelling streets near the Docks have a wicked air peculiar to themselves;[2] they give one a sensation which few even of the most dilapidated alleys on the other side of the main road can impress upon a casual wayfarer. They make one think of Méryon's Rue des Mauvais garçons:[3] that curiously suggestive etching with so curiously suggestive a name. What is it, exactly, that causes the dishonesty of a row of mere houses? Here, at all events, you meet few people, you hear no noise, you see nothing actually suspicious behind any of these dark shutters, those undrawn blinds. Yet it is with a strangely suspicious sensation that you pass doorway after doorway feeling at every step that next moment—next moment—yes, the street is quiet, but you realize that it is plotting something secretly, and you walk in suspense at this suspended villainy of things.

II

A broad dimly lighted street near the Docks. Most of the windows are dark: the street sleeps. There are few passers and they flit by like wicked shadows. As I walk slowly onwards I see a low window with neither blinds nor shutters. Attracted by the bright light, I stop and look in. It is a small poorly-furnished room that I see. In the middle is a table, covered with the remains of supper. There is a lamp on the table, and grouped around it, chatting eagerly, their faces bent forward into the circle of the light, are four people, evidently Jews. The two whom I see in profile have the long hooked noses, the black, shifty eyes, the tangled black hair of the definite tribal type. The woman who faces me is partly hidden by the lamp. But I can see her coarse black hair and the dark skin of her cheek. The one who sits with her back to the window has the bent and mountainous shoulders of a very old woman. They have finished supper, but they still sit around the table eagerly discussing something. It is not the party at the table, however, that makes me pause so long at the window. Off in a corner, almost close to the door, sits a young girl of delicately Jewish beauty. She sits motionless, absorbed, lost in some vague reveries, her head lifted, her eyes gazing into space, her lips slightly parted. She sits as Thérèse sits in Zola's play,[4] self-absorbed, unconscious of those about her—the greedy, gossiping folks around the table. Of what is she thinking, I ask myself, as at last I move on my way, haunted by the clear pallor of that strange, mystic face, those visionary eyes, that immovable attitude.

III

We heard the sound of a barrel organ, and turning the corner saw before us a large open space, which seemed almost filled with little dancing figures. The children had swarmed out from the network of streets surrounding us, some, no doubt, had followed the organ from afar. And now it was a patter of shoes on the rough pavement, the rising and falling of little petticoats in the air, the stirring of scores of little dirty-stockinged legs in time to the rhythm of the tune. They were dancing those elaborate step-dances which are the fashion just now among the street children, and, as always happens, some were teaching others how to do it, with serious airs of importance, a serious attention on the part of the learner. Soberly dressed, dressed in tawdry finery, dressed in rags; all with holes in their stockings, with frocks that lacked buttons, frocks coming undone; hatless for the most part, or swinging their hats in their hands, the children danced to the sound of the barrel-organ. Some of them, trained, no doubt, in the pantomime, twirled their legs with astonishing dexterity; all kept up the step with tireless persistence. The whole court was a heaving sea of vari-colored skirts. It was with solemn faces, without cries or laughter, that the children danced—little pale creatures, who took their amusement with profound seriousness. Around them was an outer edge of bigger girls, of women with babies, who looked on curiously. My friend, the actress, leaned back against the window-sill of a shop, drawing her cloak around her. Her face wore that tantalizing smile which it wears so often, and which melts her clear features, into so novel, so attractive a grace. Our eyes met: it was only thus that either of us confessed how both longed to be dancing with the children.

IV

At the end of the long and narrow street we had been following a broad road cut crosswise. Two public-houses stood sentinel at the corner. As we passed between them, out into the open space, one of the glass doors of the public house on our left swung open. A fine-looking woman of about thirty ("something like Ada Rehan,"[5] said the actress), leant up against the wall, putting her handkerchief up to her flushed face—so bold and handsome under its tumbled cloud of blond hair. She was quite drunk, and she sobbed in little short gasps, jerking out a few convulsive words between her sobs. A man, leering sympathetically tried to pacify her, while another man, who had followed her out of the public house, stood a yard or two away, with an air half-ashamed, half-defiant. It was he, no doubt, who had made the poor thing cry. With furtive air he approached her: perhaps he wanted some more money out of her pocket, for he made a feeble attempt to wheedle himself back into her favor. But the woman, holding herself against the wall, only plunged the handkerchief more desperately into her streaming eyes. The man shrugged his shoulders, and stepped heavily back against the swing door. It opened, closed behind him. We walked on, and turning some time after, still saw the blonde woman leaning up against the wall, with the light of the gas-lamp on her yellow hair, her handsome crimsoned face, the pocket handkerchief that had once been white. And the other man, with the sympathetic leer, was still by her side. He had come nearer.

V

Ahead of us the road is ablaze with lights. Gradually, as we came nearer, they revolve themselves into flaring naphtha-lamps, swinging from the cross-timbers of the stalls that line both pavements. It is now late; the middle of the road is strewed with vegetable refuse in which our feet sink; but there is still plenty of stuff on the stalls, there are still people passing, people pausing to scrutinize the goods. Odors of stale meat, of stale fish, of stale vegetables, mingle in inexpressible confusion with the musty smell of cast-off clothes, the pleasant savor of hot chestnuts, of hot potatoes. Butchers flourishing long knives in front of their pale, or dark-colored joints, shout one another down in voices grown hoarse with much shouting. The shrill voices of women rise from the green grocers, the fancy stalls; puckering their inflamed cheeks, the saleswomen cry their wares. And it is now a line of intent faces before a stall, the eyes all turned in one direction where the seller is offering a great bargain; and now an avid circle about a swinging lamp the light full on their open mouths, their tired, staring eyes, their wisps of untidy hair, as some cheap-jack holds up his little boxes of pills, or his cheapest knives in the market. Jews elbow past, talking in various dialects; young girls with babies drag themselves wearily along, stopping, half to look at the things, half for the sake of a rest. And there is a hubbub of voices, a confused movement, a constant flickering and alteration of lights. As we turned up one of the side streets into semi-darkness, the whole lighted scene seems to suddenly go out, as if one had extinguished it, and the noise itself, though we are but a few yards distant, drops all at once to a vague, and indistinguishable murmur.

VI

I started out the other night with the intention of going to a music hall. But I had not got far along the Strand, when I met Scaramouch, John Davidson, the poet; and Saint-Just, John Barlas, the revolutionary.[7] Scaramouch is irresistible when he insists; the three of us fancied ourselves to be poets; and when three poets meet, it is enough for one of them to have made up his mind. So presently we found ourselves in the Café Royal. Saint-Just quenched a modest thirst with a small lager; I, who can never drink beer except in Germany, ordered a vermouth; Scaramouch gratified his fantasy with an absinthe. It was not the absinthe, nor the vermouth, nor the lager: but we soon began talking metaphysics. There is a subtle influence in the heat, the glare, the reduplicating mirrors, of the golden café with its clumsy goddesses tumbling through the roof: it shuts one upon one oneself, exciting and oppressing the brain at once. We talked of London, of the impression its streets gave us. "I feel as I walk along the Strand," said Saint-Just, "how kind it would be if I were to stab every second man I meet:—I wouldn't do it for the world," he added gently. "Kind to which?" I asked, "the first or the second?" Scaramouch leaned across the table between us. "Stab *him*," he said; "he's the second man!"

So it was that we began to discuss the problem of existence. The ideal man, to Scaramouch, is Shakespeare; to Saint-Just Buddha. "Starve yourself for three weeks," said Saint-Just, with his fervent seriousness, "and then light will come to you: then you will be in a condition to receive it." "Let me rather," retorted Scaramouch fiercely, "be as Hercules when he went to call on the Danaides; only thus can one front the prob-

lems of the universe as they should be fronted." And he sipped his absinthe. For my part I confess that I have never been very anxious to
solve problems. I never succeeded in solving those of Euclid when I was
at school, and I scarcely fancy I am likely to have greater success with
more difficult ones now. Still, it is interesting, once in a while, in the
Café Royal, watching the smoke curl upward from one's cigarette, to
set the mind at work on the trick of "spiral ascensionist." As interesting
as it is useless—that we all know. So when the problems had been
examined in all their angles, and problems superimposed upon problems
till they touched the ceiling, I was rejoiced to find that the conversation
was slipping round towards art. The soul in art: that was how we slid
imperceptibly into the subject. Not that the soul in art seems to me of
much more interest than the soul in itself—at all events as a matter for
discussion. But the Café Royal in art—that, if you like, has its interest!
And we were soon confessing to one another that each of us had written
a poem about the Café Royal—something modern, modernity in poetry.
Saint-Just's was about a lady with amber gloves; my lady was in black,
black from head to feet; as for Scaramouch, he declared that poem,
title, subject, everything was copyright, so I dare not breathe a syllable
about it. Perhaps I may venture to quote my sonnet. I did not quote it
then: we are merciful and spare one another, but why spare the public?

Ambiguë

Is there a meaning in your mystery,
    Strange eyes, so cold, so mirror-like, whose smile
    Lures, but declares not? What determinate wile
Lurks in that passionate ambiguity?
How steadily your gaze from him to me
    Turns all its jewelled brilliance! For the man,
    He holds you by his purse-strings, while he can.
He holds you—as the fisher holds the sea!

Sphinx, I adore you, I am at your feet.
    (Heed not the man: I speak but through the eyes!)
    But do not hear me: change not: nay, smile thus
    Forever with that air ambiguous
What lies beneath it? Nay, I know not, sweet,
Her if the snake is in your paradise.

There is an impression, which, at all events, is after nature. Shall our theorizings decide that its being so is a merit or a defect? All art is founded upon truth, we were told once; upon lies, affirms a modern apostle. The nearest approach to nature—to nature, which may be beautiful or which may be ugly in itself; or the exclusive preoccupation with beauty—which is the legitimate aim of the artist? First principles in art—as useless a search perhaps, as the search for other kinds of first principles. It is not in the Café Royal certainly, that one can find the answer: and so we fell again to questioning other matters—religion, conduct, the present, the future. Saint-Just, like all revolutionaries, is a visionary, and he mildly but confidently asserted his power to foretell the future. "Well," said Scaramouch, "you can foresee a revolution, can you? I can foresee the Cromwell, the Napoleon, who will come after, and master the revolution. It is not very difficult to foresee the future of nations." And he began puffing his pipe vigorously. "In a million of years or so," he went on, "you'll admit that the world will be done for, used up, burnt out, a mere moon, without inhabitants, without memory of Shakespeare, without memory of Oscar Wilde, of you and me—" but here the smoke from his pipe obscured him, and I lost the conclusion from these comfortable premises. My cigarette had gone out, like our speculations, which had come to nothing—not even a conviction. And the mirrors seemed to surround us like the cold limits of the visible, showing us wherever we looked, only ourselves and our fellows; a brilliant light, a crowd, an hour's pastime. But outside, impenetrably shut off from us until our time came to rise and go forth, there was the night, there were the stars.

That lighted gulf, before which the footlights are the flaming stars between world and world, shows the city the passions and that beauty which the soul of men in cities is occupied in weeding out of its own fruitful and prepared soil.

Ernest Dowson[1]

* * * I cannot remember my first meeting with Ernest Dowson.[2] It may have been in 1891, at one of the meetings of the Rhymers' Club, in an upper room at the Cheshire Cheese, where long clay pipes lay in slim heaps on the wooden tables, between tankards of ale; and young poets, then very young, recited their own verses to one another with a desperate and ineffectual attempt to get into key with the Latin Quarter.[3] Though few of us were, as a matter of fact, Anglo-Saxon, we could not help feeling that we were in London, and the atmosphere of London is not the atmosphere of movements or of societies. In Paris it is the most natural thing in the world to meet and discuss literature, ideas, one's own and one another's work; and it can be done without pretentiousness or constraint, because, to the Latin mind, art, ideas, one's work and the work of one's friends, are definite and important things, which it would never occur to any one to take anything but seriously. In England art has to be protected, not only against the world, but against oneself and one's fellow-artist, by a kind of affected modesty which is the Englishman's natural pose, half pride and half self-distrust. So this brave venture of the Rhymers' Club, though it lasted for two or three years, and produced two little books of verse[4] which will some day be literary curiosities, was not quite a satisfactory kind of *cénacle*. Dowson, who enjoyed the real thing so much in Paris, did not, I think, go very often; but his contributions to the first book of the club were at once the most delicate and the most distinguished poems which it contained. Was it, after all, at one of these meetings that I first saw him, or was it, perhaps, at another haunt of some of us at that time, a semi-literary tavern near Leicester Square, chosen for its convenient position between two stage-doors?[5] It was at the time when one or two of us sincerely worshipped the ballet; Dowson, alas, never. I could never get him to see that charm in harmonious and coloured movement, like bright shadows seen through the floating gauze of the music, which held me night after night at the two theatres which alone seemed to me to give an amusing colour to one's dreams. Neither the stage nor the stage-door had any attraction for him; but he came to the tavern because it was a tavern, and because he could meet his friends there. Even before that time I have a vague impression of having met him, I forget where, certainly at night; and of having been struck, even then, by a look and

manner of pathetic charm, a sort of Keats-like face, the face of a demoralised Keats, and by something curious in the contrast of a manner exquisitely refined, with an appearance generally somewhat dilapidated. That impression was only accentuated later on, when I came to know him, and the manner of his life, much more intimately.

I think I may date my first impression of what one calls "the real man" (as if it were more real than the poet of the disembodied verses!) from an evening in which he first introduced me to those charming supper-houses, open all night through, the cabmen's shelters. I had been talking over another vagabond poet, Lord Rochester, with a charming and sympathetic descendant of that poet, and somewhat late at night we had come upon Dowson and another man wandering aimlessly and excitedly about the streets. He invited us to supper, we did not quite realise where, and the cabman came in with us, as we were welcomed, cordially and without comment, at a little place near the Langham; and, I recollect, very hospitably entertained. The cooking differs, as I found in time, in these supper houses, but there the rasher was excellent and the cups admirably clean. Dowson was known there, and I used to think he was always at his best in a cabmen's shelter. Without a certain sordidness in his surroundings he was never quite comfortable, never quite himself; and at those places you are obliged to drink nothing stronger than coffee or tea. I liked to see him occasionally, for a change, drinking nothing stronger than coffee or tea. At Oxford, I believe, his favourite form of intoxication had been haschisch; afterwards he gave up this somewhat elaborate experiment in visionary sensations for readier means of oblivion; but he returned to it, I remember, for at least one afternoon, in a company of which I had been the gatherer and of which I was the host. I remember him sitting, a little anxiously, with his chin on his breast, awaiting the magic, half-shy in the midst of a bright company of young people whom he had only seen across the footlights. The experience was not a very successful one; it ended in what should have been its first symptom, immoderate laughter.

Always, perhaps, a little consciously, but at least always sincerely, in search of new sensations, my friend found what was for him the supreme sensation in a very passionate and tender adoration of the most escaping of all ideals, the ideal of youth. Cherished, as I imagine, first only in the abstract, this search after the immature, the ripening graces which time can only spoil in the ripening, found itself at the journey's end, as some of his friends thought, a little prematurely. I was never of their opinion. I only saw twice, and for a few moments only, the young girl to whom most of his verses were to be written, and whose presence in his life may be held to account for much of that astonishing contrast between the broad outlines of his life and work.[6] The situation seemed to me of the most exquisite and appropriate impossibility. The daughter of a refugee, I believe of good family, reduced to keeping a humble restaurant in a foreign quarter of London, she listened to his verses, smiled charmingly, under her mother's eyes, on his two years' courtship, and at the end of two years married the waiter instead. Did she ever realise more than the obvious part of what was being offered to her, in this shy and eager devotion? Did it ever mean very much to her to have made and to have killed a poet? She had, at all events, the gift of evoking, and, in its way, of retaining, all that was most delicate, sensitive, shy, typically poetic, in a nature which I can only compare to a weedy garden, its grass trodden down by many feet, but with one small, carefully tended flower-bed, luminous with lilies. I used to think, sometimes, of Verlaine and his "girl-wife," the one really profound passion, certainly, of that passionate career; the charming, child-like creature, to whom he looked back, at the end of his life, with an unchanged tenderness and disappointment: "Vous n'avez rien compris à ma simplicité," as he lamented. In the case of Dowson, however, there was sort of virginal devotion, as to a Madonna; and I think had things gone happily, to a conventionally happy ending, he would have felt (dare I say?) that his ideal had been spoilt.

But, for the good fortune of poets, things rarely do go happily with them, or to conventionally happy endings. He used to dine every night at the little restaurant, and I can always see the picture, which I have so often seen through the window in passing: the narrow room with the rough tables, for the most part empty, except in the innermost corner, where Dowson would sit with that singularly sweet and singularly pathetic smile on his lips (a smile which seemed afraid of its right to be there, as if always dreading a rebuff), playing his invariable after-dinner game of cards. Friends would come in, during the hour before closing time; and the girl, her game of cards finished, would quietly disappear, leaving him with hardly more than the desire to kill another night as swiftly as possible.

Meanwhile she and the mother knew that the fragile young man who dined there so quietly every day was apt to be quite another sort of person after he had been three hours outside. It was only when his life seemed to have been irretrievably ruined that Dowson quite deliberately abandoned himself to that craving for drink, which was doubtless lying in wait for him in his blood, as consumption was also; it was only latterly, when he had no longer any interest in life, that he really wished to die. But I have never known him when he could resist either the desire or the consequences of drink. Sober, he was the most gentle, in manner the most gentlemanly, of men; unselfish to a fault, to the extent of weakness; a delightful companion, charm itself. Under the influence of drink, he became almost literally insane, certainly quite irresponsible. He fell into furious and unreasoning passions; a vocabulary unknown to him at other times sprang up like a whirlwind; he seemed always about to commit some act of absurd violence. Along with that forgetfulness came other memories. As long as he was conscious of himself, there was but one woman for him in the world, and for her he had an infinite tenderness and an infinite respect. When that face faded from him, he saw all the other faces, and he saw no more difference than between sheep and sheep. Indeed, that curious love of the sordid, so common an affectation of the modern decadent, and with him so genuine, grew upon him, and dragged him into more and more sorry corners of a life which was never exactly "gay" to him.[7] His father, when he died, left him in possession of an old dock, where for a time he lived in a mouldering house, in that squalid part of the East End which he came to know so well, and to feel so strangely at home in. He drank the poisonous liquors of those pot-houses which swarm about the docks; he drifted about in whatever company came in his way; he let heedlessness develop into a curious disregard of personal tidiness. In Paris, Les Halles took the place of the docks. At Dieppe, where I saw so much of him one summer, he discovered strange, squalid haunts about the harbour, where he made friends with amazing innkeepers, and got into rows with the fishermen who came in to drink after midnight. At Brussels, where I was with him at the time of the Kermesse, he flung himself into all that riotous Flemish life, with a zest for what was most sordidly riotous in it. It was his own way of escape from life.

To Dowson, as to all those who have not been "content to ask unlikely gifts in vain," nature, life, destiny, whatever one chooses to call it, that power which is strength to the strong, presented itself as a barrier against which all one's strength only served to dash one to more hopeless ruin. He was not a dreamer; destiny passes by the dreamer, sparing him because he clamours for nothing. He was a child, clamouring for so many things, all impossible. With a body too weak for ordinary existence, he desired all the enchantments of all the senses. With a soul too shy to tell its own secret, except in exquisite evasions, he desired the boundless confidence of love. He sang one tune, over and over, and no one listened to him. He had only to form the most simple wish, and it was denied him. He gave way to ill-luck, not knowing that he was giving way to his own weakness, and he tried to escape from the consciousness of things as they were at the best, by voluntarily choosing to accept them at their worst. For with him it was always voluntary. He was never quite without money; he had a little money of his own, and he had for many years a weekly allowance from a publisher, in return for translations from the French, or, if he chose to do it, original work. He was unhappy, and he dared not think. To unhappy men, thought, if it can be set at work on abstract questions, is the only substitute for happiness; if it has not strength to overleap the barrier which shuts one in upon oneself, it is the one unwearying torture. Dowson had exquisite sensibility, he vibrated in harmony with every delicate emotion; but he had no outlook, he had not the escape of intellect. His only escape, then, was to plunge into the crowd, to fancy that he lost sight of himself as he disappeared from the sight of others. The more he soiled himself at that gross contact, the further would he seem to be from what beckoned to him in one vain illusion after another vain illusion, in the delicate places of the world. Seeing himself moving to the sound of lutes, in some courtly disguise, down an alley of Watteau's Versailles, while he touched finger-tips with a divine creature in rose-leaf silks, what was there left for him, as the dream obstinately refused to realise itself, but a blind flight into some Teniers kitchen, where boors are making merry, without thought of yesterday or to-morrow? There, perhaps, in that ferment of animal life, he could forget life as he dreamed it, with too faint hold upon his dreams to make dreams come true.

For, there is not a dream which may not come true, if we have the energy which makes, or chooses, our own fate. We can always, in this world, get what we want, if we will it intensely and persistently enough. Whether we shall get it sooner or later is the concern of fate; but we shall get it. It may come when we have no longer any use for it, when we have gone on willing it out of habit, or so as not to confess that we have failed. But it will come. So few people succeed greatly because so few people can conceive a great end, and work towards that end without deviating and without tiring. But we all know that the man who works for money day and night gets rich; and the man who works day and night for no matter what kind of material power, gets the power. It is the same with the deeper, more spiritual, as it seems vaguer issues, which make for happiness and every intangible success. It is only the dreams of those light sleepers who dream faintly that do not come true.

We get out of life, all of us, what we bring to it; that, and that only, is what it can teach us. There are men whom Dowson's experiences would have made great men, or great writers; for him they did very little. Love and regret, with here and there the suggestion of an uncomforting pleasure snatched by the way, are all that he has to sing of; and he could have sung of them at much less "expense of spirit," and, one fancies, without the "waste of shame" at all. Think what Villon got directly out of his own life, what Verlaine, what Musset, what Byron, got directly out of their own lives! It requires a strong man to "sin strongly" and profit by it. To Dowson the tragedy of his own life could only have resulted in an elegy. "I have flung roses, roses, riotously with the throng," he confesses, in his most beautiful poem; but it was as one who flings roses in a dream, as he passes with shut eyes through an unsubstantial throng. The depths into which he plunged were always waters of oblivion, and he returned forgetting them. He is always a very ghostly lover, wandering in a land of perpetual twilight, as he holds a whispered *colloque sentimental* with the ghost of an old love:

> Dans le vieux parc solitaire et glacé,
> Deux spectres ont évoqué le passé.[8]

It was, indeed, almost a literal unconsciousness, as of one who leads two lives, severed from one another as completely as sleep is from waking. Thus we get in his work very little of the personal appeal of those to whom riotous living, misery, a cross destiny, have been of so real a value. And it is important to draw this distinction, if only for the benefit of those young men who are convinced that the first step towards genius is disorder. Dowson is precisely one of the people who are pointed out as confirming this theory. And yet Dowson was precisely one of those who owed least to circumstances; and, in succumbing to them, he did no more than succumb to the destructive forces which, shut up within him, pulled down the house of life upon his own head.

A soul "unspotted from the world," in a body which one sees visibly soiling under one's eyes; that improbability is what all who knew him saw in Dowson, as his youthful physical grace gave way year by year, and the personal charm underlying it remained unchanged. There never was a simpler or more attaching charm, because there never was a sweeter or more honest nature. It was not because he ever said anything particularly clever or particularly interesting, it was not because he gave you ideas, or impressed you by any strength or originality, that you liked to be with him; but because of a certain engaging quality, which seemed unconscious of itself, which was never anxious to be or to do anything, which simply existed, as perfume exists in a flower. Drink was like a heavy curtain, blotting out everything of a sudden; when the curtain lifted, nothing had changed. Living always that double life, he had his true and his false aspect, and the true life was the expression of that fresh, delicate, and uncontaminated nature which some of us knew in him, and which remains for us, untouched by the other, in every line that he wrote.

Dowson was the only poet I ever knew who cared more for his prose than for his verse; but he was wrong, and it is not by prose that he will

live, exquisite as that prose was at its best. He wrote two novels in col-
laboration with Mr Arthur Moore: *A Comedy of Masks,* in 1893, and
Adrian Rome, in 1899, both done under the influence of Mr Henry
James, both interesting because they were personal studies, and studies
of known surroundings, rather than for their actual value as novels. A
volume of "Stories and Studies in Sentiment," called *Dilemmas,* in
which the influence of Mr Wedmore[9] was felt in addition to the influence of Mr James, appeared in 1895. Several other short stories, among
his best work in prose, have not yet been reprinted from the *Savoy.* Some
translations from the French, done as hack work, need not be mentioned
here, though they were never without some traces of his peculiar quality
of charm in language. The short stories were indeed rather "studies in
sentiment" than stories; studies of singular delicacy, but with only a faint
hold on life, so that perhaps the best of them was not unnaturally a study
in the approaches of death: "The Dying of Francis Donne."[10] For the
most part they dealt with the same motives as the poems, hopeless and
reverent love, the ethics of renunciation, the disappointment of those
who are too weak or too unlucky to take what they desire. They have
a sad and quiet beauty of their own, the beauty of second thoughts and
subdued emotions, of choice and scholarly English, moving in the more
fluid and reticent harmonies of prose almost as daintily as if it were
moving to the measure of verse. Dowson's care over English prose was
like that of a Frenchman writing his own language with the respect
which Frenchmen pay to French. Even English things had to come to
him through France, if he was to prize them very highly; and there is a
passage in *Dilemmas* which I have always thought very characteristic of
his own tastes, as it refers to an "infinitesimal library, a few French
novels, an Horace, and some well-thumbed volumes of the modern
English poets in the familiar edition of Tauchnitz." He was Latin by all
his affinities, and that very quality of slightness, of parsimony almost, in
his dealings with life and the substance of art, connects him with the
artists of Latin races, who have always been so fastidious in their rejec-
tion of mere nature, when it comes too nakedly or too clamorously into
sight and hearing, and so gratefully content with a few choice things
faultlessly done.

And Dowson in his verse (the *Verses* of 1896, *The Pierrot of the
Minute, a dramatic phantasy in one act,* of 1897, the posthumous volume,
Decorations) was the same scrupulous artist as in his prose, and more
felicitously at home there. He was quite Latin in his feeling for youth,
and death, and "the old age of roses," and the pathos of our little hour
in which to live and love; Latin in his elegance, reticence, and simple
grace in the treatment of these motives; Latin, finally, in his sense of
their sufficiency for the whole of one's mental attitude. He used the

commonplaces of poetry frankly, making them his own by his belief in them: the Horatian Cynara or Neobule was still the natural symbol for him when he wished to be most personal. I remember his saying to me that his ideal of a line of verse was the line of Poe:

> The viol, the violet, and the vine;
> ["City in the Sea," *Poems,* 1831]

and the gracious, not remote or unreal beauty, which clings about such words and such images as these, was always to him the true poetical beauty. There never was a poet to whom verse came more naturally, for the song's sake; his theories were all æsthetic, almost technical ones, such as a theory, indicated by his preference for the line of Poe, that the letter "v" was the most beautiful of the letters, and could never be brought into verse too often. For any more abstract theories he had neither tolerance nor need. Poetry as a philosophy did not exist for him; it existed solely as the loveliest of the arts. He loved the elegance of Horace, all that was most complex in the simplicity of Poe, most bird-like in the human melodies of Verlaine. He had the pure lyric gift, unweighted or unballasted by any other quality of mind or emotion; and a song, for him, was music first, and then whatever you please afterwards, so long as it suggested, never told, some delicate sentiment, a sigh or a caress; finding words, at times, as perfect as these words of a poem headed, "O Mors! quam amara est memoria tua homini pacem habenti in substantiis suis":

> Exceeding sorrow
>   Consumeth my sad heart!
> Because to-morrow
>   We must depart,
> Now is exceeding sorrow
>   All my part!
>
> Give over playing,
>   Cast thy viol away:
> Merely laying
>   Thine head my way:
> Prithee, give over playing,
>   Grave or gay.
>
> Be no word spoken;
>   Weep nothing: let a pale

Silence, unbroken
  Silence prevail!
Prithee, be no word spoken,
  Lest I fail!

Forget to-morrow!
  Weep nothing: only lay
In silent sorrow
  Thine head my way:
Let us forget to-morrow,
  This one day!
            [*Verses*, 1896]

There, surely, the music of silence speaks, if it has ever spoken. The words seem to tremble back into the silence which their whisper has interrupted, but not before they have created for us a mood, such a mood as the Venetian Pastoral of Giorgione renders in painting. Languid, half inarticulate, coming from the heart of a drowsy sorrow very conscious of itself, and not less sorrowful because it sees its own face looking mournfully back out of the water, the song seems to have been made by some fastidious amateur of grief, and it has all the sighs and tremors of the mood, wrought into a faultless strain of music. Stepping out of a paradise in which pain becomes so lovely, he can see the beauty which is the other side of madness, and, in a sonnet "To One in Bedlam," can create a more positive, a more poignant mood, with this fine subtlety:

With delicate, mad hands, behind his sordid bars,
Surely he hath his posies, which they tear and twine;
Those scentless wisps of straw, that miserably line
His strait, caged universe, whereat the dull world stares,
Pedant and pitiful. O, how his rapt gaze wars
With their stupidity! Know they what dreams divine
Lift his long, laughing reveries like enchanted wine,
And make his melancholy germane to the stars'?

O lamentable brother! if those pity thee,
Am I not fain of all thy lone eyes promise me;
Half a fool's kingdom, far from men who sow and reap,
All their days, vanity? Better than mortal flowers,
Thy moon-kissed roses seem: better than love or sleep,
The star-crowned solitude of thine oblivious hours!
            [*Verses*, 1896]

Here, in the moment's intensity of this comradeship with madness, observe how beautiful the whole thing becomes; how instinctively the imagination of the poet turns what is sordid into a radiance, all stars and flowers and the divine part of forgetfulness! It is a symbol of the two sides of his own life: the side open to the street, and the side turned away from it, where he could "hush and bless himself with silence." No one ever worshipped beauty more devoutly, and just as we see him here transfiguring a dreadful thing with beauty, so we shall see, everywhere in his work, that he never admitted an emotion which he could not so transfigure. He knew his limits only too well; he knew that the deeper and graver things of life were for the most part outside the circle of his magic; he passed them by, leaving much of himself unexpressed, because he would permit himself to express nothing imperfectly, or according to anything but his own conception of the dignity of poetry. In the lyric in which he has epitomised himself and his whole life, a lyric which is certainly one of the greatest lyrical poems of our time, "Non sum qualis eram bonæ sub regno Cynaræ," he has for once said everything, and he has said it to an intoxicating and perhaps immortal music:

Last night, ah, yesternight, betwixt her lips and mine,
There fell thy shadow, Cynara! thy breath was shed
Upon my soul between the kisses and the wine;
And I was desolate and sick of an old passion,
　　Yea, I was desolate and bowed my head:
I have been faithful to thee, Cynara! in my fashion.

All night upon mine heart I felt her warm heart beat,
Night-long within mine arms in love and sleep she lay;
Surely the kisses of her bought red mouth were sweet;
But I was desolate and sick of an old passion,
　　When I awoke and found the dawn was grey:
I have been faithful to thee, Cynara! in my fashion.

I have forgot much, Cynara! gone with the wind,
Flung roses, roses riotously with the throng,
Dancing, to put thy pale, lost lilies out of mind;
But I was desolate and sick of an old passion,
　　Yea, all the time, because the dance was long
I have been faithful to thee, Cynara! in my fashion.

I cried for madder music and for stronger wine,
But when the feast is finished and the lamps expire,

Then falls thy shadow, Cynara! the night is thine;
And I am desolate and sick of an old passion,
   Yea, hungry for the lips of my desire:
I have been faithful to thee, Cynara! in my fashion.
                       [*Verses,* 1896]

Here, perpetuated by some unique energy of a temperament rarely so much the master of itself, is the song of passion and the passions, at their eternal war in the soul which they quicken or deaden, and in the body which they break down between them. In the second book, the book of *Decorations,* there are a few pieces which repeat, only more faintly, this very personal note. Dowson could never have developed; he had already said, in his first book of verse, all that he had to say. Had he lived, had he gone on writing, he could only have echoed himself; and probably it would have been the less essential part of himself; his obligation to Swinburne, always evident, increasing as his own inspiration failed him. He was always without ambition, writing to please his own fastidious taste, with a kind of proud humility in his attitude towards the public, not expecting or requiring recognition. He died obscure, having ceased to care even for the delightful labour of writing. He died young, worn out by what was never really life to him, leaving a little verse which has the pathos of things too young and too frail ever to grow old.

[Henri Toulouse-Lautrec]1

There was something in Lautrec when he was most exasperated that was singular, angular, vivid, discordant, and yet exquisitely fascinating. There was no harmony in his face, but the dwellers under this strange mask were three, and the problem was how they contrived their common life. When his speech loosened, and threw off what had tied down the very wings of his imagination, that voice rose and soared, and seemed to me at times like the wild clamours of some savage eagle, that shouted and knew why it shouted, high up in the heavens. When he was at his best he debated with one, with a certain fury and a certain conviction, as to the existence of the dregs of the soul, and as to what is the best intoxication for its petulance and wonder and mockery, and I have heard him imagine that one, risen from the dead at the day of judgment, might see an arm that reaches out, and hides the sea and the stars; or that one might have been present when Christ, hanging on the Cross, laments that the bones of his feet are stretched with extreme pain. I said to him once that in an ancient Welsh poem there is a fierce, loud complaint, in which mere physical likeness and the intolerance of age translate themselves into a limitless hunger, and into that wisdom which is the sorrowful desire of beauty. And then we spoke of the mediæval hatred of winter and cold, with a far more unbounded hatred of old age and sickness and the disasters which are not bred in the world, but in a blind part of the Universe itself; older than the world, as old as chaos, out of which the world was made. Transfiguring things fearful and fervent into forms of pure Beauty, worshipping, as he did, Beauty herself with more than a lover's devout adoration, these fervent and fearful things, turning back upon themselves, became luxurious, assumed women's forms in which one saw revealed, bodily and spiritually, the apparent innocence of the flesh (which is rarely if ever innocent) and the ignorance of the spirit (which is rarely if ever ignorant). And, like Rodin, he is possessed with the desire of seizing the unseizable, the inexplicable force of that mystery which surrounds the vital energy of the earth itself—and out of these forces in the eternal battle of sex he also has chosen for the most part the universal vivifying force of sex. And his women, at their worst, live only with the life of their animal desire, and that obsession has carried them beyond the wholesome bounds of Nature, into the violence of a perversity which is at times almost or literally insane.

Just as Lautrec, who knew Edmond de Goncourt, preferred a certain perversity in Nature, to what in Nature is natural, so both painter and novelist admired passionate and sensuous things, partly for their own sake, partly that they had to be complex with all the complexity of a deliberately depraved instinct. In any case Lautrec possessed in the extreme, what I have always possessed, an unholy fascination for forms of evil, of cruelty, of horror; for abnormalities, for the exaggeration of things to a point in which one's nerves create their own visions. What is in one's blood, remains there always; and if cruelty is to be found somewhere in one's blood, there it remains always. * * *

Lautrec's immense originality was too much a part of the man himself, yet in certain senses so wide apart from him that the man as one knew him and the painter as one admired him, were in a sense *homo duplex.* Women he loved too much (if that were possible in one's Paris!) and for reasons known equally to himself and to them: occult and abstract reasons, in all conscience; *Les Filles,* in a word, these Lamias and Cleopatras and Messalinas and Lucrezias and Lesbias and Marcellas, who at least ought to be illegitimately descended from Lilith, whose amorous mouths cry and lie and entreat and deny; who are made to prey on us and for us to prey on; as God's animals always must. And, it may be justly said that it is those of us who love them most passionately and who are most passionately loved by them in return, are the artists who love women next to their Art; who, being poets, sing of them; who, being painters, paint them; who, being sculptors, mould them in clay and fix their forms in living marble.

It is impossible to give what one calls the spiciest of the anecdotes that went raging over artistic Paris in regard to this singular—this abnormal —product of nature, Lautrec; for reasons certainly well known to those who loved him, who hated him. Yet in spite of the conflicting legends that disturbed Paris, but which rarely disturbed him—legends that meant no more to him than they did to Villiers de l'Isle Adam—no modern painter was more popular than he was from La place Clichy to La place Pigalle. Always, like Villiers, he was looked upon by most people as an amusing kind of madman, a little dangerous, whose ideas, as they floated freely over the café tables, it was at times highly profitable to steal. Lautrec's life being exasperating to himself, he loved to exasperate the general public. One anecdote can be given, the meaning of which is, perhaps, occult. One day, in the house of a friend, Lautrec wanders about the anteroom, in the act of leaving, as if he were searching for something he fails to find. Anticipating his friend's interrogation, he says to him, softly: "J'avais un petit bâton!"

Costly objects, this man of nerves simply could not exist without. And, when he wanted to, he would trail some of them from his studio to one of the evil houses he was frequenting; these houses of iniquity from which he would emerge into some wintry murk of that city of perdition which is Paris, into a world sin-steeped; out of a world steeped in sin to some house of perdition.

As for these infamous Houses of Sin, he knew them and loved them, loved them too much, with no lover's love, but with a love of women's flesh; together with a desire to escape the horrid crew of daily tiresome deeds, and to find himself in heated and perfumed rooms, where the dim alcoves add their esoteric obscurity to the room's mystery, where the winds wafted themselves down the chimney or through a crevice in door or window; where he designs all the sins on the walls and their names in scarlet letters. And, where the revels go on all night, and those lost creatures that have their souls to save give themselves, not always ignobly. I think some vision rises in those wild and mad and visionary eyes of his, eyes malign and evil, of something far beyond those tempting sins— these sins for which he pays year by year so heavy a price—of some kind of salvation, of some kind of redemption beyond the grave.

Auguste Rodin[1]

I

I met Auguste Rodin in Paris, 182 rue de l'Université, in May, 1892. The last time that I saw him was at a dinner given in Old Burlington Street in 1907. No one who has seen him can ever forget his singular appearance. There before me stood a giant of genius, with the timidity of the colossus; with a face in which strength struggled with passion; with veiled blue eyes that dilated like the eyes of a parrot when he spoke of anything that interested him deeply. He made few gestures; only when he sat, with his great hands folded on his knees, the gestures he made were for a purpose, never for an effect. I was struck by his quietness, his simplicity, a certain caution which comes from a suspicion that he is not being taken simply enough. When he talked of books or of his art or of nature there was always the same freshness and profundity.

It was in Meudon, in 1903, that Rodin spoke to me about Gustave Moreau.[2] He said Moreau was a man of science, one of a generation which was taught to study art in the galleries, and not from nature. He was a great combiner. He took colour from Delacroix, his figures from the antique. He was not a genius, not a creator, not the great artist some have called him, but he belongs to the second rank. His greatest defect was that the figures which should be the principal part of the composition were uninteresting; the detail and the surroundings took up most of his interest. *Il était froid au fond*, said Rodin. * * *

He spoke to me also of modern dress; what could be done with it? It all depends on the suggestion of the nude underneath the clothes. The beauty of woman's costume is that the woman is underneath, and lends it some of her life. It makes him sad to see old clothes hanging in shop-windows—they seem so empty of life, waiting to become alive. He spoke of the way in which the nude is suggested here, simplified by some fine sweep. He has not done it because he has been engaged in other work and so has had no time even to attempt it. It can never be as great as the nude, but the eighteenth century had shown that it can be delightful.

When I first saw him he said to me that his secret consisted in *exaggeration:* that in this way he gets his effects without any of the hardness of other sculptors. As he showed me his mysterious little statue—the man kneeling so strangely in adoration before the woman in whom is imaged the sphinx and the child—he said to me: "Tell me what it means—what is your impression?"

"*Le mystère de l'amour,*" I said.

I saw the *Danaid* slightly enlarged, with its wonderful flesh, the palpitation of the very dimples. Certainly no one but Rodin has been so tender with women in his exquisite creations; none has ever caught so much of the eternal feminine as this sculptor of Hell. I saw the bust of Puvis de Chavannes[3] in marble, wonderfully modelled; the lines of the neck coming out like real flesh, the modelling of the ear, the lines of the face. Yet in so wonderful a poise of the head one saw the ability of the expression of nullity: the look of a man who goes through a crowd and sees nothing.

When one has realized what is called the *colouring* of his statues, in a sense like that of painting, the cunning employment of shadows, the massing, the conception that begins them, the achievement that ends them, one sees little enough of the infinite secrets of this man of genius. Let me choose, for instance, the exquisitely enlaced couple where a youth and a maiden are clasped in a virginal embrace—the shadow of the hair falling along his cheeks—with so lovely and discreet a shadow, when the lips press the hair of the maiden; her face is blotted out under his cheek: one sees it, lost in ecstasy, behind. And in these who lie in a space of small rock, one sees the exquisite purity of the flesh, the daring of the pose, foot pressed amorously on foot: the very down of the flesh.

So, in the two qualities I have named, sweetness and strength, he is allied with Michelangelo. "For to his true admirers," wrote Pater, "there are sweetness and strength, pleasure with surprise, an energy of conception which seems at any moment about to break through all the conditions of comely grace, recovering, touch by touch, a loveliness found usually only in the simplest natural things—*ex forti dulcedo.*"[4]

Yet, in this epic in stone, stone becomes song, becomes music. And in its perfect proportions, in its harmonies, in its balance (composed of so many exquisite poems massed together) how lyric art becomes a great drama! And there is a definite reason for comparing this creation of Rodin's with both the lyrical and the dramatic arts. Did he not say to me, did he not write, of the architecture of the human body, "that it is architecture, and that architecture is comparable with it"? "Moving architecture," as he calls it in his book, "and so simple, if one possesses the secret of it, that it hurts one's eyes and yet one must see it."[5] But he said to me with his deep laugh, "instead of giving me my due as a sculptor—as to the quality of my work—they say I am a poet. Of course, when one is inspired one is a poet. Yet when they say that my inspiration gives a certain value to the theory of the poet neighbouring on folly, there they are wrong. *Je suis le contraire d'un exalté."*

In regard to this saying I asked him why he had represented Hugo naked, and he said: *"C'est plus beau."* Then he said: "It is for the Panthéon—a man in modern dress would not be in keeping there." * * *

II

The art of Rodin competes with nature rather than with the art of other sculptors. Other sculptors turn life into sculpture, he turns sculpture into life. His clay is part of the substance of the earth, and the earth still clings about it as it comes up and lives. It is at once the flower and the root; that of others is the flower only, and the plucked flower. That link with the earth, which we find in the unhewn masses of rock from which his finest creations of pure form can never quite free themselves, is the secret of his deepest force. It links his creations to nature's, in a single fashion of growth.

Rodin is a visionary, to whom art has no meaning apart from truth. His first care is to assure you, as you penetrate into that bewildering world which lies about him in his studios, that every movement arrested in these figures, all in violent action, is taken straight from nature. It is not copied, as you or I would see it; it is re-created, as he sees it. How then does he see nature? To Rodin everything that lives is beautiful, merely because it lives, and everything is equally beautiful.

Rodin believes, not as a mystic, but as a mathematician, I might almost say, in that doctrine of "correspondences" which lies at the root of most of the mystical teaching. He spies upon every gesture, knowing that if he can seize one gesture at the turn of the wave, he has seized an essential rhythm of nature. When a woman combs her hair, he will say to you, she thinks she is only combing her hair: no, she is making a gesture which flows into the eternal rhythm, which is beautiful because it lives, because it is part of that geometrical plan which nature is always weaving for us. Change the gesture as it is, give it your own conception of abstract beauty, depart ever so little from the mere truth of the movement, and the rhythm is broken, what was living is dead.

We speak of the rhythm of nature. What is it, precisely, that we mean? Rhythm, precisely, is a balance, a means of preserving equilibrium in moving bodies. The human body possesses so much volume, it has to maintain its equilibrium; if you displace its contents here, they shift there: the balance is regained by an instinctive movement of self-preservation. Thus what we call harmony is really utility, and, as always, beauty is seen to be a necessary thing, the exquisite growth of a need. And this rhythm runs through all nature, producing every grace and justifying every apparent defect. (The same swing and balance of forces make the hump on a dwarf's back and the mountain in the lap of a plain. One is not more beautiful than the other, if you will take each thing simply, in its own place. And that apparent ugliness of the average, even, has its place, does not require the heightening energy of excess to make it beautiful. It, too, has the beauty of life.)

There was a time, Rodin will tell you, when he sought for beautiful models; when he found himself disappointed, dissatisfied, before some body whose proportions did not please him. He would go on working merely because the model was there; and, after two hours' work, discover suddenly the beauty of this living thing which was turning into a new kind of life under his fingers. Why choose any longer? Why reject this always faultless material? He has come to trust nature so implicitly that he will never pose a model, leaving nature to find its own way of doing what he wants of it. All depends on the way of seeing, on the seizure of the perfect moment, on the art of rendering, in the sculptor's relief, "the instant made eternity."

To obtain grace, Rodin will say to you, you must begin with strength; otherwise the work will become hard and dry. "Quelque chose de puissant," he will repeat, with half-closed eyes, the hands clutching upon the imagined clay. If you remind him of Baudelaire's saying: "L'énergie, c'est la grâce suprême," he will accept the words as the best definition of his own meaning.

The later manner of all great artists, in every division of art, obeys the same law of growth. Aiming always at the utmost precision of rendering his subject matter, the artist comes gradually to take a different view of what precision really is. He begins by seeking a form which can express everything without leaving anything over; he desires to draw his circle round some separate fragment of nature, and to exhibit the captured, complete thing. Only, nature rebels. Something remains over, stays outside the circle. The breath has gone out of the body, the mystery has gone out of the soul. He has cut off his fragment, if you will, but he has cut it off from life. At this point the public accepts his work; he seems to have attained. At this point he realizes how far he is from attainment, and he sets himself to the eternal search. He breaks down the strait limits of his form, he seeks to find new links by which to attach this creature of his hands to the universal life of things. He says frankly to the spectator of his toil: you must come and help me, or I can never tell you all that I have to say. He gives a twofold burden to the lines of his work: that which they express, and that which they suggest. The lines begin to whisper something to the soul, in a remote voice which you must listen in order to hear. The eyes have something more to do than to see. The mind must collaborate with the eyes, and both must be content to share with life itself the dissatisfaction of an inexplicable mystery left over at the end.

Rodin's earlier form seemed able to say everything which he had to say; the modelling was infinitely detailed, the work lived with a vivid life of its own; and what remained over? Something remained over, the breath was not yet wholly lodged and at home in the body, the soul was not yet wholly conscious of its power of flight. He began to feel towards another form, apparently vaguer, essentially closer to the idea. He learnt how to indicate by a continually greater economy of means, by omission, by the simplification or synthesis of a great complexity of efforts; he found out short cuts which would take him more swiftly to his end; he built up his new form as much with the brain as with the hand. The Balzac is a divination; everything is there, and it is there as it must be if it is to be shown by sculpture: all depends on the sheer science of the relief, on the geometry of the observed profiles; but the life, the mystery, the thing divined, must be divined over again by everyone who looks at it. The work is no longer a block cut sharply off from nature; it is a part of ourselves, to be understood only as we understand one another.

III

In one of Rodin's finest creations, a great hand, large, strong, and smooth, holds in a paternal grasp a lump of earth, out of which emerge two ephemerides, fragile, pathetic creatures, with the delicate, insubstantial grace of passing things, who cling to each other joyously, accepting life on its terms of brief delight.[6] It is God bidding the earth increase and multiply; it symbolizes human life, in all its dependence on that unknown force in the hollow of whose hand it lives and moves. Elsewhere he has indicated the vain struggles, the insane desires, the insatiable longings, the murderous divisions, of the ephemerides, man and woman; here he indicates their not less pathetic content, the butterfly accepting its hour.

All Rodin's work is founded on a conception of force; first, the force of the earth, then the two conflicting forces, man and woman; with, always, behind and beyond, the secret, unseizable, inexplicable force of that mystery which surrounds the vital energy of the earth itself, as it surrounds us in our existence on the earth. Out of these forces he has chosen for the most part the universal, vivifying force of sex. In man he represents the obvious energy of nature, thews and muscles, bones, strength of limb; in woman, the exquisite strength of weakness, the subtler energy of the senses. They fight the eternal battle of sex, their embraces are a grapple of enemies, they seek each other that they may overcome each other. And the woman, softly, overcomes, to her own perdition. The man holds her in the hollow of his hand, as God holds both man and woman; he could close his hand upon the fragile thing that nestles there, and crush it, but something paralyses his muscles in a tender inaction. The hand will never close over her, she will always have the slave's conquest.

Rodin was studying drawing, with no idea but of being a draughts-man, when the idea of modelling in clay came to him. He had been drawing the model from different points of view, as the pivot turned, presenting now this and now that profile. It occurred to him to apply this principle to the clay, in which, by a swift, almost simultaneous, series of studies after nature, a single figure might be built up which would seem to be wholly alive, to move throughout its entire surface. From that time until now, he has taken one profile after another, each separately, and all together, turning his work in all directions, looking upward at the model to get the arch and hollow of the eyebrows, for instance, look-ing down on the model, taking each angle, as if, for the time, no other existed, and pursuing the outlines of nature with a movement as constant as her own. At the end, the thing is done, there is no need of even a final point of view, of an adjustment to some image of proportion: nature has been caught on the wing, enfolded by observation as the air enfolds the living form. If every part is right, the whole must be right.

But, for the living representation of nature in movement, something more is needed than the exact copy. This is a certain deliberate exag-geration; not a correction, not a deviation, but a means of interpretation, the only means by which the softness and the energy of nature can be rendered in clay. It is a manner of expressing in clay what nature ex-presses with the infinite resources of its moving blood. "All art," said Mérimée, "is exaggeration à *propos*." It is on the perfection of this à *propos* that everything depends, and here Rodin's training as a draughts-man gives him his safety in freedom. He, who never measures his pro-portions, can rely implicitly on the exactitude of his eye, in preserving the proportion of every exaggeration.

When *l'Age d'Airain,* the bronze which is now in the Luxembourg,[7] was sent to the Salon of 1877, Rodin was accused by the hanging com-mittee of having moulded it on a living model. He protested, there was an official inquiry, and the commissioners came to the conclusion that at least some parts of the body had been thus moulded. It was not until three years later that the charge was finally disproved and officially withdrawn; the statue was again exhibited at the Salon, a medal of the third class awarded to it, and it was afterwards bought by the State. The story is instructive, and might be remembered by those who have since brought against Rodin so very different an accusation. Turn from this statue to the marvellous little bronze of *la Vieille Heaulmière:*[8] there, in that re-incarnation of Villon's ballade, you will see the same precision of anatomical design, with an even deeper sense of the beauty of what age and the horror of decay cannot take out of the living body. Rodin has never taken a step without knowing exactly where he is going to set his foot, and he has never turned back from a step once taken. It was not until he could copy nature so exactly as to deceive the eyes of those who imagined that they knew nature when they saw it, it was not until he had the body by heart, that he began to make the body think. He had given it form; the form must be awakened. The touch of life and of thought comes, then, from an exaggeration here, an exaggeration there; a touch, inexplicable and certain, which is at once his method and his secret.

It is on these two methods that Rodin relies for the rendering of his vision of life. The art of the sculptor gives him but one means of expression; all is in relief, all depends on the power, balance, and beauty of the relief. Watching the living movement from every angle, turning about it as a wild beast turns about its prey, spying for the moment to pounce, seize, and possess, he must translate form, movement, light and shadow, softness, force, everything which exists in nature, by the cunning adjustment of his relief. "Le style, c'est l'homme," we say; "le modelé, c'est l'art," Rodin would say.

Rodin has sometime been compared with Michelangelo, but it would be more accurate to trace the principles of his art back to the Greeks. The Greeks worked directly from nature, with a fresh observation, the eyesight of the youth of the world, and its unspoilt mastery of hand. In Donatello we find the same directness, less powerful but not less sincere. Michelangelo approached nature through Donatello, so to speak, and then departed from nature, with his immense confidence, his readiness to compete with nature itself on a scale more decoratively impressive than nature's. His exaggeration is not the exaggeration of the Greeks, nor is it Rodin's, an attempt at always greater fidelity, at an essentially more precise exactitude; it deviates, for his own purposes, along ways of his own. He speaks truth, but not without rhetoric.

Every figure that Rodin has created is in the act of striving towards something: a passion, an idea, a state of being, quiescence itself. His *Gates of Hell* are a headlong flight and falling, in which all the agonies of a place of torment, which is Baudelaire's rather than Dante's, swarm in actual movement. "Femmes damnées" lean upward and downward out of hollow caves and mountainous crags, they cling to the edge of the world, off which their feet slip, they embrace blindly over a precipice, they roll together into bottomless pits of descent. Arms wave in appeal, and clasp shuddering bodies in an extremity of despair. And all this sorrowful and tortured flesh is consumed with desire, with the hurrying fever of those who have only a short time in which to enjoy the fruits of desire. Their mouths open towards one another in an endless longing, all their muscles strain violently towards the embrace. They live only with a life of desire, and that obsession has carried them beyond the wholesome bounds of nature, into the violence of a perversity which is at times almost insane.

But always, in the clay itself, there is ecstasy. Often it is a perverse ecstasy; at times, as in the Iris, as in the Muse who swoops like an eagle, as in the radiant figure with the sun in his hair who flings open the gates of the mountains in the monument to General Sarmiento,[9] it is pure joy; often, as in the Balzac, the Hugo, the Puvis de Chavannes, it is the ecstasy of creative thought. But always there is ecstasy.

In Rodin's sculpture, clay or marble, that something powerful of which he speaks has ended in a palpitating grace, as of living flesh. He feels, he translates, sensation for sensation, the voluptuous soft cool warmth of the flesh, the daintiness of the skeleton, indicated under its smooth covering; all that is exquisite in the structure of bone and muscle, in the force of man and the suppleness of woman. The flesh seems to shiver, curdle, tightening upon the bone as if at a touch; it lies abandoned, in a tender repose; it grapples, flesh upon flesh, in all the agonies of all the embraces. His hand seems to press most caressingly about the shoulder-blades and the hollows of the loins. The delicate ridge and furrow of the backbone draw his hand to mould them into new shapes and motions of beauty. His hand follows the loins where they swell into ampler outlines: the back, from neck to croup, lies quivering, in all the beauty of life itself.

In the drawings, which constitute in themselves so interesting a development of his art, there is little of the delicacy of beauty. They are notes for the clay, "instantanés," and they note only movement, expression. They are done in two minutes, by a mere gallop of the hand over paper, with the eyes fixed on some unconscious pose of the model. And here, it would seem (if indeed accident did not enter so largely into the matter) that a point in sentiment has been reached in which the perverse idealism of Baudelaire has disappeared, and a simpler kind of cynicism takes its place. In these astonishing drawings from the nude we see woman carried to a further point of simplicity than even in Degas: woman the animal; woman, in a strange sense, the idol. Not even the Japanese have simplified drawing to this illuminating scrawl of four lines, enclosing the whole mystery of the flesh. Each drawing indicates, as if in the rough block of stone, a single violent movement. Here a woman faces you, her legs thrown above her head; here she faces you with her legs thrust out before her, the soles of the feet seen close and gigantic. She squats like a toad, she stretches herself like a cat, she stands rigid, she lies abandoned. Every movement of her body, violently agitated by the remembrance, or the expectation, or the act of desire, is seen at an expressive moment. She turns upon herself in a hundred attitudes, turning always upon the central pivot of the sex, which emphasizes itself with a fantastic and frightful monotony. The face is but just indicated, a face of wood, like a savage idol; and the body has rarely any of that elegance, seductiveness, and shivering delicacy of life which we find in the marble. It is a machine in movement, a monstrous, devastating machine, working mechanically, and possessed by the one rage of the animal. Often two bodies interlace each other, flesh crushing upon flesh in all the exasperation of a futile possession; and the energy of the embrace is indicated in the great hand that lies like a weight upon the shoulders. It is hideous, overpowering, and it has the beauty of all supreme energy.

And these drawings, with their violent simplicity of appeal, have the distinction of all abstract thought or form. Even in Degas there is a certain luxury, a possible low appeal, in those heavy and creased bodies bending in tubs and streaming a sponge over huddled shoulders. But here luxury becomes geometrical; its axioms are demonstrated algebraically. It is the unknown X which sprawls, in this spawning entanglement of animal life, over the damped paper, between these pencil outlines, each done at a stroke, like a hard, sure stroke of the chisel.

For, it must be remembered, these are the drawings of a sculptor, notes for sculpture, and thus indicating form as the sculptor sees it, with more brevity, in simpler outline, than the painter. They speak another language than the drawings of the painter, searching, as they do, for the points that catch the light along a line, for the curves that indicate contour tangibly. In looking at the drawings of a painter, one sees colour; here in these shorthand notes of a sculptor, one's fingers seem actually to touch marble.

IV

Rodin will tell you that in his interpretation of life he is often a translator who does not understand the message which he hands on. At times it is a pure idea, an abstract conception, which he sets himself to express in clay; something that he has thought, something that he has read: the creation of woman, the legend of Psyche, the idea of prayer, of the love of brother and sister, a line of Dante or of Baudelaire. But more often he surrenders himself to the direct guidance of life itself: a movement is made before him, and from this movement he creates the idea of the movement. Often a single figure takes form under his hands, and he cannot understand what the figure means: its lines seem to will something, and to ask for the completion of their purpose. He puts it aside, and one day, happening to see it as it lies among other formless suggestions of form, it groups itself with another fragment, itself hitherto unexplained; suddenly there is a composition, the idea has penetrated the clay, life has given birth to the soul. He endeavours to represent life in all its mystery, not to penetrate the mystery of life. He gives you a movement, an expression; if it has come straight from life, if it has kept the living contours, it must mean something and he is but your comrade in the search for that meaning.

Yet he is never indifferent to that meaning; he is rarely content to leave any single figure wholly to the chance of interpretation. Rodin is a thinker, as well as a seer; he has put the whole of his intelligence into his work, not leaving any fragment of himself unused. And so this world of his making becomes a world of problems, of symbols, in which life offers itself to be understood. Here is a face, fixed in an attitude of meditation, and set aside unfinished, to which a hand, lifted daintily to the temples, has found its way out of another study; and the man's hand waits, giving the movement which completes the woman's head, until the hand of the same model has been studied in that position. Here two lovers, on the back of an eagle, are seen carried to the same point of heaven on the flight of the same desire. Christ agonizes in the Garden of Eden, or it may be Prometheus; he is conquered, and a useless angel, who cannot help, but perhaps comes as an angel of glory, hovers down to him. A shoal of rapid Muses, hurrying to reach the poet, swim towards him as upon carrying waves. A great Muse, swooping like an eagle, hurls inspiration into the brain of the poet. Another figure of inspiration, an Iris, meant for the monument of Victor Hugo, is seen arrested in a moment of violent action, which tears the whole body almost in two. With one hand she grasps her foot, drawing the leg up tight against the body; the other leg is flung out at a sharp angle, in a sudden, leaping curve. All the force of the muscles palpitates in this strenuous flesh; the whole splendour of her sex, unveiled, palpitates to the air; the messenger of the gods, bringing some divine message, pauses in flight, an embodied inspiration.

In a group meant for some shadowy corner of a park, among growing things dear to Pan and the nymphs, a satyr grasps a woman with fierce tenderness, his gay animal face, sharpened with desire, the eye oblique like the ears, appearing over her shoulder; his hoofs clutch the ground;

one hand catches her by the hair, the other seizes her above the knee, as
if to lift her in his arms; she pushes him away, startled, resisting the
brutality of instinct, inevitably at his mercy. Here are two figures: one, a
woman, rigid as an idol, stands in all the peace of indifference; the other
a man, tortured with desire, every muscle strained to exasperation,
writhes in all the ineffectual energy of a force which can but feed upon
itself. She is there, before him, close to him, infinitely apart, and he
could crush but never seize her. In an exquisite and wholly new rendering of the Temptation of St. Antony, the saint lies prostrate, crouched
against the cross, which his lips kiss feverishly, as he closes his pained
eyes; the shoulders seem to move in a shuddering revolt from the burden
which they bear unwillingly; he grovels in the dust like a toad, in his
horror of the life and beauty which have cast themselves away upon him.
And the woman lies back luxuriously, stretching her naked limbs across
his back, and twisting her delicate arms behind her head, in a supple
movement of perfectly happy abandonment, breathing the air; she has
the innocence of the flesh, the ignorance of the spirit, and she does not
even know what it is to tempt. She is without perversity; the flesh, not
the devil; and so, perhaps, the more perilous.

It is interesting to compare this version of a subject which so many
artists have treated, always in a spirit of perversity or of grotesque horror, with all those other versions, from Hieronymus van Bosch, with
his crawling and swooping abortions, in whom there could lie no possible temptation, to Rops, with his woman of enticing flesh spread out
mockingly upon the cross, from which she has cast off the divine body.[10]
To Rodin it is the opposition of the two powers of the world; it is the
conflict of the two rejections, the two absolute masters of the human
will. St. Antony cannot understand the woman, the woman cannot
understand St. Antony. To her, he seems to be playing at abnegation, for
the game's sake, stupidly; to him, she seems to be bringing all hell-fire
in the hollow of her cool hands. They will never understand one another,
and that will be the reason of the eternal conflict.

Here is the Balzac, with its royal air, shouldering the crowd apart, as
it steps into the final solitude, and the triumph. It is the thinker of action,
the visionary creator of worlds, standing there like a mountain that has
become man. The pose is that of a rock against which all waves must
dash themselves in vain. There is exultation, a kind of ferocity of enjoyment of life and of the making of life, in the great beaked head, the
great jaws, the eagle's eyes under the crag of eyebrows. And the rock
which suggests the man, the worker wrapped in the monastic habit of
his dressing-gown, all supple force under the loose folds of moulded
clay, stands there as if growing up out of the earth, planted for the rest
of time. It is the proudest thing that has been made out of clay.

It is Balzac, but it is more than Balzac; it is the genius and the work of Balzac; it is the *Comédie Humaine,* it is Seraphita and Vautrin and Lucien and Valérie; it is the energy of the artist and the solitude of the thinker and the abounding temperament of the man; and it is the triumph of all this in one supreme incarnation, which seems to give new possibilities to sculpture. * * *

[Music Halls and Ballet Girls]¹

I

It was through some occult sign in my Horoscope that I made the acquaintance of John Hollingshead, the manager of the Alhambra in 1892. As soon as we became friends, he called me *l'Enfant de la maison*. Indeed no better, no more significant name could have been given me, for was I not infatuated, was I not fascinated, by the Empire and the Alhambra, besides the lesser music-halls, for ten years? I am *aficionado*, as a Spaniard would say, of music-halls: they always in every foreign country in which I lived or travelled amused me; I am always grateful to anyone or anything that amuses me. For only in the music-hall is the audience a part of the performance, but it was always amusing for me to contrast La Scala with Les Ambassadeurs.² It was at such places as these and at cafés and Evil Houses that I came to understand what I had never felt before and for which I contend: that, for one thing, nothing need be without beauty, because life is a source and sap of Beauty. There was not one of those grimacing masks, those horribly pale or horribly red faces painted white and red, leering professionally across a gulf of footlights, or a café table that does not live, live to the roots of the eyes, some in the soul, I think! And if beauty is not the visible spirit of all that infamous flesh which Lautrec, for instance, painted, with all my hatred and all my admiration, of its foolish energy, I at least am unable to conjecture where beauty has gone to live in the world. * * *

Did I myself deliberately choose music-halls and the public-houses or did they choose me? I imagine they chose me. I lived in them for the mere delight and the sheer animal excitement they gave me. I liked the glitter, barbarous, intoxicating, the violent animality, the entire spectacle, with absurd faces, gestures, words, and the very odour and suffocating heat. I went there as I went to public houses, as I walked in the streets at night, as I kept company with vagabonds, such as myself, because of the craving in me which I could not quiet.

It was Hollingshead who flung wide open before me and for me—

who gave me as it were the very key that could unlock it—the gate of my Forbidden Paradise. Might I not have awakened on some fabulous night with the same wonder as Adam when he wakened out of sleep in the Garden of Eden? * * *

II

I had such an enormous amount of adventures in Fountain Court, The Temple, where I lived for ten years, besides the adventures that followed me while I was abroad—in Spain, Paris, Russia, in fact everywhere—that the most unerring memory any man might possess—(which mine is) is utterly incapable of remembering the unaccountable number of men and women one met (the names even) and of one's adventures and one's misadventures. It would be indeed unfortunate if one could. The most awful thing is when one's memory wakens one at midnight and flashes before one in visions and derisions the damnable faults we have made by mistake, the sins we ought to have committed. And worst of all when the separate hells we have traversed rise up before us and one recalls these lines of Rossetti:

> Night sucks them down, the tribute of the pit
> Whose names, half entered in the book of Life,
> Were God's desire at noon. And as their hair
> And eyes sink last, the Torturer deigns no whit
> To gaze, but, yearning, waits his destined wife,
> The Sin still blithe on earth that sent them there.
>
> > [Sonnet LXXXV,
> > "The House of Life," *Poems*, 1870]

I see no reason why in my *Confessions* I should torment my imagination, rack my brain, agitate my mind, instigate researches in my memory, when these incidents, these adventures, the recollections of men and of women, those impressions of travels and of cities have for the most part been recorded in my books of travels, in my prose, in my verse, so definitely and so finally that it might be out of the question to make use of them, except when the necessity of my narrative compels me to use them. As for the vices, the virtues, the lust of the flesh and the lust of the spirit, the desire, the passions that have possessed me, one need only turn over the pages of my verses, and if you choose imagine this, imagine that, and I assure you that you will never fathom the unfathomable gulf that exists between the writer and the reader, nor the intensity of the meaning they contain, not the intensity of the pain and pleasure, of rapture and satiety and satisfaction, which only I myself—who have lived them all and have lived through them—have the right to judge of: only myself. Is it for such a shifting guide that I am to forsake the sure and constant leading of art, which tells me that whatever I find in humanity (passion, desire, the spirit or the senses, the hell or heaven of man's heart) is part of the eternal substance which nature weaves in the rough for art to combine cunningly into beautiful patterns? The whole visible world itself, we are told, is but a symbol, made visible in order that we may apprehend ourselves, and not be blown hither and thither like a flame in the night. How laughable it is, then, that we should busy ourselves with such serious faces, in the commanding or condemning, the permission or the exemption, of this accident or that, this or the other passing caprice of our wisdom or our folly, as a due or improper subject for the "moment's monument" of a poem![3] It is as if you were to say to me, here on these weedy rocks of Rosses Point, where the grey sea passes me continually, flinging a little foam at my feet, that I may write of one rather than another of these waves, which are not more infinite than the moods of men.[4]

I thought of writing a section or sections on Alhambra nights and on Empire nights.[5] But, I asked myself, "Is there any reason in the world why I should?" Those burning nights were so vivid, so essentially a part of my vivid and burning existence, I was so inextricably mixed up with crowds of ballet girls, the people on the stage, the stage managers, the dancing masters, such as Carlo Coppi, together with the inevitable stage door, the pavements, one's hanging about, as one waited for this or that girl; small crowds on or near the pavement who had nothing to do with us, which were mightily amused by our goings-on; and most of all the hurried or lazy throng, the ballet girls as they came one after the other with much jostling, with much jolly laughter out of the stage door on to the pavement: that, if you like it in miniature, that particular, strange, original, bewildering, perplexing, exciting, passionately-coloured, whirlwind of a world in which like a scented whirlwind I existed.

III

One night I met in the Alhambra a certain neurotic doctor called Ianson, a certain man and woman I had never seen before. We returned in two cabs to Fountain Court. I gave them drinks and cigarettes in my study; the hours went on (just as they always did there) when the doctor suddenly seized a lancet he had in his pocket and tried to pierce a vein in the girl's wrist. She shrieked: the blood had to be stopped; then, furious with the man who had hurt her, she whispered in my ear that I must come home with her. We left the Temple together; I and she got into a cab and found ourselves in Chelsea.

Night after night, when I had my window curtains drawn and the light shone through them, I was more or less besieged with men and women (some of whom had seen suspicious shadows behind the curtains) who climbed up the steep stairs and began to hammer at my oak door, which was as impenetrable as the Gates of Hell. Whenever I heard a knock at the door I gazed through the muslin curtains that covered the little window in the narrow passage, as discreetly as a woman's veil conceals her face; and if it chanced to be Dowson or Yeats or certain other people, I let them in; otherwise never! Dowson was always at his best when he came alone: then we talked without end, deep into the night. Sometimes we would wander down the deserted streets near Covent Garden; where, when one drink made him unreasonable, I had to drag him bodily back from some chance encounter with the policeman. We often had breakfast in queer sorts of taverns, so the nights went on; so the days went on; and, on my part on the whole, rarely without some adventure. There were hateful nights when I had to let him in with certain vile people. I warned him never to bring them again; when he did my door remained silent, silent as death; and for all the kicking of his heels on that oak, remained so. * * *

IV

It may be noticed that, except in Poe's *Israfel,* the theme of his imagination is ruin, inevitable ruin. His genius was developed before it had attained its final mastery, by brooding over a fixed idea. It has been alleged and seems to be a fact that Poe—who had a sinister and bizarre genius, a morbid and depraved imagination—was not virile. It was curious to note that Dowson, who was morbid and neurotic, told me that he was more sexually excited by women's breasts than by any other part of woman's flesh. He was not abnormal, he was lacking in vitality; therefore he went after common whores in the worst quarters of London; these, apart from his drink, helped in killing him. When Yeats saw him for the last time, he was pouring out a glass of whiskey for himself and he said: "The first to-day." Yeats made a mistake in forgetting something I told him, "A Rhymer had seen Dowson in some café in Dieppe with a particularly common harlot, and as he passed, Dowson, half-drunk, caught him by the sleeve and whispered: 'She writes poetry. It is like Browning and Mrs Browning.' "[6] The scene took place in an awful café at Antwerp, in a disreputable street near the harbour. The harlot was just as drunk as Dowson; and, for the life of me, one could conceive of her relinquishing her profession rather than writing one line of verse.

V

Violet

The first ballet girl I ever "took up with" (as they always say) was Violet Pigott who lived in 57 Belmont Street, Chalk Farm Road, sometime in 1892. She was stupid, sensual, pretty and not perverse; she was slender and had shapely legs. When flesh means nothing more than the satisfaction of one's senses, she was nothing more to me than a thing of flesh. One could drain her empty kisses; for what one so absurdly calls "love" at that age, there was naturally no question between us. She comes in my *London Nights* as Lilian.[7] Hating as I always did to wait for such creatures, and at so far off a distance, I remember strolling up and down a street near there, and to my intense delight buying the rare first edition of *Le Livre Mystique* of Balzac of 1835 which contains the wonderful *Louis Lambert,* in which there is so much of Balzac himself. * * *

And as I write these lines I still feel that curious thrill I always had on finding before me a rare first edition; and how—at that time—such books meant—*de temps en temps*—ever so much more to me than these mere girls of the Alhambra. She was jolly; I wrote some jolly verses about her; and I had nothing much to do in those years except to wander after sensations and adventures, after women and after books. She came into my life just then, when I wanted that kind of stimulant; for I was just then spending most of my nights in the music-halls, and because one needs all kinds of queer stimulants. It was not in that year but in later years that I had to have recourse—at certain hours of the night—to "pick-me-ups" which one generally had at Heppel's shop, a chemist in the Haymarket whose shop was then open into very late hours. That meant late suppers, after theatres and after other adventures, at night clubs—such as the famous and infamous Corinthian, which went on for I don't know how many years before it came to an untimely end. I look up to the outside and into the lighted windows whenever I stroll down that street, 6 York Street, with a sort of retrospective envy, for the times that are over and gone.

Violet finally made her exit to America, and I recall with an abject horror, mixed with disgust, the hour I spent with her and some of her awful friends—men and women, one Ford, the stage manager with whom she was infatuated,[8] besides the ballet girls and strollers-on—at a public house which still bears that sinister sign of The Final. Not that it ever had any finality as far as I was concerned. This shameful behaviour on her part, on the part of these people—who actually wanted me to stay up all night at Violet's house so as to see her off next morning—that remains hateful. The whole scene was so sordid and so mean, so abominable, that it reminded me of certain scenes of Zola, who sickens you with the horrid unrealities of the horrible lives of his characters. * * * Nothing may be more charming than a frankly sensuous description of things which appeal to the senses. These inches of bare flesh which these ballet-girls always show on the stage and off the stage, which I had seen in Violet, and which I saw for the last time in that miserable public-house, remain, in a sense which one cannot explain, the sign of degeneration.

[John Addington Symonds][1]

I

How is it that letters one reads in print have so strange a fascination? It seems to me that, in reading letters of Keats, Lamb and Byron, one feels something one has never felt before, and that this something is like a magnetic current flowing subtly from them to us, and that this can only be compared with that other magnetic current which makes one shift one's centre when one loves a woman; when the centre itself is shifted, is put outside one's self. It was with a curious sense of shifting my centre when, after having finished reading the *Letters and Papers of John Addington Symonds*, collected and edited by Horatio F. Brown, these sentences I had written on Keats recurred to me: "It is to call in a passing stranger, and to say: 'Guard all my treasures while I sleep.' For there is no certainty in the world, beyond the certainty that I am I, and that what is not I can never draw one breath for me, though I were dying for lack of it."[2]

So, in a flash of memory, the last words in the last letter Symonds wrote—*Addio. A rivederci mai?*—evoked a vivid image of the man as I knew him.[3] We met in London in July, 1892. What struck me then, and afterwards, were his varied aspects: the morbid, disquieting, nervous, contorted, painful expression of his face; the abnormal, almost terrible fixity of the eyes, as restless as the man himself. Of this he was evidently aware. "I should like to go down to posterity," he wrote, "with that apprehensive yet courageous look upon the wrinkled features." I saw in his violent activity, in his vehement vitality, another aspect, that of one whose spirit, that abode so uneasily within a body its inner fires were so rapidly consuming, desired nothing more than the one impossibility— eternal youth: *L'Amour de l'Impossible*, that mystery of mysteries, Nirvana, Medusa, Hecate, Astarte.

So, not only in the book I had read but in Horatio Brown's *Life*,[4] the actual record of this "chequered, confused and morally disturbed existence" quickened my senses in its revelation of the nobility and the endlessly thwarted endeavour of a human spirit "to live resolvedly in the whole, the good, the beautiful"; but, to those who knew and loved the man, it calls up not merely the blithe companion of any hour's adventure, but the real sympathetic, suffering individuality that lay ever so much deeper, and it recalls that memory with almost intolerable vividness. He was like Rousseau in one thing only: an indefinable taint of death clung always about him, and living always under sentence of death, knowing that he was stricken by mortal disease, he asked himself how he might make as much as possible of the interval that remained, and so, aware of what Victor Hugo says—*"Les hommes sont tous condamnés à mort avec des sursis indéfinis"*—he spent all that remained to him of this "indefinite reprieve" with a feverish intentness upon opportunity which caused him to do many things hastily that would have been done better with more leisure, and to attempt a universal conquest of literature where limitation would have been an act of wisdom.

On his arrival in London, Symonds asked me to lunch with him. His exquisite charm and innate courtesy soon put me at my ease. It seemed to me wonderful—I think it seemed so to him—to have met finally after all our correspondence. We had much in common; and yet with what singular differences! In any case, two men of letters were face to face, with some of the world's enigmas to discuss, together with those men and women we knew, the books we had read, the cities we had seen, some of our travels, our sensations, our instincts, our aversions; and, as we grew more intimate, our conversation turned, naturally enough, on our prose and verse. After I had referred to some of my adventures with Verlaine, I quoted this line of Baudelaire:

> *Nous avons dit souvent d'impérissables choses;*
> ["Le Balcon," *Les Fleurs du Mal,* 1857]

which excited him; it incited him to tell me many of the details of his Autobiography, which he had very much at heart.[5]

I asked Symonds to visit me whenever he liked in Fountain Court, The Temple, where I was living. One morning—it was fairly late, as I had returned in the early hours—I heard a knock at my door. I jumped out of bed and saw in the court below Angelo, that magnificent gondolier, who was his lifelong friend, who always travelled with him. I opened the door and apologised for the state of undress I was in—the strange situation pleased him and amused him—and I asked him to wait for me in the study. After some time he signalled to Angelo, who came up and joined us. Never shall I forget the impression Angelo gave me then, and afterwards in Venice: a man so utterly alive and, just then, so utterly out of his surroundings, whose vivid and passionate glances, whose wild gestures, whose intense excitement, whose rapid interchange of words sent waves of sensation over me. It might almost be said that he spoke with his eyes. I said to Symonds that I had invited some of the ballet-girls of the Empire to tea on the following afternoon; I asked him if he would join us. There sprang from his lips: "Certainly, I shall be most delighted!"

I was certain that he knew that his world could never be mine. I had lived in the world of art from my youth onward; I had just then begun to live, not only in the world of art, but in the world of the music-halls. One, I was certain, was almost a form of religion; the other, I knew, was a form of depravity. I told him then that I was one of several men of about my age who worshipped the ballet. As for Dowson, neither the stage nor the stage-door had any attraction for him; he came to the tavern because it was a tavern and because he could meet his friends there. I never could get him to see that charm in coloured and harmonious movement, like brilliant shadows seen through the flashing gauze of the music, which held me night after night at the two theatres which alone seemed to me to give an amusing colour to one's dreams.

On the following afternoon Dowson turned up, then the ballet-girls one after another, whose laughter and whose youth always enchanted me; then Symonds, whose entrance seemed to disturb them; they began to be curiously nervous, and he by being for a few minutes nervously shy. Yet when, with the gravity of a Doge, he handed round the tea, and I the cakes and the cigarettes, we suddenly became quite at home. Later on we tried the effect of haschisch—that slow intoxication, that elaborate experiment in visionary sensations, which to Dowson at Oxford had been his favourite form of intoxication, which, however, had no effect on him, as he sat, a little anxiously, with, as his habit was, his chin on his breast, awaiting the magic, half shy in the midst of that bright company of young people, of which I was the host and the gatherer, whom he had seen only across the footlights.

After the others had left Symonds and I remained alone. That night he dined me at the Café Royal and I took him with me to the Empire. He admitted to our mutual excitement, to the entire novelty of that situation; he ended by saying—over our dinner—that he would never forget that afternoon, that it was one of the most amusing and successful of his various adventures. He said to me then that he never feared anything so much as his own self—in spite of the means he tried, again and again, to escape from that self of his; never "truly reconciled either with himself or with life," he intimated to me that he had chosen to write his *History of the Renaissance* rather than the impossible one of writing the history of his own soul; yet, there and then and always when I was with him, I felt, with a certain reciprocal heat, that it was the personality that gave him his real interest, his extraordinary fascination: strange, contradictory as he was in all things.

II

With the permission of Horatio Brown I am printing one of Symonds's letters:—

March 21, 1889.

Dear Mr. Symons,

I have been very bad toward you, shut up here in this mountain valley of oblivion, and you have been very good toward me in many mindful ways. Last of all, you have sent me your volume of poems, some of which, you know, I already possess in your handwriting. I have been reading them slowly through during the last days and now I should like to say something to you about them. But the older an old critic grows, worn with the continuous flowing over him of floods of literature, the less can he rightly say to a young eager poet. It is best, I think, for such a man as I am, not to utter opinions upon this or that of your poems, but to tell you that the net result left upon my mind after sympathetic and critical reading of your book is—that you *are* a poet.

If I were to pass from this generality to particulars, I should tell you that I rate highest in the scale—looking at the poems of *Days and Nights*—the transcripts from life; realistic and penetrated with strong human emotion; next the sonnets (the form of which in many cases seems to me of admirable quality); afterwards the translations from the French. I have no hesitation in urging you to go forward in the path of poetry. It seems to me that you might taket a great stride on that path, if you were to concentrate your powers of sympathetic intuition, analysis, dramatic presentation, and poetical treatment, upon some central theme—viewed by you as artist more objectively than you have as yet viewed anything. This is tantamount to saying that I believe you have the gifts to produce a substantial work of art, if you will gird your loins up to what is the supreme adventure. I speak in all humility, knowing that what I indicate is the touch-stone of attainment in our art of writing, and confessing that such an adventure would have always been beyond the scope of my own faculty. But I think you have the stuff in you to make it worth your while trying to gather all your forces together for some comprehensive deeply meditated poem.

I do not believe that much can be done with the drama in

this age. Yet there are forms which serve as substitutes for the drama. And I submit as a mere opinion that you would find yourself braced up to the best by attempting some work planned upon a big scale— a large canvas.

Do not think ill of me because of my long silence. Distance only. Diurnal drudgery deadens. Besides, we have not yet touched hands or exchanged the magnetism of spoken words.

Believe me very sincerely and unforgettably yours,

J.A. SYMONDS.

There is an intense honesty in many of Symonds's letters. I admire him the more for the "crudity of his expressions"; nor do I wonder that he began to yawn over my immature productions and some of his own he least cared for; and as he yawns remembering those lines of Byron:—

And that which after all my spirit vexes,
Is, that I find no spot where man can rest an eye on,
Without confusion of the sorts and sexes,
Of beings, stars, and this unriddled wonder,
The world, which at the worst's a glorious blunder.
[Canto 11, stanza 3 of *Don Juan*, 1824]

So I can imagine him in Venice, in Davos, anywhere, puzzling his soul out over the perplexing facts of our most bewildering universe: in which, indeed, we can, with Byron in Florence, "get drunk with beauty," cry out with him—as Dante and Shakespeare cried—for life, life in its entirety, for the naked contact of humanity, as the only warmth in the world; or, as it were in vision, become lost among throngs of spectral beings as real as those Blake and Shelley believed in—whirled from the actual contact of the world itself somewhere into void space between loneliness and utter darkness. * * *

III

* * * The idea of beginning an Autobiography occurred to Symonds in March 1889. He wrote:—

But, such is the oddness of man's nature, I have chosen this particular moment to begin a new literary work of the utmost importance—my "Autobiography." It is interesting work but I see that it tends *ad infinitum*, and that it will be hardly fit to publish. According to my conception of such a work, the years of growth are the most important, and need the most elaborate analysis. It is a fascinating canvas, this of a *Leibensschilderung*, for a man who has been hitherto so reticent a writer, and who is so naturally egotistical and personal as I am. Heaven knows what will come of it and what will be done with it.[6]

"What has been done with it?" has often been asked. Symonds himself knew; he told me, he mentioned in his letters, that the MS. in its entirety could only be privately printed: yet that he was anxious to have it published.

This Autobiography of Symonds, the original manuscript of which has been preserved, intact, by his literary executor, Horatio Brown, would, if it were ever given to the world, be not only his self-defence, his self-confession, but his defence against the world—and chiefly against that minor part of the world which, as he supposed, was at watch on him, and with no very favourable intentions. He did not wish to explain himself like Rousseau: he must have felt, with Cellini, that it shocked him to think of going down into his grave without having made the whole world hear those inner voices of his.

It seems evident, from all we know of him, and from all we have read of him, that Symonds was physically very sexual; that he was to a certain extent abnormal; that those morbid and neurotic strains in his vigorous personality became more obvious year by year: He knew himself to be, neither finally nor fatally, an *homo duplex;* unlike Rossetti, who was the slave of his imagination—an imagination of a power and dominance never equalled—over which he had not the slightest command. As restless as Rossetti, Symonds at Davos would begin to talk with some intimate friend who was staying with him; he would begin to sip his favourite wine at ten o'clock, then steadily into the early hours of the morning; and all the while wandering from topic to topic, interminably, passing from Aretino to Aristophanes, from Petronius to Rabelais, until the very senses of the listener began to reel. "I was a very nervous child," he wrote, "and subject to many physical ailments, which made me no doubt very disagreeable to the people around me. Being sensitive to the point of suspiciousness, I imagined that I inspired repugnance in others, and my own condition not unfrequently made me noisome to myself. I became unreasonably shy and timid. Dreams and visions exercised a far more potent spell. Nigh to them lay madness and utter lack of self-control."

In regard to the question of pathology, some have wondered whether Symonds was altogether sane. Abnormal he was: much of his finest work is abnormal, as in *The Age of the Despots;* where he dwells on the question of the blood lusts of those ferocious and insane tyrants—Alexander VI., Cesare Borgia, the Malatestas, the Medici, the Orsini—and on that age which makes the history of it the fountain head of tragic motives. In regard to these questions I must refer to a significant incident in the youth of Symonds. In January 1863, when he was at Oxford, an incident happened which proved of most serious consequences to one whose temperament was febrile and sensitive: a certain friend sought, by means of garbled letters, to damage Symonds's character at Magdalen. He entirely failed in his object. "But," writes Brown, "the unexpectedness of the blow, and the treachery of a man he had trusted, the annoyance at home, the odious necessity of defending himself, so preyed on his nerves and brain, worn by a perpetual internal conflict, and excited by the strain of two fellowship examinations, as to precipitate a physical crisis which was already imminent. After three weeks this crisis arrived, Symonds's health gave way suddenly, and as he said, 'I have never been such a strong man since.' "[7]

The meaning of this is quite evident. It has been said, or supposed, that he might have had a dangerous influence; that he may have subconsciously used other men's vitality for his own excitement: a mere supposition. In 1888, it is curious to note, he was dining with Browning at Venice, in the Palazzo Barbaro, when some tedious person interrupted the conversation by talking to him of the dearth of young poets. "You must ask God who made them," said Browning; "I don't know." This leads me to the certainty that an artist lives a double life, in which he is for the most part conscious of the illusions of the imagination, of the illusions of the nerves; so, before any of those common disturbances which might jangle the toneless bell of his nerves, might not any artist descend into his own proper hell, taste hell's venom, and from thence arise with an immense effort, a changed man, as Dante was, when

> Hell's reek
> Has crisped his beard and singed his cheek,

and, without so much as lifting one finger, become an instrument of God's vengeance? * * *

[Arthur Henry Bullen]¹

* * * From the time when I first met [Bullen], in 1892, till the last time when I came on him unawares at the performance of Dryden's *Marriage à la Mode* given by the Phoenix in the Lyric Theatre, when he was so humourous, so kind-hearted, so friendly, so attentive to the play itself, just as he always used to be, the charm he had for me has never left me—a charm that could turn to fascination. Both Celtic, we had certainly much in common; yet we were apt at times to quarrel furiously—then to forget all that in his genial laughter.

He had a vivid personality, and was loveable enough as a man, in spite of his eccentricities. "He seemed not wholly our contemporary," writes Charles Whibley.² He was and he was not: in much the same sense as Charles Lamb was and was not wholly of his own century. Bullen never felt as Lamb did the genius of places; he felt the genius of books. * * *

I shall never forget Bullen's restless manner of walking up and down a room, the animal's restlessness, the animal's nerves, either in his house in Stratford-on-Avon or in his rooms in town, or in the old Cottage where he stayed with me, in Kent;³ smoking his pipe, stopping, waving his hands, reciting verses with a poet's rhythm, scanning Latin lines as only a Latin scholar can scan them. His ear was almost as unerring as mine; so much so that the boldest of his ascriptions in regard to the question of two Elizabethan dramatists can never be challenged. His reverence for these texts was only equalled by his reverence for Latin poetry and Latin prose. He would quote, whenever I asked him, long passages from Lucretius and from the prose of Tacitus. He even converted me to a liking for Robert Bridges's verses, after a heated discussion, as we both walked to and fro in his room. Together with his sardonic humour he had a great power of hating and of expressing his aversions in Rabelaisian phrases.

He had an imagination of a curious kind—one that came and went, as when the winds toss winter leaves. He had a passion for many things; but, apart from his passion for his rather singular existence, all his ardency went into a deep devotion for the dramas and lyrics of the Elizabethan Age. His whole nature was in certain senses almost Elizabethan, so deeply it seemed to me rooted in that rich and abundant soil. * * *

In all of Bullen's Selections and Prefaces he sorted and stored, with his delicate intellectual Epicureanism—he had so much of that rare quality himself!—the choicest perfumes and the most odorous scents of those lyrics he rescued from forgetfulness. And for one thing, had it not been for him, we should never have had a complete edition of Campion.[4] In Campion the art of the song-writers seems to concentrate itself, become individual, become conscious. He sums up, in a single name, the many nameless writers of perfect words and airs. It is difficult to distinguish between many of his lyrics and the lyrics of different unknown writers. Only, we must suppose that what is really many-sided in him is in them the whole expression of a temperament or character, which he multiplies, so to speak, in himself, as the man of genius does who is also a versatile artist. Bullen's edition of Campion should be on every bookshelf which holds a Blake or a Rossetti. It is a book to take down, linger over, and read for mere idle pleasure, as one might listen to music played softly on a clavichord.

When I was staying with Bullen at Stratford-on-Avon he had nearly finished the work of so many laborious years, the *Stratford Town Shakespeare,*[5] which came to us from a printing-press set up in a house that Shakespeare must have visited, the Tudor house, which stands two doors from New Place, where Shakespeare's house stood, the house in which he died, and in which he had lived for at least the most mysterious years of his life, the five years in which he wrote nothing. And yet to live at Stratford and to write nothing becomes somewhat less mysterious when one is actually there.

Any dreams might have been dreamed in Stratford-on-Avon, any work written there in the intervals of life in London; any dreams might have seemed enough in themselves to give up London for, and even, who knows? poetry. I am not at all sure that Shakespeare had really given up work and ambition during those last years in which he was seeming to do nothing. May he not have been meditating, may he not have actually begun a revision of his old work which he may well have hesitated to carry far? Shakespeare revising Shakespeare: it suggests an ambition beyond anything that a man has conceived.

At Stratford Shakespeare seems a likely miracle. No theory is needed to explain so rare a growth out of so delicately prepared a soil. The return thither becomes inevitable, and the actual employment of a supreme mind, which had absorbed life and which was itself imagination, a matter of indifference. "Ripeness is all."

I can only recall one man whose memory was even more incredible, even more abnormal, than Bullen's: Richard Garnett. I believe he had read everything, and he seemed to have forgotten nothing. He talked always—as Bullen in his most excitable moods always did—with gusto. Garnett was the only man I ever knew who talked like a book. His sentences flowed on, unhesitatingly, in lengthy periods, all the commas and semi-colons almost visible to the eye. Bullen, luckily for him and for me, had no sense of semi-colons nor of commas; yet, when he liked, he could become irreverant, mocking, macabre, sinister. Only, he lacked, among many other things, what is to be found only in Poets, in Creators: the certainty that every corner of the world is alive with tempting and consoling and terrifying beauty.

Only, as I think of him as I always knew him; with his Irish humour, his full-blooded way of talking, so ripe and rich and learned were his expressions: discoursing of many things with a better sense of what those things were to him—of what they were to me—than most of his contemporaries; when I look backward—as one looks "backward into the Abyss of Time"—to indirect touches of his own work, to those innumerable letters I have had from him; when I remember the fine casuistries of his conversations long after midnight, suddenly, the man's likeness emerges.

A Study in Morbidity:
Herbert Horne[1]

I

One counts one's evil days as one might calculate mathematics; one counts one's good days as one might calculate the dates on the calendar. It was no evil day when I came on Selwyn Image[2] at Fitzroy Street, there were many links between us, as for instance, in our mixed blood. Then there were the allurements of the music-hall. From there certain of us went to the Crown. As Image alone knows the mystery of its reincarnation and hideous revival, I give this letter of his, March 26, 1921.

My dear Symons,

I was indeed glad to see your handwriting again, and hear of your welfare and doings. Forgive my not answering at once, but this week I have had to be out of town, and when in it over-burdened with exacting engagements.

The dear old Crown of many blessed memories was in Charing Cross Road north of the Alhambra stage-door—just north of Coventry Street. One would never know it nowadays. For some years it has been turned into an elaborate, crowded, much-bedecked Hotel. I suppose they'll call it—as unlike as chalk from cheese from its old retirement. I often think—and talk with Janet over what it once was to some of us—and of the company that used to gather there night after night year in and year out. All of 'em scattered—how many of 'em dead?

Indeed for myself I grow very old and tired—and practically never go out o' nights unless compelled. But I will try shortly—when things get a bit slacker—to meet you one lunch-time at the C[afé] R[oyal] and have a long chat. I shall be most interested to hear about the Confessions you speak of.[3] I fear I shouldn't dare to write down my own, if I had to be as honest over the business as—say Samuel Pepys Esq.

This is my narrative of a conversation between Image and myself during the dinner on the 3rd of January, 1924. He said, "I met Horne when he was eighteen.[4] His father was a regular bad lot, dissipated, shady, cruel, selfish.[5] He was for many years the member of a certain club: finally they found him out, he had done something shady in regard to money; they ejected him and removed his portrait from their walls. He had left his children, two sons and a daughter, to their own devices; the results of which was the sons had a terrible bringing up." * * *

"Yes," said Image. "I know all about that. I found that Horne was abnormally cruel, utterly self-absorbed, full of sudden furies and revolts. When insanity betrayed itself was when he fell into frantic furies; then his bad blood surged into his evil eyes, made his lips quiver, convulsed his whole face. And, for instance, his insanity showed itself in a most vexatious manner when, annoyed and made furious by some commission he had wanted to have and which was given to me, we had a fierce quarrel. He disappeared for two years, no one knew whither. It appeared that he had gone so as to escape from charges of the worst kind against him to some part of Italy. He never wrote me one letter, in fact I heard nothing about him until he came back. Then we returned to our former friendly relations." I said, "You remember those nights when Horne would become ghastly, livid, atrocious; the spirit of revenge which had lived always in him sprang to the surface and showed its hideous visage; the baser animal appeared in a baser fashion."

Image said, "A feminine trait in Horne was his adoration of flattery. Whenever he was flattered he literally expanded. The most extraordinary thing happened when Randall Davies[6] showed me among the manuscripts Horne had bequeathed to him a huge package, piles and piles of cardboard, on which he had pasted every drawing I had given him, my letters, scraps of envelopes, I know not how much else. It seemed to me tragic, then ridiculous. There is one point I must emphasise: that Horne was the most secretive man I have ever known, absolutely and always. And this was one of the worst qualities in his sinister nature. He avoided more than anyone I have ever known the least reference to what he did with his nights, let alone what he did with his days." He added: "I had no inkling of Horne's homosexuality. You are probably right in what you have said. So abnormal, so self-centered a man with a taint of insanity in his veins, is as often as not [not] responsive of the actions he commits. That is of course only a side issue to this sinister question."

II

It was my evil genius, like Casanova's, who deluded me into entering the same house where Image lived, where I encountered Herbert Horne, whose shifting and treacherous eyes were one of the certain signs of what was inimical in the man. He was short,[7] dark, neat, very worldly looking. His manner was cold and restrained, with a mingling of insolence and diffidence. He never mentioned the word "love" except to jest at it; and yet there could be no doubt as to his meaning. His whole attitude was of patient waiting. Such women were set apart in his carefully arranged life from matters which absorbed him in other senses. He was one of those critics who could do any man's work but their own. When he sat down to write something dry and hard came into the words. He always chafed a little under what seemed an unnecessary devotion. On principle, he did not like clever women. He had his own very deliberate theory of values, and one value was never allowed to interfere with another. A devoted, discreet, amateur of women, he appreciated women really for their own sex.

For several years we were on rather friendly terms. I rarely called on him in his rooms in Kings' Bench Walk, not far from where George Moore lived. He had a terrible habit of calling on me in Fountain Court when I least wanted to see him. We were most friendly when he was keeping Muriel Broadbent.[8] It was with a Latin solemnity Selwyn Image and myself signed a legal document—for the rent of the place in which she stayed—that she was an honest woman. She was frightfully nice and kind to me; one of those women who are sensual and excitable though not passionate. There was something bright and attractive about her, apart from her erotic nature. She had a curious way of taking off her stays—which made such red marks on her flesh—whenever she could; and in the matters of the flesh she was fairly diffident. She often took refuge with me when her men made her exasperated; and when I opened the door after she had knocked on it, she burst in, flushed and feverish, then flung herself on the sofa and became hysterical. She got mixed up in an indiscriminate fashion with young lords and with younger poets, with Jews and with Gentiles, with painters and prose writers; and to such an extent that they all got mixed up and jumbled together in that queer head of hers. When finally she had to marry a man of good position,[9] there were terrible scenes between her and her keeper. Once I was walking with him in Chelsea when Muriel waved her hand to us from a cab; his face became livid and furious; and in his surly voice he said, "Let us turn down the next street and escape her."

Horne exacted more from the women he was mixed up with than any man has a natural right to exact. Outwardly, he was the animal on the prey; but in his complex character, inwardly, one divined his abnormal passion for men: he was at once a hard liver, a Sadist and a Pervert.

Horne was fiendishly jealous, cold, cruel, calculating; always aware of the insidious ambushes into which he might fall, which he took an immense trouble in avoiding. Sexually endowed to an excess which was morbid, an abominable sense of his fascination when he was least so came over him. Intensely avid in following up sinister adventures by which he hoped to profit, he let me in to some of his cunning plots which so often to his disgust were abject failures. He was unpassionate; he never had any passionate adventures; whatever passion he had went in the wrong direction; he was literally incapable of inspiring either love or passion in women's hearts; and if by chance he wakened a spark of it in any of them, that was soon extinguished. He raised in many of these women such an aversion that he became to them literally insupportable. This was his lifelong grievance.

Such a man as Horne who never marries, never could have, and who lives, as one phrases it, alone for the greater part of his life must have resources of his own, not an inner contentment, from which he imbibes as from drugs and drinks ineffable sensations. All lovers and all mistresses have partaken of the waters of Lethe: some have drunk oblivion, some death, some everlasting memory. And to all this must be applied Meredith's fundamental, elemental, primitive line, "Lethe had passed those lips and he knew all." * * *

In lives such as these, there is a kind of aching *Sterility*, which may or may not make them barren of success. Then the nausea of a series of disgusts, the odour of corruption; satiety, disillusion; and in these cases the absolute need of a prodigious mental activity, an aloofness from the atmosphere of the common world; in which these create an atmosphere of their own, which might be peopled with mocking and contemptuous shadows and phantom shapes. I am inclined to end this study in morbidity with a quotation from Pater, in his somewhat cynical review of *The Picture of Dorian Gray* by Oscar Wilde. "But his story is also a vivid, though carefully considered, exposure of the corruption of a soul, with a very plain moral pushed home, to the effect that vice and crime make people coarse and ugly."[10]

Paul Verlaine in London[1]

On Sunday, November 19, 1893, Muriel [Broadbent] and I make up the spare bedroom and get it into order for Verlaine's coming.[2] Next day no boats can cross on account of the storm. Instead of coming at 7:40 in the morning the train arrives about one after midnight. At 2:30 I go down below, and there, coming slowly through Fountain Court, a vague, mysterious figure, carrying a tiny valise and leaning on a stout stick, is Verlaine.

I take him upstairs; we sit on the sofa, a box of biscuits between us, and a little gin, and talk till five. Next day, lunch together at Court's Restaurant, Verlaine walking very painfully, leaning on my arm. In the afternoon he shows me the MS. of his lecture and asks my advice about some points, and I promise him my copy of *Sagesse* to read from. All through the day people arriving for tickets. About four Horne and Muriel come, and Mu makes tea for us. At seven, Verlaine and Horne and I go to dinner at a private room in the Roma with Heinemann;[3] then on to the lecture afterwards, at Bernard's Inn. Verlaine sits quietly at the table and reads in a low, agreeable, but rather indistinct voice. It is a great success, everyone is charmed; many people come forward and are introduced to him afterwards, as he sits in the picturesque chair on the little raised platform. Then we go back to the Temple, walking this time; Heinemann and Image come with us. We stay chatting and drinking, then Heinemann goes; we settle up our accounts, they go about two o'clock, and I write my little notice for the *Star*.[4]

Next day Image comes to breakfast, then I take Verlaine to the doctor to have his foot seen to; then Image takes us to lunch at the Holborn; then Verlaine and I go on to the Bodley Head,[5] getting back to the Temple to find Miss Belloc, the lady interviewer, waiting on the stairs. Then visitors arrive: Lane, Horne, Muriel, Crackanthorpe,[6] Dowson, Dolmetsch.[7] Mu makes and serves the tea, and at seven the four of us drive to the Globe, where we are to dine with Heinemann. Gosse is there, too, and we have a charming dinner. Then the Alhambra (Verlaine dates all his misfortunes from a woman he met on coming out of there twenty years ago); we see the Phantos and the Chicago ballet. Verlaine finds it just as it was before. Afterwards we go to the Crown, which is more rowdy than we have ever seen it before. Crowds of people, including a good many of our friends. Then the usual four drive back to the Temple which we enter grandly, the gates opened for us. Next morning I put Verlaine in the train for Oxford, get into the train for Cornwall, and here I am, watching the sea down below, tossing in the bay.

Verlaine's memory of London was wonderful. He recognized everything he had seen before, and every change. Twenty years ago he spent a year in England; stayed with Rimbaud in Howland Street. The woman he is living with now used to be a woman of the streets. "Elle n'est pas jolie, mais c'est une bonne femme; je l'aime; elle m'aime. . . . Nous nous querellons, nous béquetons, quelquefois elle me lance une claque à la figure, elle me traite comme un enfant; elle me fait pleurer, et j'aime ça" (he added, with a subtle smile). "Je ne suis pas beau; elle ne m'aime pas pour ma littérature; mais elle sait que je suis quelqu'un. . . ."

Perhaps if Verlaine's wife had made him weep he would still have been with her. "Mais elle était sotte." She got a divorce and married again; neither she nor their son George will have anything to do with him. He is deeply wounded by both. "Mon fils se permets de me juger." . . . This woman ("la grosse femme"), whom he addresses as Madame Verlaine, has had a considerable influence upon him. For a long time he lost all interest in women, and all pleasure from their company. It was this woman who, as he says, "redeemed" him. "J'ai vécu enormement," he said of his life with her.

I remember an odd thing he said to Horne: "I like to read Shakespeare, but I prefer to see a ballet."

[Lillie Langtry and Oscar Wilde][1]

When I was living on Judge's Walk,[2] several interesting things happened. Yeats was then finishing with Edwin John Ellis[3] a vast edition of the works of *William Blake, Poetic, Symbolical, Critical* which was printed in 1893. Ellis informed me that Mrs. Langtry had asked him to design the decorations for her performance of *Antony and Cleopatra* which had satisfied her; and he added, "Would you care to come with me to the rehearsals?" I said: "I should be most delighted." I went with him to every rehearsal. Lillie Langtry had not then passed the zenith of her superb beauty, and in her profile she always suggested to me Antinoüs.

Perfect bodily sensitiveness; the joy and sadness which are implicit in mere human breathing; a simplicity of sensation which comes at once into the delightful kingdom of things, which we are so painful in our search for, and thus attain a sort of complexity, or its equivalent, without knowing it; life takes on its own terms, and without reference of moment to moment: it is all this that I find in the grave and smiling and unthinking, and pensive head of Antinoüs, in that day-dream of youth, just conscious enough of its own felicity for so much the more heightened enjoyment of that passing moment. When I was in Rome in 1897, I saw another aspect of Lillie Langtry. In the Capitoline Museum of Rome, in a room filled with busts of the emperors, there is one bust, that of Julia, the daughter of Titus, which has for me precisely the charm and pathos of those fragile things to which this kind of art gives something of the consecration of time. The little fashionable head, so small, eager, curled so elaborately for its life of one fashionable day, and seeming to be so little at home in the unexpected, perpetuating coldness of marble: what has such as this to do with the dignity of death? In his famous portrait of Lillie Langtry, Watts gave some of that passionate life infused into Joachim,[4] or the soul itself, fluttering a faint body as a flame is fluttered by the wind (as is the portrait of Swinburne) : for the portraits grow before us, building up man out of dust and breath, as in the first creation. I have referred to the dignity of death. The pagan sentiment should surely be ours: man would remain at home forever on the earth if he could: as it loses its colour and the senses fail, he clings ever closer to it; and yet the mouldering of bones and flesh must go on to the end. * * *

When Rossetti wrote on Mrs. Morris,[5] "Beauty like hers is genius," he thought only of her supreme beauty, of her perfect body, of her languid and to him responsive flesh. She had no genius, no more has Mrs Langtry. [Mrs. Langtry] was never a great actress; she was always too inanimate, too cold when she ought to have been ferociously passionate. And of course the quality of her voice told against her. When she spoke with one in private, when she spoke her lines on the stage, one's nerves were jarred by the harsh, almost masculine voice. Yet I can imagine that deep voice of hers might have been really attractive to many of her lovers.

I suppose I have always been vain—not to excess—of what is supposed to be one's personal beauty. I was quite certain then from the intensity of her gaze on me that she was struck by me. I wrote some verses on her which I sent her. I have them here where I write, written hastily in pencil on one leaf of the paper bound copy of *Antony and Cleopatra*, which had my introduction.[6]

To Mrs Langtry as Cleopatra (written during rehearsal, Nov: 16th 1894)[7]

> I would that Shakespeare could behold in you
> As I, the Cleopatra of his dreams;
> For I have known, this deathless night, it seems,
> A joy the soul of Shakespeare never knew.
>
> And could he see you, serpent of old Nile,—
> The rapturous languor of your witching eyes,
> The sweet malicious magic of your smile—
> The heart of Shakespeare were with Antony's.

* * * One night before the first night when I was wandering through the corridor to the wings, I came on Oscar Wilde, huge in height, with insolent eyes, in evening dress, with the traditional green carnation in his button hole, conversing with some of the made-up girls. He might have been waiting for Lillie Langtry who, I was told, never cared much either for Wilde or for his poetry.[8] * * *

If ever any man of my generation indulged in unreal passions, and to excess, and with a kind of Asiatic luxury—passions, to begin with for women; these passions, utterly extinguished, passion for men and boys; these, to the end, unextinguished, these leading him to an open proclamation of his peculiar and sinister Vice, to an obvious and evident, however carefully or carelessly concealed, advertisement of his Male Prostitution; who trailed with him, or after him, a series of painted boys, and with these was as shameless as Nero or Tiberius—it was Oscar Wilde. Unreal always, no seeker after unrealities, when his tragic death fell upon him he saw, I imagine, nothing before him but the unreal ghost of his unreal Passions.

[Frank Harris and Oscar Wilde][1]

I

When I wrote certain annotations on "Some Problem Plays" I said in reference to Shaw's *Mrs Warren's Profession*:

> Humanity, as Shaw knows, does not move by clockwork and the ultimate justice will have to take count of more exceptions and irregularities than Shaw takes count of. [. . .] Shaw's logic is sterile, because it is without sense of touch, sense of sight, or sense of hearing. Tolstoi's logic is fruitful, because it understands, and because to understand is, among other things, to pardon. In a word, the difference between the spirit of Tolstoi and the spirit of Shaw is the difference between the spirit of Christ and the spirit of Euclid.[2]

Now, it occurs to me to ask: what is the spirit of Frank Harris compared with the spirit of Tolstoi and of Shaw? Harris has a marvellous understanding of humanity, and, being pitiless, he can pardon; like Tolstoi he is abnormally normal and therefore he can express every feeling without having to allow for any personal deduction; he feels to the roots of the emotion: he strikes at civilization, patriotism; he strikes in the same direction as the Nihilists and from the same impulse. His convictions carry him against these barriers; he acts on his convictions; so does the Nihilist. Shaw says in one of his letters, with some lapse in the matter of taste, in answer to the question: "What was wrong with Harris?" "It is necessary to reply: 'He was simply the most impossible ruffian on the face of the earth.' "[3]

Now, supposing that someone had asked me the same question, I would have replied: "On the contrary, during the seven years when I was on really intimate terms with Frank Harris, he seemed to me a man with a prodigious talent which he too often misused: he had an immense vitality, an intense vanity and vivacity and violence; he was endowed with the most vibrant voice I have ever heard, which reminded me of a beaten eastern gong, he was the best and the least exacting Editor I have ever come across, both as Editor of *The Fortnightly Review* and of *The Saturday Review*."⁴ * * * Last June [1925] when I was in Paris I read his privately printed book, *My Life and Loves*, and I was sorry that such a man could have written it. No one could be "agog to know how far our guesses corresponded with the facts." The book is beneath contempt. And yet I do not think he would find any quiet in his grave if he had not divulged what he has divulged. * * *

II

I have before me *Oscar Wilde: His Life and Confessions* by Frank Harris; and, not only from the fact that for at least seven years Harris was one of my intimate friends, but also from the personal and from the literary point of view, I must confess that these two volumes have almost the making of a masterpiece. This book is written with love and hatred, with malice and cruelty and enthusiasm; it is in every sense a living document, and a document of a most amazing and of a most startling kind. Harris refers to Wilde's aversion for Beardsley, which I believe Beardsley shared, and to Wilde's dislike of his illustrations of *Salome;*⁵ besides this he says crudely: "The curious thing about the boy was that he expressed the passions of pride and lust and cruelty more intensely even than Rops." Then comes the inevitable lunch at the Café Royal where Oscar declares he will drink nothing but absinthe. "Absinthe" he declares, "is to all other drinks what Aubrey's drawings are to other pictures; it stands alone: it is like nothing else; it shimmers like southern sunlight in opalescent colouring; it has about it the seduction of strange sins. [. . .] It is just like your drawings, Aubrey; it gets on one's nerves and is cruel. [. . .] When I have before me one of your drawings I want to drink absinthe, which changes colour like jade in sunlight, and makes the senses thrall, and then I can live myself back in imperial Rome, in the Rome of the later Caesars."⁶

I forget in exactly what year I met Oscar Wilde; probably in 1894; certainly one night in an apartment at the top of a house, 64, Margaret Street, that had been taken for the season by Edgar Fawcett and Edgar Saltus.⁷

I was standing in a corner of the room talking with Saltus when I saw enter a man I had often heard of, but did not know by sight. Saltus said: "That is Oscar Wilde." I need not describe his appearance; that is too well known; but, I admit, he puzzled me. I am uncertain now if I felt an instant repugnance at the first sight of so famous a writer, of so prodigious a wit. I gazed at him with curiosity, as I always did when I met strangers. Finally, I saw his eyes fixed on mine, in that insolent fashion he always had. He made Fawcett introduce me to him. He was effusive in his way of shaking hands, a manner he never got over. We sat down and talked for more than an hour.

I had read most of what he had written; it appeared that he had read much of my verse and prose. I remember that we chiefly talked on Paris, France and French literature, and on living French writers. What I liked in him was, first of all, his wit; a kind of brilliant sudden gymnastic, with words in which the phrase itself was always worth more than it said; it was not a wit of ideas in which the thing said was at least on the level of the way of saying it, that I found years afterwards in Whistler's conversation; for with Whistler, it was really a weapon, used as seriously as any rapier in an eternal duel with the eternal enemy. What I liked also in Wilde was his instinct for receiving other people's opinions; which often enough, the moment after he heard them, he claimed as his own.

Much younger as I was than Wilde, I found, gradually, that, with all his reading of French books, he could not—I think he never did—fathom in any essential sense the genius of Verlaine and of Villiers de l'Isle-Adam. He saw things on the surface; was often the dupe of himself. Feeling always after *la nuance,* he never attained it. Not being creative, he never, I think, really understood the ultimate difference between the amazing and bewildering and unachieved things that he wrote and what is creation. Yet, to show his readiness in instantly accepting me for what I was, he asked me to write an article on Villiers de l'Isle-Adam, for *The Woman's World* he was then editing; and this, the first essay written in English on Villiers, he printed.[8] * * *

Once at a Private View in the New Gallery, as I came downstairs, I came on Wilde, in the midst of his admirers, showing more than ever his gift of versatility. Seeing me he made a gesture, and as I went up he introduced me to John Gray, then in what is called "the zenith" of his youth. The adventure was certainly amusing. I was not aware that he was supposed to be the future Dorian Gray of Wilde's novel.[9] * * *

Dorian Gray had many origins. The actual story is a fantastic invention, taken, I imagine, from Balzac's *La Peau de Chagrin,* an unsurpassable masterpiece, in which every scrap of skin from a wild ass shrinks at every will and wish of its possessor. Only in Wilde's—the first essentially French novel written in English—lust and vice and cruelty and abnormality and unnatural passions are treated in a way which one never finds in Balzac. * * *

Sex and Aversion[1]

I suppose I was born wicked and wanton: these stanzas of Blake are
symbolic of my youth and to a certain sense are symbolical of my later
life:

> My mother groaned! my father wept.
> Into the dangerous world I leapt:
> Helpless, naked, piping loud,
> Like a fiend hid in a cloud.
>
> Struggling in my father's hands,
> Striving against my swaddling bands,
> Bound and weary I thought best
> To sulk upon my mother's breast.
> ["Infant Sorrow,"
> *Songs of Experience*, 1794]

My early imagination, which was in embryo, was stirred and obsessed
by people and places, by still sleeping sensations. And of all this I must
have been sleepily half aware. The first imagination of a child in regard
to Lamb, for instance, and to myself, are evidently wonderful: one
dreams, my eyes wander like a cat's inscrutable eyes in which visions
come and go. * * *

I must admit that wanton and wicked people, that most forms of wickedness and wantonness, have inevitably appealed to me. Certain incidents
or accidents, certain divinations of the mind and the spirit, certain incredible desires which make one's blood boil and one's veins palpitate
and one's heart throb wildly, scents, presages, omens, the stupor of noon:
who can number the infinity of these infinitudes? What is born in the
blood remains in the blood, always. I, therefore, have come to the conclusion that I must have a strong constitution—my father had it who
lived to a great age, both my grandfathers had it—which, together with
my nervous energy, has carried me through more perils, imprisonments,
calamities, joys and raptures, violent passions, and immense exaltations
in travelling abroad (apart from those millions of small things that make
up part of one's existence) than any man I have ever heard of. I must

not, of course, forget Casanova; Casanova's escape from the *Piombi* in Venice was miraculous.² Casanova was never a model of virtue; nor was I, as passionate after sensations as Casanova, my passions in regard to them have always varied. I also—what real lover has not?—tasted the forbidden fruits of the earth; but certainly with less gluttony than one finds in Casanova's enjoyment of them. As for one's past, that's a question much too difficult to solve. * * *

It is simply incredible for us to forget our past; and of all poets and painters whose existence was so tragic and so passionate, whose life, as Pater said, "was a crisis at every moment," one who lived the life of the imagination at the same time that his immense mesmerism was exerted over women, who endured the eternal tragedy of those who have loved the absolute in beauty too well, and with too mortal a thirst: Rossetti, surely, was the most unlikely of all men to forget his past. At the same time, hypnotic as he was to an amazing degree, I could imagine that he could hypnotise himself. I have always known that I am mesmeric, but not hypnotic. I have exerted my mesmerism so many times—either unconsciously or deliberately—perhaps one uses both at once—and, as a matter of fact, it has never failed.

Sex—the infernal fascination of Sex—even before I actually realised the meaning of its stirrings in me—has been my chief obsession. One's own Vitality: that is a centre of Life and of Death. It is also the centre of Creation. Without the possession of women, how can one create? I know not how many artists have created or invented who are sexless: yet there is always something lacking—the essence, the quintessence of the ultimate, the achievement—in such painters, as Watts, in such writers as Ruskin and Carlyle. There seems to me in such cases as these a kind of sterilization. I find in Ruskin a feverish rhetoric and an almost unimpassioned eloquence. De Quincey's style carried further with less imagination becomes the style of Ruskin and what is frankly called prose poetry, a lucky bastard glorying in the illegitimacy of its origin. Carlyle, with his enormous and Teutonic energy which makes his volumes on the French Revolution a magnificent masterpiece, was a poet in prose as Ruskin never was. Thus when Ruskin wrote verse, it was lamentable, not because it was uncouth like Carlyle's few uneasy fragments, but because there was no poet at work in it. Carlyle has said supreme things about a few great poets whom he cared for most; he has shown a sense of what poetry really was, under a cynic's cloak of rugged contempt.

* * * Wilde's vices were not simply intellectual perversions, they were physiological. This miserable man had always been under the influence of one of those sexual inversions which turned him into a kind of Hermaphroditus. That distress which he tried to express in his writings after his condemnation had nothing virile in it; and his best known

tragedy *Salome* reveals in its perversion of a legend his own sexual perversion. As he grew older the womanish side of him grew more and more evident. Lautrec saw him in Paris, and in the appalling portrait of him he shows Wilde, swollen, puffed out, bloated and sinister. The form of the mouth which he gave him is more than any thing exceptional; no such mouth ought ever to have existed: it is a woman's that no man who is normal could ever have had. The face is bestial. A man with a ruined body and a ravaged mind and a senseless brain does not even survey the horror of his hideous countenance in a mirror: this thing that is no more a thing gazes into the void.

My morbid and abominable sense of aversion, for I know not how many people, began when I was a mere child, when I used to sob and shrick when I was carried in my mother's arms to see people I hated and to enter houses I loathed, has if anything increased. Hating temperamentally to remain one whole day under any roof in which I am one with the Wandering Tribe—and never going out without lighting on men, girls, and artists by what is called my "flair" or my "genius" for such encounters, which always delight me; or without coming across odious creatures. There are not a few of these odious creatures I have met, mostly men, sometimes women, I would willingly hate out of existence. There are so many people who have no manners at all, who intrude into one's privacy, who enter one's house or one's room with all the insolence of the parvenu, as if either the house or the room belonged to them; who are literally eaten up with self-conceit; who are as much a nuisance as a pestilence or a plague; who, as a matter of fact, deserve to be kicked, flung down stairs, as Landor certainly did, as Richard Burton[3] certainly did, as Rossetti certainly did. To those of us—most artists, that is, who are at once gifted and punished for their sensitive nerves, such as Pachmann[4] and [Augustus] John—an intruder, one to whom one is hostile, whose very voice one hates, gives us nothing but jars to the nerves.

I have in me a spirit of revenge, of unforgetfulness, of an implacable insolence which resents any insult which might perhaps not have meant to have been an insult, as much as it resents the interference of any living being with my own liberty. Among the many passions of Emily Brontë, the dominant one was to live, "where she may be alone with liberty." She is alone with her "chainless soul" as I am alone with my "chainless soul." She forgot nothing; that sense of personal identity which aches in all her poems, in all her prose, is a sense, not of the delight, but of the ineradicable sting of personal identity. A quenchless will is part of her pride: like Shelley she echoes the useless rebellions of the earth. So this woman, one of the greatest women who ever lived, was self-consumed by the disease which sapped her constitution, by the burning fire of her imagination. That ineradicable sting has always meant to me not the final sting of death, but the sting of all the sins I have committed. It is the serpent's sting; it is a sting of the nerves.

Then again the terror of meeting those we have to meet and hate to have to meet. I explain nothing: that explains itself. Call it exasperation, suspense, call it whatever name you like, it remains always at the root the same, in the sense of the roots of the weeds. In certain night-vigils or in waking dreams, I remember not without some of Baudelaire's cynical amusement and sardonic irony, the various well-known men who—being aware not only of my verses but of the fact of the immoral life I was certainly then leading, that I was a danger to Society—deliberately snubbed me in the street. These insults, just then, I neither forgot nor forgave.

I was then certainly under no delusions nor indeed under any illusions on the question that my own life; living as I did always what manner of existence best suited me, was my own affair, absolutely; and that neither friend nor foe had the least reason for interfering with any act of mine, with any spoken word; and that whether my life was moral or immoral, depraved or degraded, insolent or isolated, that remained as literally my own secret as Baudelaire's, who having cultivated his hysteria—as I was supposed to have cultivated my own hysteria—with all the casuistry of a Confessor, did actually become a confessor of sins, who has never told the whole truth.

One thing must always be taken for granted: that no sooner has a poet printed a book of Erotic Verses, no sooner has a painter painted various Erotic Subjects—whether it be a question of Rodin or of Verlaine, of the Marquis de Sade in his prose, of Aretino in his avowed obscenities—a man's work and a man's existence are mixed together in an extricable fashion; certainly not to be imaged by the knots of serpents who are literally strangling one another with terrified struggles to escape from Medusa's brain, but by the innate corruption of what is in such cases a mere parody of the Original Sin. * * *

My Planets[1]

These are my Planets under which I was born near on midnight at Milford Haven, Wales, on the 28th of February, 1865.[2]

> If the astrologers speak truth, and tell
> That the stars make for us our heaven and hell,
> My passionate and perverse horoscope,
> Where the intellectual forces may not cope
> With Scorpio, Herschel, Venus and the Moon,
> Marked in my life that love in me should swoon
> Into the arms of strange affinities
> It was myself looked at me with your eyes,
> Where Venus and the Moon with Herschel strove
> In some ambiguous paradox of Love.[3]
> ["Mundi Victima, II," *Amoris Victima,* 1897]

In my horoscope, which was made by George Pollexfen, an uncle of Yeats at Rosses Point, Sligo, Ireland, every detail marked out from my signs in the Zodiac, was foreseen from my youth onward and up to that point in 1896, and up to the present year, 1925, with a sinister certainty in regard to what has been good and evil in my nerve-tormented existence which literally bewilders my imagination. There are signs of it in *Days and Nights,* 1889; there are signs of it in all my books of verse, down to *Lesbia* and *Love's Cruelty.*[4] Pater never said anything more fundamental in regard to me than in th[is] sentence: " 'J'aime passionnément la Passion,' " he might say with Stendhal. * * *

I have loved Passion—in my own way—as passionately as Catullus and Villon and Verlaine. And yet there are such infinite ways as well as entanglements by which one apprehends Passion. Verlaine was more passionately in love with life than any man I ever knew and yet I do not imagine that he loved Passion for Passion's sake—nor as amorously as Villon and Catullus loved passion for Passion's sake. * * *

I sometimes think, that in many of my poems on the subject of harlots, I have given evidence of the purity of my intentions, apart from the supposed or imaginary impurity of such subjects as these. One requires in such verses the simple sudden sound of plain lines which should show, at least, one's absolute poetic power upon words. * * *

In April 1893 when I found myself in the Casino Eden in Antwerp with Dowson and Smithers,[5] my experiences were awful enough, apart from my stupefaction. The result of this were these verses:

Eyes that caught my eyes, and hungered, as a fire;
Hands that sought and caught my hands in their desire;
Hands and eyes that clipt and lipt me as a hungering fire!

But I turned away from your ecstatic eyes
But my heart was silent to your eager sighs,
But I turned to other eyes from your imploring eyes.

Hands that I rejected, you were fain to give;
Eyes that for their moment lived me, as I live;
Mouth that kissed me: Flora of the Eden, O forgive! . . .
["Flora of the Eden: Antwerp," *London Nights,* 1895]

The creature who to my horror kissed me and who caught hold of me with the bestial ferocity of a wild beast was insatiable: so that she reminds me of the immortal Hysteria, "the monstrous, indifferent, insensible Beast, poisoning all that go near to her, all that look on her, all that she touches; she that has become the symbolic deity of indestructible Lust, chosen among many by the catalepsy that has stiffened her limbs that has hardened her muscle."[6] I imagine that the creature was under the spell of some form of catelepsy; never in my life have I been so tormented and so furiously and ignobly attacked as by Flora; a vampire of the worst imaginable kind. She might even have been a Succubus. I have before me a learned book entitled *Demonality or Incest and Succubi* by the Rev. Father Sinistrari of Ameno, written originally in Latin. "For the Incubus is by reason of his body more noble because more subtle; consequently, when having an intercourse with an Incubus, man does not degrade; and, taking that into consideration, Demonality cannot be more than Bestiality. Incubi and Succubi have therefore body and soul, and consequently are animals." He refers to the *Lamia,* out of whose legend Keats created one of his most wonderful poems, which is consummate; it is a passionate, almost morbid expression of the conflict between those antagonistic forces which fought their battle out continually within his breast: it is flame-like and its colours dazzle one's eyes with their brilliance.

He, sick to lose
The amorous promise of her lone complain,
Swooned, murmuring of love, and pale with pain.
[I, 287–89]

Keats is a Decadent before Baudelaire: like him he is Neo-Latin in
his insistence on the physical symptoms of his lovers, the bodily translations of emotion. All that trembling and swooning of his lovers would at
all events be very much at home in modern French poetry, where love is
again, as it was to Catullus and Propertius, a sickness, an exhausting
madness, or a poisoning. And in love, doubt is part of that torture
without which few persons of imagination would fling themselves quite
heartily into the pursuit. And that is the poet's business amid the cloudy
splendour of natural things: to have no identity, to be a voice, a vision.[7]
I have come to * * * one of my studies in strange flesh, and I have
chosen one because it is peculiarly pure and because for that reason it
is one of my favourites: "Dawn."

Here in this little room
You sleep the sleep of innocent tired youth,
While I, in very sooth,
Tired, and awake beside you in the gloom,
Watch for the dawn, and feel the morning make
A loneliness about me for your sake.

You are so young, so fair,
And such a child, and might have loved so well;
But now, I cannot tell,
But surely one might love you anywhere,
Come to you as a lover, and make bold
To beg for that which all may buy with gold.

Your sweet, scarce lost, estate
Of innocence, the candour of your eyes
Your childlike, pleased surprise,
Your patience: these afflict me with a weight
As of some heavy wrong that I must share
With God who made, and man who found you, fair.
[from *London Nights*]

I have the exact date of that event: January 12th, 1893. She was one
of the youngest and one of the most beautiful girls I have ever met. Her

youth, her rare beauty, her amazing and absolute innocence, her delicious sense of surprise because I had both pleased and surprised her—I had come upon her in the promenade of the Empire—and that joy of life which was part of the freshness and the fairness of her youth: all that, which was not exactly new to me, instilled into my very blood a sense of pity which I had never felt before in all my intercourse with harlots.

Now that was exactly what I had seen, when she was undressing so slowly and so daintily before me: the insidious manner in which such a girl—unexperienced as she was in most of the nets and arts of love—undoes (or lets one undo) a series of buttons, and, if she wears stays these have to be undone; then she lets fall her dress which coils around her feet; the petticoat soon follows the dress: then one gets the glimpse of those tempting and clinging white drawers which invariably excite one's senses, knowing exactly what they conceal, but not yet aware of the shapeliness of the legs. Those moments of expectation which makes one's heart beat so rapidly are as it were the moments before and after a crisis. One is reluctant to unveil immediately one of the woman's last disguises. The bodice slips off on its own accord: the breasts palpitate under the chemise. And it is then that she laughs and blushes and becomes shy and puts out her tiny hands as if to ward one off. It is I who remove her chemise. Then she laughs merrily and lets me kiss her breasts and the hollows between them. That excites her: her eyes glow and her cheeks crimson: nervous shivers run all over her body. She makes a great effort and draws back. Then she sits down and takes off her shoes, then her stockings, and in an instant the drawers are on the floor. That instinctive manner she has of leaning over on herself excites one's flesh almost to a boiling point. One sees the naked back, one sees the small breasts round as apples stand out most invitingly in the effort she makes even in the undoing of her shoe-laces. Then the girl I refer to rose to her feet, without the least shame, but excitedly, let me devour passionately all that there is in such pure and perfect nakedness. She was a masterpiece of flesh.

But "God do so unto me, and more also"—whatever that Scriptural imprecation may mean—"if ever again I lend anything more valuable than money to a woman or an artist," wrote Swinburne, who, at least in private and when I was with him, had a curious passion for imprecations. They lift a weight off one's mind, they relieve the tension of one's spirit, they are most beneficial for the nerves. We are in such haste to be doing, to be writing, to make our voices audible for a moment in the derisive silence of eternity, that we forget one thing, of which we are only the parts—namely, to live and to exist.

[Marcelle and Other Parisian Diversions]¹

I came on Marcelle—who, for one thing, was a Lesbian—in the Moulin Rouge; I went back with her that night, and many another night after that; she lived at the top of a house that gave on la Place Pigalle: She comes into *London Nights* in "Hands" and "Mauve, Black and Rose." The first is an evident imitation of one of Verlaine's poems in *Sagesse*. Its first stanza reads:

> The little hands that once were mine,
> The hands I loved, the lovely hands,
> After the roadways and the strands,
> And realms and Kingdoms once divine.
> ["XVII: Les chère mains . . . ," 1881]

and mine:

> The little hands too soft and white
> To have known more laborious hours
> Than those which die upon a night
> Of kindly wine and fading flowers.

The second is Latin and decadent and perverse; it has an intricate and erotic meaning: every image used is symbolical of some of the things she wore and of parts of her body.

> Mauve, black, and rose,
> The veils of the jewel, and she, the jewel, a rose.
>
> First, the pallor of mauve,
> A soft flood flowing about the body I love.
>
> Then, the flush of the rose,
> A hedge of roses about the mystical rose.

Last, the black, and at last
The feet that I love, and the way that my love has passed. * * *

There used to be a famous and infamous Night House in Paris, on the Boulevard des Capucines, above either the Café de la Paix or the Americain; and exactly on the opposite side of the street Juliens, where one had delicious ices. This I frequented, with others, night after night; we got there after the theatres were over and remained there until one saw dawn, pallid as the moon, through the windows. It was one of the most riotous and rowdy places of that kind in Paris; room after room, men and women coming up and down the stairs, at times an interminable throng; there were the usual drinks and the usual dancers, besides some of the women who lived there. The heat was suffocating. * * *

In all that there is a purely Parisian kind of luxury—*une soif des femmes*—and with this the much more material fact that these women are there, as they are everywhere else, to excite men's desire, and to excite their own, to kill time—as far as time ever can be killed—and to be men's merchandise. As people took turns at the piano, I often took mine; and, with the atrocious heat that went from my head to my heels and to the end of my finger-tips, I made mad music rise out of those notes I touched, which maddened the dancers, and which made me perhaps too often turn my head to observe their furious extravagances.

When we went down that narrow staircase to the Boulevard des Capucines there was only room for two, and one got confused in the midst of those over-dressed women, with some of the over-dressed men; until, on the sudden, the cold wind struck our heated foreheads and made us pause. The chances were that on certain nights I slept alone in my hotel in the Latin Quarter; that on certain nights I slept out.

On one of those memorable nights when at the Moulin Rouge I had conversed with Lautrec, who was seated at his usual table, several women seated beside him, and had left him to join the avid circle that tightens like a snake who tightens his coils around the chahut dancers, while, being tall, I looked over the heads of the others, then got through them, and watched greedily these licentious dancers: suddenly the band stopped and they stopped, and La Mélinite flung herself into my arms.[2] We rejoined Lautrec, and I finally went home with her: she lived not far from the Moulin Rouge. Famed as she was as a Lesbian, she had also an almost cruel passion for men. That night of all the nights I spent with her is one of my most memorable nights. There was nothing that girl could not do: sterile as she was, but one who could exhaust others when she herself was not exhausted. At times she hardly breathed, she trembled all over, shivered, shuddered: rained her kisses on me as she embraced me: her mouth on mine that ached with heat. Then her hands seized my hands, she strained them as her lips sucked at my lips. Then, as they closed inextricably, her abandoned body that was abandoned to mine became rigid with sterile ecstasies, as one sudden shiver knitted my flesh with hers. Then was she deathless and divine, and equal flame-like with my fires. The whole obscure universe that had gathered itself together between the walls of her room divided itself. Then, I know not how long after that, the fascinations of her flesh snared me, as Circe's snare men's souls—I breathed in a web of burning fire. * * *

In Paris I got utterly tired of that eternal refrain: "Couchez-avec," always with a note of interrogation. Sex in Paris is an obsession, and often to a point of sheer abnormality. In Paris, in the Cafés, the grand Boulevards, in those of the Quartier Latin, and elsewhere, one's conversation is inevitably mixed with Sex and the Sexes; that rarely happens in London, except in the Café Royal, the Eiffel Tower, and in certain night haunts. In Paris one can talk for hours that never seem endless on all imaginable topics—Sex being always the under current. When I used to sit at nights on the terrasse of the Café d'Harcourt, which was the chief haunt of that Quarter and of their fugitive and faithless lovers, I never anywhere enjoyed anything like the conversation that went on between them—whether I joined in their conversations, as I often did, with some Suzanne on one side of me and some Jean on the other side, nothing seemed to matter. Our conversation might easily become lewd and licentious; but the free and easy way in which we discussed our invariable, variable, inevitable, stupid, atrocious, vile, ignoble, delicious and malicious topics, was as pure as one's breath. Most of these young unsophisticated girls were fearfully fascinating; in the summer so lightly clad that you could almost divine their nakedness under their dresses; bodies which seemed always so willing to offer their most intimate charms to anyone who wanted to go home with them; faces so eager and wild, so wicked and so innocent, so impure and so pure; ripe red lips that might suck your soul out of you; mouths so amorous and at the same time so full of laughter; voices, of course that varied, which were rarely beautiful, which, fairly often, were hoarse from the effect of too much brandy. Gay, light hearted, hot-blooded, vicious, passionate, morbid, cruel, jealous, implacable, shifty, crafty, perverse, exasperated, furious and insatiable: there they were, for one's choice, when they were not as they mostly were, the mistresses of the men who were with them; even in these cases it depended entirely on the girl's sudden whim or caprice.

One always had the strange feeling that there might be something perilous in them: the sex gone wrong, corrupted, tainted; for these daughters of Sin and of Death bear always in their wombs the seeds of Eve, which like woman's first temptation by the Serpent have in them the seeds of birth and the seeds of death. * * *

Hugues Rebell[1]

Hugues Rebell, a Breton by birth, born in 1868, died in Paris in March 1905, at the age of thirty-seven. He was violent in every sense of the word, as violent as his animality, and he was one of the most astonishing figures of our generation, and one of the most original. He made his appearance in Paris in 1892, in the Latin Quarter, where I frequently met him in houses and in cafés. He was always dressed in black, clean-shaved, somewhat fat in body and in face; there was in his aspect a mixture of the formidable and the feminine, which at once drew one's attention to the man: one saw the ardent passion in his eyes, that reminded me of what I must call the furnace of a soul, and an inner fire which seemed to infect his face with all the violence of his blood. At times a strange timidity made him hesitate: but when he spoke the words burst out of his mouth with a vengeance. * * * His force was frantic, almost elemental: like one of those vital forces which are driven this and that way by the four winds from the four quarters of the world. He could be shameless in his speech. An insensate thirst intoxicated him with the desire to drink in all the perfumes and all the madness and all the vice and vehemence that exist upon the earth, together with a frenzied appetite and an audacity which reminded me when I saw him now of Nero, now of Tiberius, now of Caligula, gave to the man himself an exasperation which showed at least the atrocity of his nerves. * * *

He was one of those to whom love and hate were interchangeable words. * * * And yet he was not always dominated by his passion: it was when he was most logical and most certain of himself that passion itself seemed to take the words out of his mouth. There was nothing he hated more than Democracy: he had a repugnance to it which—were one to venture to use the word before him by hazard—raised what I might call the howl of a lion. His vocabulary certainly never equalled Verlaine's: but, as for his invective, you might turn over a dozen pages of Verlaine's *Invectives* and you would find nothing like them. In these pages there is a devouring rage—as in the case of Rebell—which must flame itself out, not a subtle malice, justifying its existence, as the serpent does by the beauty of its coils. Rebell apparently took the greatest possible care of himself, but he seemed in some sinister manner to disregard his health, which was magnificent.

He ignored so many things which are literally essential. As for the conventional division of time, as to our relative submission to the alternatives of day and night, he ignored them. He ruined his health because he fatally ignored the fact that sleep and rest must of necessity interrupt the intoxication of one's work. His days, and the greater part of his nights, were spent in this fashion: he would sit before his table writing, and all around his room were immense bookshelves which overflowed with books, and opposite to him was a virile engraving of Montaigne between two portraits of Wagner and Nietszche. At night he lighted his candles which he replaced as soon as the wicks were extinguished, and this went on for endless hours. He literally—and he himself showed it— ignored fatigue; thirteen hours of uninterrupted work never tired him.

Rebell, being rich, had a passion for travelling: he went to Spain, England, Germany and Italy; he learnt the dialects of Venice and Naples; he knew Spanish and Italian and English. He went to Madrid with the intention of writing a book on Goya, which never appeared. He wrote a study of Rops, but not with the tremendous instinct of Huysmans for what is bestial and obscene in the work of a man who had in him Belgian and Hungarian blood.[2] * * *

Rebell had a prodigious passion and lust for the flesh of women: therefore his most creative work is bestial and sexual and enigmatical and exotic and Satanical and monstrous and intensely imaginative. And, I must confess, that the main part of his prose was as abnormal as the man himself. He was an absolute type of Abnormality. He was an impure Pagan and he had his cult for Venus: he praised her as an offended Goddess, as a God against whom man sins every day of his life. On one side was nature, instinct, the universal attraction of the Sexes: on the other side, pure imagination; nor did he ever fix his gaze upon the brilliant face of this double Image without the other appearing to him a sinister and exciting altar of repose. As he rendered homage to Woman and to her Sex he seems to have fought the inevitable battle between the Flesh and the Spirit which is part of our inevitable Destiny. * * *

Are there not certain sexual perfumes which are said to be capable of annihilating the Sex? The Gods are perfidious: one must not offer too much incense before the shrine of Aphrodite, one must not be misled by the divine malice of certain of these Divinities. Even when he spoke of love there awakened in him the idea of a faith he might impose upon one. He was Breton and Catholic: making love, speaking of love, writing of love, he knew what he had to sacrifice, he knew the occult sense of the sacrifice. * * *

He was an Immoralist and Moralist: therefore in his absolute fashion he treats of love, now as a lover, now as a passionate Sensualist, always luxurious and often licentious. He is a depraved Prelate who says the Black Mass on the naked body of a Harlot, and who says it with not so much with the spirit of Satan as with the fervour of a Saint.

La Nichina, 1897, is his masterpiece: a resurrection of Venice, in the 16th century, which does honour to his learning, his exactitude, and to the intensity of his vision of a life which actually did exist in that dissolute century, which was violent and vehement, frantic, luxurious, furious, pitiless and at times languid. His conception is derived from the *Raggiomenti* of Aretino; and it is just as turbulent, exotic, in the immensity of its adventures. It is a singular and sinister work of art, and its fire and flame and shamelessness, its vivacity, its voracity, its Bacchic raptures, its insane perversities, and homosexuality, remind me in a sense of the *Memoirs* of Casanova in their licence and passion for debauch and for excesses and amusements. In the case of Rebell, his creation is complete, it is a world invented out of his capricious desires, which is to a certain extent *cérébrale.* * * *

Rebell's last years were unutterably miserable and his troubles became worse during the tortures he endured from his malady. If he did not die of hunger, that was because Maurice Barrès and Ernest-Charles[3] saved him from starvation: they put aside for him six hundred francs which they gave Louise· Favier,[4] for her to present to the proud and easily offended novelist. She glided these notes among the flowers she had brought him, one afternoon, [in the] boulevard des Batignolles. I certainly knew those rooms and their contents, nor have I forgotten the warmth of Rebell's welcome, nor the immense and marvellous fascination of his conversations. He was a Breton gentleman, animal to a degree, and he told me that his ancestors were Corsairs of Nantes (I had not then visited Nantes) and he added that this explained the violence of his blood which stirred all his senses. * * *

The facts are that Rebell, being obliged to escape from his creditors, went to a kind of hiding place in the Marais, where he was followed by a vile couple of outcasts of Montmartre, who, for some time previous to his ruin, had entirely subjugated him. The refined and marvellous artist had sunk to be (so I was told) the submissive slave of this bully and his worse paramour. It was said that they actually subjected him to violence: he who had always been so violent and who, in spite of this (as I knew) remained to the end an erudite scholar and a dandy. One day when he was wandering furtively about the streets he fell down in a fit, and was removed to the accident ward of the Hôtel Dieu, where he died. This was found out by his task-masters, and they, for reasons of their own, concealed it. Only ten days later was the fact of his death discovered. It was found in the *État Civile* that Rebell had expired in the ward and also the date of his death, so that his family regained possession of his body, which they buried in his native Brittany.

Jean Lorrain[1]

To have met Jean Lorrain, alone or with Gourmont at the Folies Bergères, or with Retté[2] in an Evil House, was a furrowing lesson in life; he was abnormally vicious, depraved and infamous. He was a scandal monger, a gambler; he was, without attempting to be so, preposterously prodigious: and to have seen, as I did, this painted dandy standing rigid beside one of the pillars in the promenade, to have gazed into his tormented eyes, when he was talking with some harlot or with some Sodomite; to have seen him mingle in the crowd and never to see him again, was one of the customary events in Paris. When I spoke with him his replies were venomous: his words stung, hurt one, they were cruel, merciless: they hit like corrosive iron. He, who was a mixture of vices and of aversions, of lusts and of abnormal passions, in whom a really artistic sense got mixed up with all that is ironical and hateful, was always spasmodically alert and alive; he was an irritable creature born with a depraved imagination and a depraved body.

No sooner had Lorrain arrived in Paris—having taken some rooms high up on the Quai Voltaire, where he lived a disorganised life, from which his prose suffered—a sense of weariness, of lassitude, crept over him; he had won the reputation of one who was bitter, sarcastic, sinister and original. He had always on him some unpleasant odour, "une mauvaise odeur de mangeaille et de pierre d'évier."

When he began to decline invitations, these refusals were evidently a sign of his degradation, of his insolence. One suspected him of keeping mistresses, but as no one ever saw them when they were with him, it seemed evident that his passion went in the direction of young men, so that those who were fascinated by art reproached him for preferring these evil creatures to women. He was calumniated, and for certain reasons he left the Quartier Latin with the idea that he might lead a more regular life on the other side of the Seine. He was soon disabused. There were no more for him the gluttonous kisses and the cheap caresses of the whores he had frequented, no more of the painted girls in the Taverns; he found another class of whores, vicious and adulterate, flowers of literature and of disease, unsexual or oversexual, and with these—with those whose eye-lashes were too black, whose mouths were too red, souls too desperately naked—he tasted ether, cocaine and opium. He gave himself up to these aphrodisiacs, out of curiosity, and he never gave them up. Inevitably his nervous system began to fail; he was

undermined, he had become more and more corrupt. Certain vigils
given up to experiments in the theories of Poe, De Quincey and
Baudelaire, during which he noted down his tormented symptoms, were
interrupted by dizziness. He became inert, as if his heart had ceased to
beat, thinking he was dead. His doctors wanted him to leave Paris. He
gave up ether and began to use morphine. He was famous: he worked
terrifically, and, as he had no choice in his hours of work, he wrote
during the night till dawn. He took strong drinks, so as to provoke his
excitations, and no sooner had he finished his work than he had recourse
to stupefying drugs. He wandered at night in the direction of the
Giunguettes of Chaton, and the *Bastringues* du Point du Jour; one found
him in the brothels of the Place Maubert (which Guys used to haunt),
and he chose by preference, so that he might study the crowd. * * *

One night in Paris when Lorrain, during a crisis, fell on the floor,
his arms thrown out both ways, implored those who were near him to
friction him, or to massage him, so as to bring back the circulation of
the blood, they undressed him completely, they took off his rings, and
when he returned to himself, pitiful to behold, his eyes half open, the
heavy eyelids filled with unshed tears, he found himself naked, in a
whore's bed where someone had taken the trouble to convey him.
Lorrain had come into the interloping world out of sheer animal
curiosity, without antipathy or disgust: in a certain sense that of the
born artist, for he had a prodigious talent and a marvelous style and a
remarkable power of invective.

It was the mixture of the artist and the Sadist which drove him into
these perilous enterprises: he was forced by his animality to study these
whores and their men with an intense attentiveness. He came to know
them absolutely. He became one of the clients of these various brothels,
where the women assailed him with their shameless solicitations: and all
this naturally awakened the suspicions of the police. All these *vedettes*
of crime and crapulence Lorrain had known through men older. Thanks
to these Lorrain was well provided for: the debauched women of the
banks of Bettancourt, the prostitutes of the Place Maubert, the trulls
of the brothels of the Barrièrs, took great care of him. One night he had
the audacity of asking certain hatless girls to join him in a night house
who were not lacking in that charm which is appropriate to these corners
of the fortifications but whose presence that night showed as it were
a shattering impertinence. They came from Grenelle, and dressed as
they always are they arrived at the door of the establishment, where they
were refused entrance, so that they had to wait at the bottom of the
staircase until Lorrain appeared, in his impeccable costume, and who,
mentioning the known names of these women, escorted them to the
dining room with its flashing lights where their impertinence was

warmly welcomed. Introduced with imaginary names such as: Le Môme Poil dru, la Marquise de X, they seated themselves at the tables, and I can at least imagine what that night really was: a Parisian orgy and an intoxicated one. Apart from this, one of the whores of the Point du Jour, with whom he would have nothing to do, swore that she would have her revenge by having him castrated. Therefore Lorrain did not remain inflexible towards this jolly girl, not only on account of his fear of her, but because she had accused him of calling her by a cruel name. * * *

Lorrain, on the sudden, became "l'homme du jour" and remained so for I know not how many years. He was immensely popular. His fame was based on his sinister and infamous novels. * * *

Monsieur de Phocas is the most monstrous, perverse, abnormal, cruel, venomous, infamous modern novel I have ever read. It is a long confession of the Duc de Héneuse who has assumed the name of Monsieur de Phocas. One of its originals might be in the *A Rebours* of Huysmans, Des Esseintes, who, like Phocas, is the last descendant of an ancient family, his impoverished blood stained by all sorts of excesses, who, appearing to be eternally young as he is eternally old—finds himself, "Sur le chemin, dégrisé, seul, abominablement lassé!" And in both books the same fantastic banquets and bizarre and malevolent amours, the reincarnation of the Sphinx, the episodes of evil boys. Both are hallucinated, obsessed, cruel, and nervous; both are *détraqué;* and there are morbid horrors and menaces and the offsprings of unnatural adulteries: there are the opium dreams, the disturbing visions; and a sense that grows upon them of terror and suspense; both have nervous maladies, are spasmodic, are haunted by sounds, are at times morbidly hysterical and have in them a kind of mystical Corruption. * * *

During the last fifteen years of his life he was seized with the passion of wandering: his imitator being Uzanne.[3] He wrote from Venice, "On the night of my arrival my emotion was so intense before San Marco and the Ducal Palace that I nearly wept. Venice is the most intense and the rarest emotion of my life. I don't want to return to France. I feel here the vivid existence of two guilty beings flame and blaze in me." * * * Wherever he went—to Nice, Venice, Bayonne, Monte Carlo, Marseilles, the Riviera—his Legend went with him: and his Legend, as he himself assured me in Paris, was stupendous, infamous, criminal. * * * And he had wandered enormously, over Algeria, Spain, Italy, Corsica, Besière, Toulon, Hyères, Saint Jean-de-Luz, Bayonne, Biarrits, returning from time to time to Paris. At last he found a villa at Nice, on the Boulevard de l'Imperatrice de Russie. * * * He became intimate with the fishermen, he wandered with Raouba Capeau or Lazaret.[4] He dressed simply with the intention of getting on with the sailors, the *débardeurs,* and *les gouapes.* He seemed to them infamous. He began to paint his face. As powder and cold cream would have given his complexion that ghastly livid hue of *La Goulue,*[5] he touched up, with rouge, his cheeks, and ears; sometimes, if the painting had been too harshly done, above the ear and underneath the lobe, some of the rouge which had melted, stained the cheeks and revealed the *Maquillage.* The lips livid and dry moistened with *raisin,* the edge of the nostrils just touched with rouge, the line of the eyebrows barely outlined with a greasy pencil, and sometimes his eyelids made heavier than their wont with rimmel: all that was done imperceptibly, with light judicious touches. The most indulgent among these brutal and simple common folk said *"Quelle Grue"* and Lorrain, disdainful, unconcerned, went his way. Lorrain evoked Byzantium with his words, his rings, his feverish and intoxicated eyes, his hallucinated eyes, with disquieting eyelids, his eyes which reflected no ecstasy, but what is inert in worn out jewels. He had the death he deserved: "le suicide d'une humanité lasse de voir toujours le désir mûrir implacable dans le fastidieux verger de la Volupté."

Édouard Dubus[1]

Poe, the victim of his heredity, his nerves, his drink and his drugs, was found stupefied in a rum shop in Baltimore on October 3, 1849, on the day of the Election, having evidently been drugged by those who made him vote,[2] he was taken to hospital, where he remained, save for a few brief intervals, in a state of delirium. Before he expired, he said: "Lord, help my poor soul." He was only forty. Dubus, in June 1899, was found stupefied on the place Maubert; he was taken to a hospital where he expired almost at once, at the age of thirty-two.[3] Retté assigned one of the causes of his death to the nefarious influence over him of Stanislas de Guaita, the Occultist, the Morphomaniac.[4] * * *

It amuses me to read in *The Savoy* of April 1896 Sir Edmund Gosse's witty and piquant account of the three exciting days and nights which he spent in the Latin Quarter in April 1893.[5] Dining, which was inevitable, in the Café d'Harcourt, where Moréas was in the chair and where Gosse had the honour of giving his arm on his way there to a most amiable lady, the Queen of Golconda, whose exact rank among the crowned heads of Europe is, he feared, but vaguely determined. They wanted to find Verlaine. "I was losing all hope, and we were descending the Boulevard, our faces set for home; the Queen of Golconda hanging heavily on my arm, and having a flattering misconception as to my age, was warning me against the temptations of Paris, when two young poets, a male and a female, most amiably hurried up to meet us with the intoxicating news that Verlaine had been seen to dart into a little place called the Café Soleil d'Or." Long before that Café changed its name and at the same time lost its reputation I incessantly haunted it. Dubus was often to be seen there, always late at night and often in the company of Louise Lacour who, after her contact with so many poets, assumed the name of Diana Morello. She was insatiable, small, as sinuous as a snake, from whose skirts emanated electric currents; she fascinated those who had loved her between two sheets. Her dark eyes flamed with desires; those she had welcomed on her immense divan have never forgotten her. No more have I. But the point I have arrived at is this: that she was too often flanked with a fair haired woman to whom Retté had given the nickname of *La Reine de Golconda,* the same one who had hung on the arm of Gosse: the same who used to hang not so heavily on mine; the same who, flattering

or not, as far as I was concerned, never for a moment ventured to warn
me against the perilous snares and temptations of Paris, nor against the
insurgent memories of those visions and shadowy loves, that are as vital
in their veins as in ours, and that turn Chastity (Saint Augustine's)
into a vain mockery: it might mean to some no more than "the crackling
of thorns under a pot." It was Diana, not the chaste Diana, nor the
Goddess of the Moon, but the woman Dubus conceived under the image
of Diana who inspires men with madness: one sees her image, naked
and luxurious, in some of his most adorable verses.

> In her image of an Empress Byzantine
> Haloed by the caressing shadows of her brows,
> Like a dawn rebellious and malign
> Riots a laughter where Torment has left its vows.
>
> The pride of her divine regard represses
> Flames from the cruel azure of July,
> And, under the frivolous pride of her lovely dresses,
> With broken wings her soul sleeps uneasily.
>
> Oh dreams of vessels that are slowly sailing
> Toward voluptuous shores where all else is unavailing,
> Save the splendour of the Suns of the Abysses,
>
> While as she tosses her rebellious tresses,
> White lilies swoon at her barbarian caresses
> And die under the red perfume of her kisses.
>   [Symons trans., *Quand les violins sont partis*, 1892]

Dubus, tall, thin, impeccably dressed, wandered over life with the
pallid face which reminds me of the *filles* of Watteau; his strange dark
eyes scintillated mischievously. Once having met Dubus you could
never forget him. He was a mixture of a dandy and a devil. His eyebrows slanted sideways, and there was always the effect of a grimace on
those vivid features: so irregular and so animal. * * *

Lydia[1]

I

When I first met Lydia she was nineteen. She had had the invariable flirtations, such as all ballet girls have; but, as I found out later, these came to nothing. She had a tremendous sense of her supreme beauty, a tremendous pride; and, what was wonderful, a tremendous sense of what was literally her Chastity. She was no more innocent than the other girls in regard to the question of Sex; she was aware of almost all that went on and the adventures of the others. She confessed to me in Fountain Court that her curiosity was so intense that she never let these girls alone: she insisted on their confessing to her certain casual sins. When one came to be married, she was inexorable in her insistence on their sexual connections which she had never had; she drank in all that with her youthful sensuality. Yet, deep down in that inexplicable creature, there was a primitive element.

Before she met me she was not perverse; I made her perverse. Never for one moment was she depraved. Her imagination, her senses and her sensations were—certainly in no sense as responsive as her body always was to me—but in certain ways responsive to what is depraved. She had some evil blood in her veins, her purple veins, without which she could never have been so passionately, so implacably, devoted to me; bone to bone, flesh to flesh. There was something evil in both of us, which caused such terrible quarrels. She was absolutely seductive, fatally fascinating, almost shamelessly animal. She was to me a form of the modern Venus, born of fire and dew; amorous, passionate, exacting. She always had a way of trying to exact more from me than I exacted from her; and like me, she was always excitable. She was nervous, restless, her eyes roved like mine, her wonderful black eyes. Many a time she fell into strange stupors, when, after immense physical fatigue, she fainted, fainted dead. She could be silent and sombre, sullen and sulky; she could make herself hateful, with deliberate malice; she could invent as many lies as I did. She believed implicitly everything that was said against me; she defended me with love's fury against my assailants; and, no sooner had she panted out these confessions, held passionately in my arms, than she disbelieved them.

* * * Sin was with us in my rooms; the Flesh was with us always; the Arch-demon arose from Hell whenever I evoked him and certainly my Venus and I came near, night after night, afternoon after noon, hell's mouth. There, after much mad dancing of my senses, I sought and found the Cloven Hill. Alas and alas for the sweet and eternal hell wherein to spend my Eternity in the arms of Venus!

Certainly this House of mine was hot with heat, the sun's ardent heat, with the ardent heat of our bodies, where some scented, dusty day-light burnt the air; where night fell like fire; where the stars went out, where the blood in both our bodies shook like flame. * * *

It was always to me a matter of absolute certainty that Lydia was the illegitimate daughter of a Spaniard who had some Gypsy blood in him; for she had in her the mixture of those two races, together with a third part that was English on her mother's side. She had no resemblance whatever to her daughter; she was plain featured, looked peevish. And then Lydia used to tell me terrible stories of her mother's detestable behaviour to her whenever she herself came in:—"Always, Arthur," she said to me in her impetuous fashion, "wondering if there might be a letter from you"—to the effect that her mother would scowl, look furious, say some words—which I can imagine, were meant to infuriate this amazing Child: then hand her one of my letters which the girl, flushing crimson, snatched out of her fingers, turned her back, rushed up the stairs to her bedroom, locked her door: sat down on her bed and tore open my letter.

That my lazy, languid, passionate Mistress had on the whole a bad time in that strange family circle, was evident: the more so that she only referred to it when she was boiling with rage. I don't mean with me: I was not then in the position of Catullus with his Lesbia.

> When her husband is with us Lesbia speaks harshly to me,
> Whereat the fool of a man is filled to the brim with glee.
> Ass, don't you see? were she silent, and could she forget all about
>   me.
> Then, were she heart—whole to you; but, now to nag and flout
>   me
> Isn't to merely remember; but what is the worst of the lot,
> She is angry, and that is a sign she is burning and boiling hot.[2]

Sometimes after my inevitable assiduity in the wings and on the pavement with Lydia, when I was waiting for her, or bringing her back with me to the stage door, it was bruited about by the girls at the Empire that she was my Mistress. This she began by indignantly denying. Proud as she was of her own beauty, of her singular beauty, part of her pride was also in her knowledge of how much I was admired, and how I was admitted everywhere: and it was no lessening of her pride that we were known to be lovers. The more she denied it the more she adored it. And what was so curious in her was the fact that the greater part of the girls fell under the spell of her fascination; nor did I wonder: she was in every sense so extraordinary a Child, so excitable, so neurotic, that they could not resist her.

No one who has haunted the music-halls as I have, can forget the hideous figure of the French Jew Nicols,[3] who had for his property the Empire and the Café Royal. He was enormous in size. He was a monster of lust; but being a Jew had a wonderful flair for wine. Every night that man, sitting inside his private box on the right of the stage, smoked his cigar and kept his eyes fixed on the stage.

He had of course behind the wings his private room; that room was literally infamous: there he sat in his arm-chair before his table: there he arranged his affairs with the manager Higgins. This room, the Jew's, always over-heated, was to my mind a torture-house. Nicols was supposed to have his choice of any ballet girl, most of all the new ones who turned up, who were obliged to obey his commands. Every girl, except the older ones who cared for nothing, shivered whenever they were summoned to his den. They blushed under their paint: they looked at me imploringly; they returned after I know not what interval with feverish faces and dilated eyes; they passed me without uttering one word.

Finally, Lydia's turn came. She had been warned of it times out of number; she had always refused insolently. I was on the stage when she came up to me and told me she was obliged to enter the Jew's room. She gave one glance out of those proud eyes of hers, then she went slowly in the direction of that room. I looked at my watch. When I saw her returning, she had been there just under ten minutes. She took me aside and said quite simply: "Arthur, dear, of course the hideous Jew tried to tempt me, tried to embrace me, tried to make me drink drugged wine. I kept all the time at arm's length from him and just told him what I thought of him. He squirmed in his chair. His cheeks puffed out. He dared not touch me. I turned my back on him, slammed the door behind me—and here I am, Arthur." She had quelled him. After that he left her alone; after that, she was never molested.

II

Shall I ever forget you? You, whom I first saw on the stage of the Empire? Never, nor you: never. Tired enough after loving a mere plaything, just enough flesh and blood to be unutterably amusing, I went as usual to the Empire. I sat in my usual seat that gives on the stage. The curtain went up. I saw the ballet. Suddenly I saw a beautiful girl whose face was strange to me. She was exotic, with passionate lips and eyes, magnetic. Then she—that is you—fixed her eyes on mine without surprise, without hestitation. As if drawn by some instinct, your eyes fixed on mine at every turn you made as you danced with the others; that is, in the circle. Then you smiled up at me; a pained, enigmatical, nervous smile. I smiled down at you as you passed me next.

When the ballet was over I went around to the stage door. I waited a long time. Then you came out very slowly under the gas light. Of course you knew I was there, or your eyes would not have been so active as they gazed through the depth of their unimaginable darkness into the night. Then I lifted my hat and spoke to you. We shook hands. You were horribly shaken with nerves and so was I. I suppose we had a drink afterwards at some tavern and that I walked back with you to the door of your house. You had so many houses, you know. Neither of us had the faintest notion that either of us just then had the least idea of falling in love. That, certainly, was fixed in our stars; that which was long in coming to us; that which, of necessity, submerged our bodies and our souls on the storm tossed waves of an infinite sea.

Doubting myself as one often has to, one has to doubt others, men and women: is any woman—was any woman in this world, from Lilith to our own generation—ever absolutely faithful to her lover? Was any lover in this world, from the first created serpent to now, ever absolutely faithful to his mistress? In all love, doubt is part of that torture without which few imaginative men would fling themselves quite heartily into the pursuit. * * *

There was something curiously abnormal in Lydia from the hour when I met her to the fatal hour when she finally abandoned me. She was far and away the most amorous and the most exacting girl I have ever known. On certain nights when she was least enigmatical and most malicious, she loomed before my vision like Astarte. When her passionate, adorable flesh became most feverish, at times my fever went out of me, and I quieted her fever. She believed in nothing, literally in nothing, neither in God nor the devil, neither in hell nor in heaven. Only, she clung on to two things, two things only: her supreme beauty of which she was always jealous; and the desire in her to be desired—to be always desired.

She taught me a few things. I taught her an immensity of things, even before I had seduced her. All the time I deliberately perverted her with that intolerable persistence I possess in matters of the flesh. Her subtle body made for love became that of Artemis, the goblin goddess who desires blood as she desires wine; who gloats over the doomed and the dead. She gathered from the divine gardens of Hades, the black-hearted poppy, the soothing and sleep-giving poppy, the poppy that drugs one's senses, which stupefies one's limbs. She had the spells that bind or devote certain creatures to the infernal gods; and with these no scent nor colour of the mystical earth. And when she had sent me half asleep, after her intolerable caresses, with her smiling face bent over me as I lay on the sofa, her image wavered before me. As Hecate, she was compact of sleep and death and flowers; sometimes she was compact like Demeter of the narcotic juices of the poppies, the emblems of death and sleep, of the dreams that intervene between sleeping and waking. Then, woven of fire and of the fruits of the fire which are the fumes of smoke, she would hold out to me one partly consumed morsel of pomegranate, the fruit of those who so quickly go down into hell. This vanished, and there flashed between us the image of the God who had drunk of the bitterness of wine to whom the sea water of the grapes of Lesbos become brackish in the cup. I had Pater's books on my shelves, I read this sentence to Lydia, "The Bacchic women are literally like winged things, they follow their new, strange romantic god. Himself a woman-like god, it is on women, on feminine souls, that his power mainly fell."[4] Then she interrupted me, "Do you mean me as one of those Bacchic women dancers? You are certainly not a god: but with women—including myself, who am more a girl than a woman—you seem to me to have some of that almost woman-like fascination that excites them and exasperates them." I glance at her and say nothing; then I go on reading: "Dionysus has sent the sting of his enthusiasm into them, and has driven it into a sort of madness." She arrests me again, gazes at me with those animal eyes of hers, "Why, Arthur, do you so often read of madness, speak of madness? I know I am not like other girls. I know you are not like other men, you have said to me I'm not quite normal: that's true, no more are you. There is something—oh, ever so many things!—in you that I can't make out. You are so inhuman. Then you become human: then back again comes your inhumanity. No, no, I also, am not altogether human." "Am I really inhuman?" I queried. "Why not? What's the use of being merely human?"

III

Her raven's hair had in it a whole midnight, storm tormented; her nerves extended into her tresses, which thrilled to my touch, which hissed when she combed them, like black rebellious snakes. Her nocturnal eyes possessed in their depths a glittering splendour, a marvellous mischief. Chaos may have conceived her, for all I know, out of some wild will-o'-

the-wisp that hallucinates the lonely wanderer in dark woods near sterile streams. She had the smouldering splendour of certain sunrises; she had the smouldering passion of certain sunsets. When her heart's blood flushed her pale cheeks pale as pale ivory, she was like a sombre night-moth. In her voice, which had some of the harshness of the voices of Spanish women, there was, as it were, the voice of the restlessness of water, the voice of restlessness which is a sea-gull's, that poise and drift to and fro between sea and land. There was in her imagination that aching loneliness which scars such young flesh as hers; and which, out of that loneliness, desires one thing only, that desire which is part of the body's desire and part of the desire of the flesh—to be loved to madness. There was nothing abstract in her desires: they were passionate and cruel; they were abnormal and relentless; there was nothing that was spiritual in them; spiritual only when body and spirit are in unison.

She was elemental, primitive. Animal she knew herself always to be. Yet with less than a woman's experience in material things she remained eternally young. Certainly, she suffered horribly from certain materialities that weighed heavily on her. Feverish, fatal, she was the most unholy mixture of complex propensities, of enigmatical surprises and surmises, of infinite perversities, of any girl I have ever known. She had the undulating grace of a tigress. Had she been perfect, how I would have hated her and cursed her, as Baudelaire did! She was rarely vindictive, rarely spiteful. Veritably, her body was imaginative. That I fascinated her before she fascinated me is so much of a certainty that she, herself, finally came to admit it. That she began by liking me frightfully, then started to tormenting, teasing, and perplexing me; that she set herself, as it were, out of sheer malice, to hate me as hell hates heaven, and that, because her blood was like mine in a state of revolt, that blood that beat so violently in her veins, that flamed in her cheeks; that, certainly, was inevitable. How she herself came to love me, how far her passion began for me before she loved me, is one of the eternal mysteries of the flesh and of the spirit. "And why," wrote Meredith, "this man should have come to his end through love, and the woman who loved him have laid her hand in the hand of the slayer, is the problem we have to study, nothing inventing, in the spirit and flesh of both."

"If you will do this for me," she would often say, "I'll be—something to you." Now that "something" said in that perverse accent she could assume when she chose, often meant much more than what she had intended. Feline and feverish to her finger tips, she had a kind of Asiatic luxury, the luxury of Oriental blood. There was an unholy magic in her fingers, which she only became aware of after she had tried them on me, which always had the effect of mesmerism and nervous exasperation. Times out of number, by the mere touch of her fingers up my arms, she made me shudder from head to foot.

Then on certain of her tragic nights, she would sob and cry, "I know that we shall not, cannot love like this always, Arthur, dear. I am not so much younger than you are; but there are times when, alas, I imagine that I am ever so much older than you. Many a man's love has been a curse to him. Will you ever curse me? You, who are so cruel, so passionate and so amorous. You who can love when you like to love and hate when you like to hate." Then after her lies and evasions that made me furious, she would turn suddenly on me and in wild repentance she would say: "What sin have I done that you should think so ill of me?"

This proud Beauty of mine had a curious, enigmatical fashion of lifting her deep, stormy and passionate eyes to the moonlight, either as we saw it from the square below Fountain Court, or shining into the window of my room; where, when it was dusk, the moon's shadow on the floor, which shadowed both of us, was magic and mystical. Then she would sigh that tragic sigh of hers which was the premonition of I knew not what, the depth of her slumbrous beauty, which too often was the equivalent of a shudder, a shudder that made her body tremble from head to foot, as a snake shivers as its coils contract in hot sunshine. She was always full of an indescribable and passionate curiosity which seemed to have no limits; it was that of a wild animal. It was perverse, excitable, unreasoning, sexual and sensual; it was literally erotic. Living as we lived for years in a state of almost utter immorality, never did her life seem so natural to her, never did my life seem so natural to me, as then. Yet, when I use the word Immorality, I must add the word Abnormality. To be entirely normal, as the majority of the world is supposed to be, is to be lacking in what is most essential in Love and in Passion. The lust of the Flesh, the lust of the Eyes, are the primary qualifications of those who are furiously passionate, furiously animal. For, as the stars of the Zodiac fight in their courses, so what is most amorous in one's mistress and in one's self stirs one's blood in revolt against the stars that fight in other's destinies. That's one reason why we become so madly jealous where the madness of love attains its zenith. * * *

The more I lusted after Lydia, my wayward passion, the more she lusted after me with an intolerable lust: the desire of possession, of being possessed by me, when she was actually possessing me, increased in us as the winter nights became more monstrous under the malignant menaces of my merciless moon. As a Vampire, she sucked the blood out of me; as Circe, she gave me the wine that I drank at her matchless lips; as Helen of Troy, she cast into the very marrow of my bones that sweet and adulterous poison no antidote can ever alleviate.

IV

I often wonder if my Lilith was entirely human; there was so curious a mixture in her veritable blood of the human and the inhuman, that on certain nights when her breath on my breath shook my soul like a feather, an unholy fascination seized on her. "And fire is my body," she might have cried then, having given me to drink the wine of Circe. Nay, not in her magical island Calypso "where the dishevelled seaweed hates the Sea," but where Hecate gives Lilith the crimson rose of passion and the wine coloured poppies, slumbrous with their inner fire, like sleeping kings of Lethe.

As I write these lines, the wind howls like a wild beast, storm winged and furious, destructive and visible; his voice is the voice of the wind, the voice that wanders as the wind wanders always, as it asks in an unknown tone infinite, unimaginable things. I adore the wind: the wind at night makes me uneasy, for being condemned for I know not what reason, from birth onward, to have had but little peace at heart, but little quietude in the soul, to have been always restless, a wanderer over the earth's surface and over the sea's shining and tormented surface, to have been passionate, to have been passionately loved, it might be that some part of the penance which I have to pay for my sins is what drives the lovers of the winds to be hunters of the Impossible.

> Who go by night into the woods with nets,
> To share the shadow of the moon in pools.
> [Symons, "The Lovers of the Wind,"
> *The Fool of the World*, 1906]

Lydia was fabulous, almost Asiatic in the languor of her movements; Spanish in her gravity and dignity; sombre and sensitive; whole world, I would willingly have thrown it away so that her return should have been actually her return. I was obliged to make the excuse that there was a woman I hated in my room. Lydia burst out into an atrocious fit of laughter, which seemed to me, as it might have seemed to her, to be expressed in the words of the Italian in "A Last Confession":—

> If you mistake my words
> And so absolve me, I am sure the blessing
> Will burn my soul. If you mistake my words
> And so absolve me, Father, the great sin

Is yours, not mine: mark this: your soul shall burn
With mine for it. I have seen pictures where
Souls burned with Latin shriekings in their mouths:
Shall my end be as theirs? Nay, but I know
'Tis you shall shriek in Latin. Some bell rings,
Rings through my brain: it strikes the hour in hell.
[Rossetti, *Poems,* 1870]

With that Lydia left me, and went slowly down the stairs. On the exact stroke of eleven I was at the stage door of the Empire. Lydia came out, she showed no surprise. That night we made it up. A few nights after that I wrote "The Return" which I gave her.[5] It has in it a purity of passion.

V

I give two instances in my experiences of the illegitimate love over-coming the legitimate. I had a letter from Katherine Willard[6] asking me to dine with her in a certain house where she would be alone. I went there: she was unchanged, the same amusing American girl essentially different from the English Tennyson type. We talked of the good old times, of our adventures. We sat in the garden after the dinner, watching the stars. She reminded me of a tragic incident that had occurred on the Atlantic Liner which had taken us from Hamburg to La Havre. Her brother[7] went on shore with other men of his kind. Before then at Hamburg, we had seen an awful lot of emigrants of every nation, wait-ing huddled up before they came on board the steamer. He spent much of his time with them on the quarter deck. They were all terribly ill, in rags and poverty, with a few bundles, all heaped together. As soon as Willard had gone on shore, Katherine and I had one of our wonderful conversations. She spoke of the way her brother was addicted to drink and the fatal results it had on him. Quite late in the night I had to retire to my room in the cabin, and there was Willard reeling drunk, just able to ask me to explain to Katherine the state he was in. I went back with great hesitation; she saw the trouble in my eyes; she implored me to tell her the truth, the awful truth. I don't even know now why I deliberately lied to her, why she made believe to disbelieve me. Next day we landed at La Havre; she lent me some money. I had spent too much of mine in Berlin and she said good-bye. To my horror I found that I had only enough money, just a little over, to pay my home passage. So I wandered, had a meagre supper in a café; then, not having enough cash in my purse, I was literally forced to try to sleep in the bathing cabin. The thing was ridiculous enough in all conscience; my limbs ached preposterously, and as soon as it was dawn, I crept out and wandered back to the town. Seated outside the café, having breakfast, to my amazement both of them turned up, because the steamer had to be repaired. I went back with them to the steamer. They smuggled some food and wine for me to have on deck. I returned on shore and had the worst crossing I ever had.

To return to that dinner of ours in London, she knew little enough of the depraved life I was then living. Inevitably I began to get agitated as the hour of eleven approached. During those years, I had to lie diabolically. I thought that she disbelieved in me; as with her eyes on mine, she smiled a broken smile, without one word of reproach. So loyal was she to me even then. We said good-bye. She was leaving next day for America. I walked hurriedly to the stage door of the Empire. I got there just in time, luckily for me!

VI

My other misadventure was of a stupid kind. I had to endure the intrusions in my room of a girl of no importance (I use Wilde's phrase) who generally bored me; who imposed herself on me in quite an objectionable manner. Prosaic, common-place, she was one of those who have huge ideas of their own importance. She wrote asking me to take her to the Lyceum to see *The Bells*.[8] I simply had to dine her at Gatti's and take her with me to the theatre. Irving was inimitable in his part; thrilling and magnificent. He gave me the intense illusion of the suspense of the increasing, the menacing tragedy; of the nervous tension of the Criminal; he was unsurpassable in the scene of the Hallucination, the Dream, the Obsession, the horrible vision of the Tribunal; an evocation of sheer stage craft. Then, as he always did, he made me shudder.

I suppose this stupid creature enjoyed what was for her a new sensation. Of course for the same reason and abruptly I had to make a sudden excuse, getting up just as suddenly, leaving her in an awful state of disappointment. I rushed back to the stage door. Again fortunately for me the ballet-girl who expected me there every night never asked me questions as to how I spent my time when I was away from her.

Now you see, the same reason that always impelled me to do these things; the over-powering attraction of the sharp unwholesome savour over the delightful and the normal. I have noted these salient incidents exactly as they were. The whole thing—more than the half of my life just then being given up to one woman, the rest [to] my Art—was nothing more than the animal in me in quest of another animal. * * * Then take these lines of Rossetti from "A Last Confession":—

> A woman laughed above me. I looked up
> And saw where a brown-shouldered harlot leaned
> Half through a tavern window thick with vine.
> Some man had come behind her in the room
> And caught her by her arms, and she had turned
> With that coarse empty laugh on him, as now
> He munched her neck with kisses, while the vine
> Crawled in her back.

There, in the man's startled senses, all in one hushed suspense of exasperated nerves, one gets the whole sensual sensation, dramatic and pictorial, of the woman, the man, the vine, the tavern: Italian and universal!

VII

Last night I dreamed that a girl I had known came to me, after a long lapse of years, offering herself over again to me. Dreams may become realities. Why not? So I note here certain details.

Somewhile after she had married quite an old and ugly man (against her will) she wrote me a passionate letter, saying that she must meet me again; but not in Fountain Court, as that might be too dangerous for us—but anywhere else that I could find. I spent ever so long a time wandering into remote corners of London; finally I came on just what I wanted. It was No. 7, Knox Street, Euston Road, and I found that a room was vacant for lodgers. I went in, made my enquiries, saw an immense room on the first floor, that suited me; gave a name that was not my own; hired the room for an indeterminate number of weeks.

I made a point of going there several times, so that the landlady might see that I brought with me books, ink and paper; and I spent several hours a day there. I mentioned to her vaguely that a woman (I told a lie as to who she was) might from time to time call on me. I had a ruled account book of the weekly sums I paid her; I kept that for many years as a curiosity.

Then from Fountain Court I wrote a letter to the married woman, giving her the address (for I always knew she was very secret in regard to my letters) in which I fixed an afternoon in the next week; not there, I said—for the first time—but somewhere down Euston Road.

As she had almost always been punctual in her assignations with me, I had not long to wait (as I wandered up and down) before I saw her tall figure dressed in black, with a veil over her face, emerge not far beyond where I was. We shook hands without a word, went slowly along (no longer, as we used to be, the admired of the crowd) and I let her in with my latchkey. She looked all round the room, sank on a chair, took off her veil; and as I kissed her her kisses were feverish, furious: and I saw that she was trembling all over.

Then she poured out to me miserable agonizing stories of her misfortunes with the man she had married; her repugnance to him, in many senses. A man—she said over and over again as she had always said to me after he came into our life—she never loved, never could; hated; yet dared not run the risk of repenting her rash acceptance of one who (as I knew) simply had bought her; with gold, with costly gifts, certainly never with love.

I had warned her in vain, she said: "What could I have done?" "What could I have done?" I said to her with a touch of passionate irony.

"And was it I?" she said—this line I had written on her⁹ she quoted against me in sardonic accents.

"Lydia,"¹⁰ said I, "what's virtue? A quality so long since forgotten that we banished it out of our lives, even before you had ceased to be a Luini saint. It is your mouth that thirsts hotly, with the old supreme warmth, for what is no more a sterile ecstasy. Your cheeks are whiter than ever, you hardly breathe. Do I not feel your pulses leaping in your throat?"

"The wine of Circe!" she sobbed in a sudden thrill of intoxication. "Give *me* the wine of Circe!"

Her hands were around me, as they used to be (ah, for how many years!) her mouth one flower of desire. Never since what we thought was to have been the last night we ever slept together had she been so wonderful. It was more than a revulsion against her hated new existence; it was a return to her utter abandonment to me; even, I think, she strove to give me more than she had ever given me. Was it a vain striving? we thought not then. An unutterable agony came over us; and it was that agony so eternally repeated by lovers that even the word eternity is not explicit enough to express it.

Hours passed, of which we were wholly unaware; so inscrutable, so inevitable, was this return of passion's unspent desires; this insensate crying of the flesh of men for women, of women for men; this hatred, born of too much love, of too much isolation: in a word, that rage in one's heart, that forgets rarely, that remembers always "that thing that hurts and is love." And I think it was Catullus who first gave utterance to this final fundamental curse on women, and on Lesbia, his mistress:

> I hate and I love: you ask me how one can do it?
> I know not: I know that it hurts: I am going through it.
> [Symons, *From Catullus*, p. 57]

This one Latin word *excrucior* [to torment] is as modern now as it was in his age: it is that intense exasperation of one's whole senses and sensations, when, after one has kissed a woman to the bone, the taste still longs for it.

No words of mine can give any idea of what we felt, that woman and I, when the time came for her to leave me. Time, of course, ought to mean nothing to such people as we were. Yet:—there is so often that detestable yet! We made another appointment for next week; neither of us, perhaps then, quite believed in its possibility. Imagine our situation for a moment: how, without her, unutterably lonely was I; she without me.

One never knows how much the man she belonged to (odious name!) knew about her absences; her lies, her evasions, her escapes. For at times, a hindrance came in our way; she was unable to get away from him. In these cases she often sent me a wire; which made me more furious than even these written words can confess. So when we met next I showed my temper against her—"the most unhappy bride the sun shone upon"; but for how little a while. She never reproached me, nor herself; never did. And, as before, her seductiveness was simply overwhelming. And, to admit the absolute truth: once a man has been enslaved by such a woman, he might as well try to forget her, as long as he lives, as to forget his own existence.

Aubrey Beardsley[1]

It was in the summer of 1895 that I first met Aubrey Beardsley.[2] A publisher [Leonard Smithers] had asked me to form and edit a new kind of magazine, which was to appeal to the public equally in its letterpress and its illustrations: need I say that I am defining *The Savoy?* It was, I admit, to have been something of a rival to *The Yellow Book,* which had by that time ceased to mark a movement, and had come to be little more than a publisher's magazine. I forget exactly when the expulsion of Beardsley from *The Yellow Book* had occurred;[3] it had been sufficiently recent, at all events, to make Beardsley singularly ready to fall in with my project when I went to him and asked him to devote himself to illustrating my quarterly. He was supposed, just then, to be dying; and as I entered the room, and saw him lying out on a couch, horribly white, I wondered if I had come too late. He was full of ideas, full of enthusiasm, and I think it was then that he suggested the name *Savoy,* finally adopted after endless changes and uncertainties.

A little later we met again at Dieppe, where for a month I saw him daily. It was at Dieppe that the *Savoy* was really planned, and it was in the café, which Mr. Sickert has so often painted, that I wrote the slightly pettish and defiant "Editorial Note," which made so many enemies for the first number.[4] Dieppe just then was a meeting-place for the younger generation; some of us spent the whole summer there, lazily but profitably; others came and went. Beardsley at that time imagined himself to be unable to draw anywhere but in London. He made one or two faint attempts, and even prepared a canvas for a picture which was never painted, in the hospital studio in which M. Jacques Blanche painted the admirable portrait reproduced in the frontispiece.[5] But he found many subjects, some of which he afterwards worked out, in the expressive opportunities of the Casino and the beach. He never walked; I never saw him look at the sea;[6] but at night he was almost always to be seen watching the gamblers at *petits chevaux,* studying them with a sort of hypnotized attention for that picture of *The Little Horses,* which was never done. He liked the large deserted rooms, at hours when no one was there; the sense of frivolous things caught at a moment of suspended life, *en déshabillé.* He would glance occasionally, but with more impatience, at the dances, especially the children's dances, in the concert room; but he rarely missed a concert, and would glide in every afternoon, and sit on the high benches at the side, always carrying his large, gilt-leather portfolio with the magnificent old, red-lined folio paper, which he would often open, to write some lines in pencil. He was at work then, with an almost pathetic tenacity, at his story, never to be finished, *Under the Hill,* a new version, a parody (like Laforgue's parodies, but how unlike them, or anything!) of the story of Venus and Tannhäuser.[7] Most of it was done at these concerts, and in the little, close writing-room where visitors sat writing letters. The fragment published in the first two numbers of *The Savoy* had passed through many stages before it found its way there, and would have passed through more if it had ever been carried further. Tannhäuser, not quite willingly, had put on *abbé's* disguise, and there were other unwilling disguises in those brilliant, disconnected, fantastic pages, in which every sentence was meditated over, written for its own sake, and left to find its way in its own paragraph. It could never have been finished, for it had never really been begun; but what undoubted, singular, literary ability there is in it all the same!

I think Beardsley would rather have been a great writer than a great artist; and I remember, on one occasion, when he had to fill up a form of admission to some library to which I was introducing him, his insistence on describing himself as "man of letters." At one time he was going to write an essay on *Les Liaisons Dangereuses,*[8] at another he had planned a book on Rousseau. But his plans for writing changed even more quickly than his plans for doing drawings, and with less profitable results in the meantime. He has left no prose except that fragment of a story; and in verse only the three pieces published in *The Savoy.*[9] Here, too, he was terribly anxious to excel; and his patience over a medium so unfamiliar, and hence so difficult, to him as verse, was infinite. We spent two whole days on the grassy ramparts of the old castle at Arques-la-Bataille, near Dieppe; I working at something or other in one part, he working at "The Three Musicians" in another. The eight stanzas of that amusing piece of verse are really, in their own way, a *tour de force;* by sheer power of will, by deliberately saying to himself, "I will write a poem," and by working with such strenuous application that at last a certain result, the kind of result he had willed, did really come about, he succeeded in doing what he had certainly no natural aptitude for doing. How far was that more genuine aspect of his genius also an "infinite capacity for taking pains"?

It was on the balcony of the Hôtel Henri IV at Arques, one of those September evenings, that I had the only quite serious, almost solemn, conversation I ever had with Beardsley. Not long before we had gone together to visit Alexander Dumas *fils* at Puy, and it was from talking thoughtfully, but entirely, of that Parisian writer, and his touching, in its unreal way so real, *Dame aux Camélias* (the novel, not the play), which Beardsley admired so much, that we passed into an unexpectedly intimate mood of speculation. Those stars up yonder, whether they were really the imprisoning worlds of other creatures like ourselves; the strange ways by which the soul might have come and must certainly go; death, and the future: it was of such things that I found him speaking, for once without mockery. And he told me then a singular dream or vision which he had had when a child, waking up at night in the moonlight and seeing a great crucifix, with a bleeding Christ, falling off the wall, where certainly there was not, and had never been, any crucifix. It is only by remembering that one conversation, that vision, the tone of awe with which he told it, that I can, with a great effort, imagine to myself the Beardsley whom I knew, with his so positive intelligence, his imaginative sight of the very spirit of man as a thing of definite outline, transformed finally into the Beardsley who died in the peace of the last sacraments of the Church, holding the rosary between his fingers.

Anima naturaliter pagana, Aubrey Beardsley ended a long career, at the age of twenty-six, in the arms of the Church. No artist of our time, none certainly whose work has been in black and white, has reached a more universal, or a more contested fame; none has formed for himself, out of such alien elements, a more personal originality of manner; none has had so wide an influence on contemporary art. He had the fatal speed of those who are to die young; that disquieting completeness and extent of knowledge, that absorption of a lifetime in an hour, which we find in those who hasten to have done their work before noon, knowing that they will not see the evening. He had played the piano in drawing-rooms as an infant prodigy, before, I suppose, he had ever drawn a line; famous at twenty as a draughtsman, he found time, in those incredibly busy years which remained to him, to deliberately train himself into a writer of prose which was, in its way, as original as his draughtsmanship, and into a writer of verse which had at least ingenious and original moments. He seemed to have read everything, and had his preferences as adroitly in order, as wittily in evidence, as almost any man of letters; indeed, he seemed to know more, and was a sounder critic, of books than of pictures; with perhaps a deeper feeling for music than for either. His conversation had a peculiar kind of brilliance, different in order but scarcely inferior in quality to that of any other contemporary master of that art; a salt, whimsical dogmatism, equally full of convinced egoism and of imperturbable keen-sightedness. Generally choosing to be paradoxical, and vehement on behalf of any enthusiasm of the mind, he was the dupe of none of his own statements, or indeed of his own enthusiasms, and, really, very coldly impartial. I scarcely except even his own judgment of himself, in spite of his petulant, amusing self-assertion, so full of the childishness of genius. He thought, and was right in thinking, very highly of himself; he admired himself enormously; but his intellect would never allow itself to be deceived even about his own accomplishments.

This clear, unemotional intellect, emotional only in the perhaps highest sense, where emotion almost ceases to be recognisable, in the abstract, for ideas, for lines, left him, with all his interests in life, with all his sociability, of a sort, essentially very lonely. Many people were devoted to him, but he had, I think, scarcely a friend in the fullest sense of the word; and I doubt if there were more than one or two people for whom he felt any real affection. In spite of constant ill-health, he had an astonishing tranquillity of nerves; and it was doubtless that rare quality which kept him, after all, alive so long. How far he had deliberately acquired command over his nerves and his emotions, as he deliberately acquired command over his brain and hand, I do not know. But there it certainly was, one of the bewildering characteristics of so contradictory a temperament.

One of his poses, as people say, one of those things, that is, in which he was most sincere, was his care in outwardly conforming to the conventions which make for elegance and restraint; his necessity of dressing well, of showing no sign of the professional artist. He had a great contempt for, what seemed to inferior craftsmen, inspiration, for what I have elsewhere called the plenary inspiration of first thoughts; and he hated the outward and visible signs of an inward yeastiness and incoherency. It amused him to denounce everything, certainly, which Baudelaire would have denounced; and, along with some mere *gaminerie*, there was a very serious and adequate theory of art at the back of all his destructive criticisms. It was a profound thing which he said to a friend of mine who asked him whether he ever saw visions: "No," he replied, "I do not allow myself to see them except on paper." All his art is in that phrase.

And he attained, to the full, one certainly of his many desires, and that one, perhaps, of which he was most keenly or most continuously conscious: contemporary fame, the fame of a popular singer or a professional beauty, the fame of Yvette Guilbert or of Cléo de Mérode.[10] And there was logic in his insistence on this point, in his eagerness after immediate and clamorous success. Others might have waited; he knew that he had not the time to wait. After all, posthumous fame is not a very cheering prospect to look forward to, on the part of those who have worked without recompense, if the pleasure or the relief of work is not enough in itself. Every artist has his own secret, beyond the obvious one, of why he works. So far as it is not the mere need of earning one's living, it is generally some unhappiness, some dissatisfaction with the things about one, some too desperate or too contemptuous sense of the meaning of existence. At one period of his life a man works at his art to please a woman; then he works because he has not pleased the woman; and then because he is tired of pleasing her. Work for the work's sake it always must be, in a profound sense; and with Beardsley, not less certainly than with Blake or with Rossetti. But that other, that accidental, insidious, significant motive, was, with Beardsley, the desire to fill his few working years with the immediate echo of a great notoriety.

Like most artists who have thought much of popularity, he had an immense contempt for the public; and the desire to kick that public into admiration, and then to kick it for admiring the wrong thing or not knowing why it was admiring, led him into many of his most outrageous practical jokes of the pen. He was partly right and partly wrong, for he was indiscriminate; and to be indiscriminate is always to be partly right and partly wrong. The wish to *épater le bourgeois* is a natural one, and, though a little beside the question, does not necessarily lead one astray. The general public, of course, does not in the least know why it admires the right thing to-day though it admired the wrong thing yesterday. But there is such a thing as denying your Master while you are rebuking a servant-girl. Beardsley was without the very sense of respect; it was one of his limitations.

And this limitation was an unfortunate one, for it limited his ambition. With the power of creating beauty, which should be pure beauty, he turned aside, only too often, to that lower kind of beauty which is the mere beauty of technique, in a composition otherwise meaningless, trivial, or grotesque. Saying to himself, "I can do what I like; there is nothing I could not do if I chose to, if I chose to take the trouble; but why should I offer hard gold when an I.O.U. will be just the same? I can pay up whenever the money is really wanted," he allowed himself to be content with what he knew would startle, doing it with infinite pains, to his own mind conscientiously, but doing it with that lack of reverence for great work which is one of the most sterilising characteristics of the present day.

The epithet *fin de siècle* has been given, somewhat loosely, to a great deal of modern French art, and to art which, in one way or another, seems to attach itself to contemporary France. Out of the great art of Manet, the serious art of Degas, the exquisite art of Whistler, all, in such different ways, so modern, there has come into existence a new, very modern, very far from great or serious or really exquisite kind of art, which has expressed itself largely in the *Courrier Français,* the *Gil*

Blas illustré, and the posters. All this art may be said to be, what the quite new art of the poster certainly is, art meant for the street, for people who are walking fast. It comes into competition with the newspapers, with the music-halls; half contemptuously, it popularises itself; and, with real qualities and a real measure of good intention, finds itself forced to seek for sharp, sudden, arresting means of expression. Instead of seeking pure beauty, the seriousness and self-absorption of great art, it takes, wilfully and for effect, that beauty which is least evident, indeed, least genuine; nearest to ugliness in the grotesque, nearest to triviality in a certain elegant daintiness, nearest also to brutality and the spectacular vices. Art is not sought for its own sake, but the manual craftsman perfects himself to express a fanciful, ingenious, elaborate, somewhat tricky way of seeing things, which he has deliberately adopted. It finds its own in the eighteenth century, so that Willette[11] becomes a kind of petty, witty Watteau of Montmartre; it parodies the art of stained glass, with Grasset[12] and his followers; it juggles with iron bars and masses of shadow, like Lautrec. And, in its direct assault on the nerves, it pushes naughtiness to obscenity, deforms observation into caricature, dexterity of line and handling being cultivated as one cultivates a particular, deadly *botte* in fencing.

And this art, this art of the day and hour, competes not merely with the appeal and the popularity of the theatrical spectacle, but directly with theatrical methods, the methods of stage illusion. The art of the ballet counts for much, in the evolution of many favourite effects of contemporary drawing, and not merely because Degas has drawn dancers, with his reserved, essentially classical mastery of form. By its rapidity of flight within bounds, by its bird-like and flower-like caprices of colour and motion, by that appeal to the imagination which comes from its silence (to which music is but like an accompanying shadow, so closely, so discreetly, does it follow the feet of the dancers), by its appeal to the eyes and to the senses, its adorable artificiality, the ballet has tempted almost every draughtsman, as the interiors of music-halls have also been singularly tempting, with their extraordinary tricks of light, their suddenness of gesture, their triumphant tinsel, their fantastic humanity. And pantomime, too, in the French and correct, rather than in the English and incorrect, sense of that word, has had its significant influence. In those pathetic gaieties of Willette, in the windy laughter of the frivolities of Chéret,[13] it is the masquerade, the English clown or acrobat seen at the Folies-Bergère, painted people mimicking puppets, who have begotten this masquerading humanity of posters and illustrated papers. And the point of view is the point of view of Pierrot—

le subtil génie
De sa malice infinie
De poète-grimacier—
[Verlaine, "Pierrot gamin,"
in *Parallèlement,* 1889]

Pierrot is one of the types of our century, of the moment in which
we live, or of the moment, perhaps, out of which we are just passing.
Pierrot is passionate; but he does not believe in great passions. He feels
himself to be sickening with a fever, or else perilously convalescent; for
love is a disease, which he is too weak to resist or endure. He has worn
his heart on his sleeve so long, that it has hardened in the cold air.
He knows that his face is powdered, and if he sobs, it is without tears;
and it is hard to distinguish, under the chalk, if the grimace which
twists his mouth awry is more laughter or mockery. He knows that he is
condemned to be always in public, that emotion would be supremely out
of keeping with his costume, that he must remember to be fantastic if he
would not be merely ridiculous. And so he becomes exquisitely false,
dreading above all things that "one touch of nature" which would ruffle
his disguise, and leave him defenceless. Simplicity, in him, being the
most laughable thing in the world, he becomes learned, perverse, intel-
lectualising his pleasures, brutalising his intellect; his mournful contemplation of things becoming a kind of grotesque joy, which he expresses
in the only symbols at his command, tracing his Giotto's O with the
elegance of his pirouette.

And Beardsley, with almost more than the Parisian's deference to
Paris, and to the moment, was, more than any Parisian, this "Pierrot
gamin." He was more than that, but he was that: to be that was part
of what he learnt from France. It helped him to the pose which helped
him to reveal himself; as Burne Jones had helped him when he did the
illustrations to the *Morte d'Arthur,* as Japanese art helped him to free
himself from that influence, as Eisen and Saint-Aubin[14] showed him the
way to the *Rape of the Lock.* He had that originality which surrenders
to every influence, yet surrenders to absorb, not to be absorbed; that
originality which, constantly shifting, is true always to its centre.
Whether he learnt from M. Grasset or from Mr. Ricketts,[15] from an
1830 fashion-plate, or from an engraved plate by Hogarth, whether the
scenery of Arques-la-Bataille composed itself into a pattern in his mind,
or, in the Casino at Dieppe, he made a note of the design of a looped-up
window-blind, he was always drawing to himself, out of the order of
art or the confusion of natural things, the thing he wanted, the thing
he could make his own. And he found, in the French art of the moment,

a joyous sadness, the serving of God or Mephistopheles, which his own temperament and circumstances were waiting to suggest to him.

"In more ways than one do men sacrifice to the rebellious angels," says St. Augustine; and Beardsley's sacrifice, together with that of all great decadent art, the art of Rops or the art of Baudelaire, is really a sacrifice to the eternal beauty, and only seemingly to the powers of evil. And here let me say that I have no concern with what neither he nor I could have had absolute knowledge of, his own intention in his work. A man's intention, it must be remembered, from the very fact that it is conscious, is much less intimately himself than the sentiment which his work conveys to me. So large is the sub-conscious element in all artistic creation, that I should have doubted whether Beardsley himself knew what he intended to do, in this or that really significant drawing. Admitting that he could tell exactly what he had intended, I should be quite prepared to show that he had really done the very contrary. Thus when I say he was a profoundly spiritual artist, though seeming to care chiefly for the manual part of his work; that he expresses evil with an intensity which lifted it into a region almost of asceticism, though attempting, not seldom, little more than a joke or a caprice in line; and that he was above all, though almost against his own will, a satirist, a satirist who has seen the ideal; I am putting forward no paradox, nothing really contradictory, but a simple analysis of the work as it exists.

At times he attains pure beauty, has the unimpaired vision; in the best of the *Salome* designs, here and there afterwards. From the first it is a diabolic beauty, but it is not yet divided against itself. The consciousness of sin is always there, but it is sin first transfigured by beauty, and then disclosed by beauty; sin, conscious of itself, of its inability to escape itself, and showing in its ugliness the law it has broken. His world is a world of phantoms, in whom the desire of the perfecting of mortal sensations, a desire of infinity, has overpassed mortal limits, and poised them, so faint, so quivering, so passionate for flight, in a hopeless and strenuous immobility. They have the sensitiveness of the spirit, and that bodily sensitiveness which wastes their veins and imprisons them in the attitude of their luxurious meditation. They are too thoughtful to be ever really simple, or really absorbed by either flesh or spirit. They have nothing of what is "healthy" or merely "animal" in their downward course towards repentance; no overwhelming passion hurries them beyond themselves; they do not capitulate to an open assault of the enemy of souls. It is the soul in them that sins, sorrowfully, without reluctance, inevitably. Their bodies are faint and eager with wantonness; they desire more pleasure than there is in the world, fiercer and more exquisite pains, a more intolerable suspense. They have put off the common burdens of humanity and put on that loneliness which is the rest of saints and the unrest of those who have sinned with the intellect. They are a little lower than the angels, and they walk between these and the fallen angels, without part or lot in the world.

Here, then, we have a sort of abstract spiritual corruption, revealed in beautiful form; sin transfigured by beauty. And here, even if we go no further, is an art intensely spiritual, an art in which evil purifies itself by its own intensity, and by the beauty which transfigures it. The one thing in the world which is without hope is that mediocrity which is the sluggish content of inert matter. Better be vividly awake to evil than, in mere somnolence, close the very issues and approaches of good and evil. For evil itself, carried to the point of a perverse ecstasy, becomes a kind of good, by means of that energy which, otherwise directed, is virtue; and which can never, no matter how its course may be changed, fail to retain something of its original efficacy. The devil is nearer to God, by the whole height from which he fell, than the average man who has not recognised his own need to rejoice or to repent. And so a profound spiritual corruption, instead of being a more "immoral" thing than the gross and pestiferous humanity or Hogarth or of Rowlandson,[16] is more nearly, in the final and abstract sense, moral, for it is the triumph of the spirit over the flesh, to no matter what end. It is a form of divine possession, by which the inactive and materialising soul is set in fiery motion, lured from the ground, into at least a certain high liberty. And so we find evil justified of itself, and an art consecrated to the revelation of evil equally justified; its final justification being that declared by Plotinus, in his treatise *On the Nature of Good and Evil:* "But evil is permitted to remain by itself alone on account of the superior power and nature of good; because it appears from necessity everywhere comprehended and bound, in beautiful bands, like men fettered with golden chains, lest it should be produced openly to the view of divinity, or lest mankind should always behold its horrid shape when perfectly naked; and such is the supervening power of good, that whenever a glimpse of perfect evil is obtained we are immediately recalled to the memory of good by the image of the beautiful with which evil is invested."

In those drawings of Beardsley which are grotesque rather than beautiful, in which lines begin to grow deformed, the pattern, in which now all the beauty takes refuge, is itself a moral judgment. Look at that drawing called *The Scarlet Pastorale.* In front a bloated harlequin struts close to the footlights, outside the play, on which he turns his back; beyond, sacramental candles have been lighted, and are guttering down in solitude, under an unseen wind. And between, on the sheer darkness of the stage, a bald and plumed Pierrot, holding in his vast, collapsing paunch with a mere rope of roses, shows the cloven foot, while Pierrette points at him in screaming horror, and the fat dancer turns on her toes indifferently. Need we go further to show how much more than Gautier's meaning lies in the old paradox of *Mademoiselle de Maupin,* that "perfection of line is virtue"? That line which rounds the deformity of the cloven-footed sin, the line itself, is at once the revelation and the condemnation of vice, for it is part of that artistic logic which is morality.

Beardsley is the satirist of an age without convictions, and he can but paint hell as Baudelaire did, without pointing for contrast to any contemporary paradise. He employs the same rhetoric as Baudelaire, a method of emphasis which it is uncritical to think insincere. In that terrible annunciation of evil which he called *The Mysterious Rose-Garden,* the lantern-bearing angel with winged sandals whispers, from among the falling roses, tidings of more than "pleasant sins." The leering dwarfs, the "monkeys," by which the mystics symbolised the earthlier vices; these immense bodies swollen with the lees of pleasure, and those cloaked and masked desires shuddering in gardens and smiling ambiguously at interminable toilets; are part of a symbolism which loses nothing by lack of emphasis. And the peculiar efficacy of this satire is that it is so much the satire of desire returning upon itself, the mockery of desire enjoyed, the mockery of desire denied. It is because he loves beauty that beauty's degradation obsesses him; it is because he is supremely conscious of virtue that vice has power to lay hold upon him. And, unlike those other, acceptable satirists of our day, with whom satire exhausts itself in the rebuke of a drunkard leaning against a lamp-post, or a lady paying the wrong compliment in a drawing-room, he is the satirist of essential things; it is always the soul, and not the body's discontent only, which cries out of these insatiable eyes, that have looked on all their lusts, and out of these bitter mouths, that have eaten the dust of all their sweetnesses, and out of these hands, that have laboured delicately for nothing, and out of these feet, that have run after vanities. They are so sorrowful because they have seen beauty, and because they have departed from the line of beauty.

And after all, the secret of Beardsley is there: in the line itself rather than in anything, intellectually realised, which the line is intended to express. With Beardsley everything was a question of form: his interest in his work began when the paper was before him and the pen in his hand. And so, in one sense, he may be said never to have known what he wanted to do, while, in another, he knew very precisely indeed. He was ready to do, within certain limits, almost anything you suggested to him; as, when left to himself, he was content to follow the caprice of the moment. What he was sure of, was his power of doing exactly what he proposed to himself to do; the thing itself might be *Salome* or

Belinda, Ali Baba or *Réjane,* the *Morte d'Arthur* or the *Rhinegold,* or the *Liaisons Dangereuses;* the design might be for an edition of a classic or for the cover of a catalogue of second-hand books. And the design might seem to have no relation with the title of its subject, and indeed, might have none: its relation was of line to line within the limits of its own border, and to nothing else in the world. Thus he could change his whole manner of working five or six times over in the course of as many years, seem to employ himself much of the time on trivial subjects, and yet retain, almost unimpaired, an originality which consisted in the extreme beauty and the absolute certainty of design.

It was a common error, at one time, to say that Beardsley could not draw. He certainly did not draw the human body with an attempt at rendering its own lines, taken by themselves; indeed, one of his latest drawings, an initial letter to *Volpone,* is almost the first in which he has drawn a nude figure realistically. But he could draw, with extraordinary skill, in what is after all the essential way: he could make a line do what he wanted it to do, express the conception of form which it was his intention to express; and this is what the conventional draughtsman, Bouguereau,[17] for instance, cannot do. The conventional draughtsman, any Academy student, will draw a line which shows quite accurately the curve of a human body, but all his science of drawing will not make you feel that line, will not make that line pathetic, as in the little, drooping body which a satyr and a Pierrot are laying in a puff-powder coffin, in the tailpiece to *Salome.*

And then, it must never be forgotten, Beardsley was a decorative artist, and not anything else. From almost the very first he accepted convention, he set himself to see things as pattern. Taking freely all that the Japanese could give him, that release from the bondage of what we call real things, which comes to one man from an intense spirituality, to another from a consciousness of material form so intense that it becomes abstract, he made the world over again in his head, as if it existed only when it was thus re-made, and not even then, until it had been set down in black line on a white surface, in white line on a black surface. Working, as the decorative artist must work, in symbols almost as arbitrary, almost as fixed, as the squares of a chess-board, he swept together into his pattern all the incongruous things in the world, weaving them into congruity by his pattern. Using the puff-box, the toilet-table, the ostrich-feather hat, with a full consciousness of their sug-gestive quality in a drawing of archaic times, a drawing purposely fantastic, he put these things to beautiful uses, because he liked their forms, and because his space of white or black seemed to require some such arrangement of lines. They were the minims and crotchets by which he wrote down his music: they made the music, but they were not the music.

In the *Salome* drawings, in most of the *Yellow Book* drawings, we see Beardsley under this mainly Japanese influence; with, now and later, in his less serious work, the but half admitted influence of what was most actual, perhaps most temporary, in the French art of the day. "Pierrot gamin," in *Salome* itself, alternates, in such irreverences as the design of "The Black Cape," with the creator of noble line, in the austere and terrible design of "The Dancer's Reward," the ornate and vehement design of "The Peacock Skirt." Here we get pure outline, as in the frontispiece; a mysterious intricacy, as in the border of the title-page and of the table of contents; a paradoxical beauty of mere wilfulness, but a wilfulness which has its meaning, its excuse, its pictorial justification, as in "The Toilette."

The *Yellow Book* embroiders upon the same manner; but in the interval between the last drawings for the *Yellow Book* and the first drawings for the *Savoy*, a new influence has come into the work, the influence of the French eighteenth century. This influence, artificial as it is, draws him nearer, though somewhat unquietly nearer, to nature. Drawings like the *Fruit Bearers,* in the first number of the *Savoy,* with its solid and elaborate richness of ornament, or the *Coiffing,* in the third number, with its delicate and elaborate grace, its witty concentration of line; drawings like the illustrations to the *Rape of the Lock,* have, with less extravagance, and also a less strenuous intellectual effort, a new mastery of elegant form, not too far removed from nature while still subordinated to the effect of decoration, to the instinct of line. In the illustrations to Mr. Ernest Dowson's *Pierrot of the Minute,* we have a more deliberate surrender, for the moment, to Eisen and Saint-Aubin, at yet another manner is seen working itself out. The illustrations, as yet unpublished, to *Mademoiselle de Maupin,* seemed to me, when I first saw them, with the exception of one extremely beautiful design in colour, to show a certain falling off in power, an actual weakness in the handling of the pen. But, in their not quite successful feeling after natural form, they did but represent, as I afterwards found, the moment of transition to what must now remain for us, and may well remain, Beardsley's latest manner. The four initial letters to *Volpone,* the last of which was finished not more than three weeks before his death, have a new quality both of hand and of mind. They are done in pencil, and they lose, as such drawings are bound to lose, very greatly in the reduced reproduction. But, in the original, they are certainly, in sheer technical skill, equal to anything he had ever done, and they bring, at the last, and with complete success, nature itself into the pattern. And here, under some solemn influence, the broken line of beauty has reunited; "the care is over," and the trouble has gone out of this no less fantastic world, in which Pan still smiles from his terminal column among the trees, but without the old malice. Human and animal form reassert themselves, with a new dignity, under this new respect for their capabilities. Beardsley has accepted the convention of nature itself, turning it to his own uses, extracting from it his own symbols, but no longer rejecting it for a convention entirely of his own making. And thus in his last work, done under the very shadow of death, we find new possibilities for an art, conceived as pure line, conducted through mere pattern, which, after many hesitations, has resolved finally upon the great compromise, that compromise which the greatest artists have made, between the mind's outline and the outline of visible things.

Charles Conder[1]

I

I had seen Charles Conder before he went to Dieppe in July 1895; he urged me to go with him, which was at that time, for me, impossible. He sent me several urgent letters, saying he had taken a room in 2 la rue de l'Oranger, opposite l'Eglise Saint Jacques; and that there was one over his which was vacant. My opportunity came on me suddenly. I sent him a wire to say I was coming. My intention was to stay at Dieppe from Saturday to Monday. Two months after I began to wonder why I had not yet returned to London: nor was I the only one to fall under this inexplicable fascination. I came there in the company of two strange people: my cynical publisher, Smithers, with his diabolical monocle; Ernest Dowson, the fantastic poet, who had the face of a demoralised Keats, curiously accentuated by a manner that was exquisitely refined.

Conder's genius was essentially French; he had French blood in his veins; and it was in Paris, where he studied in Julien's studio, that he found his way in life and in painting. He had the good luck of coming in immediate contact with two great artists: Toulouse-Lautrec and Anguetin.[2] I can imagine that Lautrec had a certain influence over Conder: there was something curiously similar in their vision a certain perversity, a touch of the morbid and of the bizarre.

Charles Conder's fascination was in every sense different from Augustus John's; he had nothing like John's animality; his genius was more delicate and perverse, more exquisite, fantastic and erotic (in the French sense of the word) than John's turbulent, depraved, cruel and virile genius—passionately original.

Conder's individuality was intensely and profoundly sensitive; in his conversation I found certain subtle superficialities. In Dieppe it was like an education in the Fine Shades to be with him. We were certainly not in the satirical situation of the Pole Ladies in *Emilia in England;*[3] who "supposed they enjoyed exclusive possession of the Nice Feelings, and exclusively comprehended the Fine Shades. If with attentive minds we mark the origin of classes, we shall discern that the Nice Feelings and the Fine Shades play a principal part in our human development

and social history." On the contrary, we were often on the back of
Meredith's famous Hippogriff in mid-air.[4] Still, there was an electric
current between us, which at times shot out very dangerous sparks—
which we never shared with the strangers who flitted to and fro between
Dieppe and Paris and Monte Carlo; not even with Cléo de Mérode,
who fascinated us by her perversely enigmatical air—a most unsacred
Madonna.

Our temperaments, the Painter's and the Poet's were, in many senses,
curiously alike. Both, for one thing, had foreign blood;[5] both were
given up to sensations and to amorous adventures; both lived chiefly by
our senses; both had an ardent adoration of beauty, out of which he
created his pictures and I my verses. So, naturally, Beardsley's temperament was utterly alien to us; who certainly troubled us, morbid as we
were then, by his feverish bitterness, his *bizarrerie;* and by that fact that
all three were aware of: that he had the fatal speed of those who are to
die young; that disquieting completeness of knowledge, the absorption of
a life-time in an hour, which we find in those who hasten to have done
their work before noon.

Conder lived a wild life in Paris; no one who has lived there can
escape it: it is inevitable. He was sensual, casual in his *leves amores;*
drawn incessantly into the thralls of modern Liliths, ferocious and over-
nervous creatures, that "subtly of themselves contemplative" spell a man
by soft-shed kisses and sensuous scent, weaving their lives into the
meshes of their enchanted webs. Certain are gifted with that wonderful
quality, *le diable au corps:* which Balzac defined for all of us. For, as
Gautier said in his exquisite book on Balzac (1859) which I have before
me: "There is in his work an odour of women: *odor di femina;* when
one entered one heard behind the doors that shut on the secret staircase
the rustle of silk and the creaking of shoes."[6] * * *

At Dieppe, for more than a month, Conder and I rarely used the
word in regard to one's *grandes passions.* However, one night, in his
room, I quite inadvertently began telling him of certain adventures of
mine in Paris; of having been fascinated, at a concert of Saint-Saëns,
by a certain beautiful girl, Min Linsella, who had red hair; that after
that I saw her at an exhibition in the Champ de Mars: Rodin had given
me a ticket for the Private View. Finally, I said, I had been—at my
request—introduced to her at the house of Dr John Chapman, 46
Avenue Kleber; and that—at her request—I had stayed two nights
longer in Paris to dance with her at a ball, given by the Chapmans.

After that there were no more secrets between us as to the two
women—both absolutely young and strangely fascinating—who had sent
us into exile. The American girl that Conder imagined he had loved
was painted by Whistler; as for mine, she lives in my verses.[7] * * *

III

I never saw in Conder the slightest trace of jealousy. He rarely spoke of other men's pictures: he was not even critical in regard to his own art. He was essentially a painter; he was a lover of women and of wine, of scent and perfume and things exotic; of women's dresses, of their fans: of Spain, of the bull-fights, of the Spanish dancers and the Spanish music-halls; of Paris and of the Moulin Rouge, of Toulouse-Lautrec, whom he adored; of Verlaine, whose verse he adored; of Baudelaire, Balzac, Gautier's *Mademoiselle de Maupin,* that matchless masterpiece; the Goncourts, Rabelais, Pater and Meredith. His conversation was never wonderful; he was often silent; he loved to hear others talk; he rarely said anything that was really original: he had none of John's intense originality. He was lazy and luxurious; no ascetic, no actual libertine, no saint, no splendid sinner. He never paraded his passions or what might have been called his vices. Such things, or such confessions as these, would never have occurred to him. He could be an exquisite dandy, he could be Bohemian; he could astonish one with his paradoxes, bewilder one with his sinister mystifications—after the manner of Poe and Baudelaire. He had no deep emotions. He was morbid, narcotic: when he was most erotic he revealed himself in his subtlest and most perverse paintings. I have seen him furious, I have seen him intoxicated: I have seen him make love to women with an infinite grace and charm in the Casino at Dieppe and on the beach at midnight to the sound of the howling wind and the storm-tossed sea. He had always the same courtesy, half feminine and half masculine, both for men and for women. His vitality, which carried him into I know not how many excesses, was a consuming flame: he was so fascinating, so vague, so elusive, that women easily fascinated him—at least he always believed that they did—and to such an extent, that he became feverish and febrile: he let his will be dominated by their will; he was never swept away by any consuming passion. When he was most excitable I noticed how soon his state of excitement was followed by exhaustion. No scented whirlwind ever swept him off his feet. Among all his mistresses, among all the women he had possessed, I do not for a moment imagine that any of them could have given him absolute satisfaction.

Conder could capture the dramatic crises in *La Fille aux Yeux d'Or* of Balzac; he could evoke the colours and the atmosphere of one of Verlaine's *Fêtes Galantes* or those of a café in Montmartre; he could evoke a *bal masqué.* His genius, which was by no means absolute—it was uncertain and wayward—often passed into the region one names the abnormal. He had no passion for the horrible; in this he was unlike

Poe and Baudelaire and Lautrec—only in Lautrec the sense of the horrible was always mitigated by a sense of pity which often merged into contempt. What painter has ever achieved the miracle of an imaginary spider's web woven out of frozen dew on some morning, except the Japanese? Did Conder ever desire really to perpetuate—in Pater's words—"that clear perpetual outline of face and line, which is but an image of ours, under which we group them—a design in a web, the actual threads of which pass out beyond it?" * * *

"Conder's women are not timeless," wrote Charles Ricketts, "they have forgotten their age: but this, like beauty, is often a mere matter of opinion! We shall find their histories on the stage of Beaumarchais: they have passed into the realms of immortality not in the paintings of Watteau but in the melodies of Mozart. * * * But what can have detained Donna Anna? It is so late, the 'Queen of the Night' has sung her great aria, the air is close—there are too many roses!"[8] To Conder I know not how many roses grown in hot-houses appealed more than the red roses that flourish and fade and finally wither. In any case these lines of Browning struck his fancy:

> It was roses, roses, all the way,
>   With myrtle mixed in my path like mad!
> The house-roofs seemed to heave and sway,
>   The church-spires flamed, such flags they had,
> A year ago on this very day.
>
> Thus I entered Brescia, and thus I do!
>   In such triumphs, people have dropped down dead.
> "Thou, paid by the world—what dost thou owe
>   Me?" God might have questioned: but now instead
> 'Tis God shall repay! I am safer so.
>   ["The Patriot," *Men and Women*, 1855]

The whole poem contains an ironical tragedy, somewhat obscure; it might mean: "The wages of sin are Death." After too much sinning comes Death. Conder's last years were nothing less than a prolonged agony of intense suffering: there were many lucid intervals in his madness; these were no more to those who watched over him than the faint flickering of a candle some vaguely scented breath of wind might extinguish.

I need not refer to the tragedy of Conder's last years. They were, in a certain sense, not unlike those of Baudelaire; essentially, they were different. Both were cruelly deprived, by sinister circumstances, of the very arts by which they lived, by which they created; in Conder's case of the dainty delicacies and exquisite perversities of his paintings in silk, in oils. And his fans; in Baudelaire's case of all that was extraordinary in his genius: his verse, his creative criticism, his imaginative prose and his marvellous gifts as a translator. Both were lovers of evil, almost in an abnormal sense; and such persistent love of evil, combined as it were with an equal adoration of beauty, must, in the end, have its revenge, nature's revenge on the unnatural. Baudelaire willed all his life to get all he wanted, and did, as a matter of fact, get nearly all he wanted— leaving aside the question of debts and of a certain poverty and of an insistent agitation of spirit. Conder, on the contrary, had very little will- power; his desire was for certain perfections, which he attained, and for success, which he got, and for pleasures which were, generally, within his reach. He often had too faint a hold upon existence to be very sensible of what he was doing or saying or going to do. Both, least likely to have done so, succumbed finally to the destructive forces within them, that pulled down, upon their heads, the house of life.

Conder, who, as I have said, had a passionate admiration for Verlaine's poetry, did, for my sake, a beautiful water-colour drawing for my version of "Mandoline":[9] almost a Watteau, with much of his daintiness, frivolity, evanescence, his instinctive sense of music. These painted puppets of his creation live and breathe and have their days and nights, their tragedies, comedies, light loves and more ardent passions. One almost heard the touch of the player's hand on the mandolin—himself half a vision and half a shade. * * *

Conder is the painter of disillusion: his imaginary figures wander from where, only in Watteau, *le frisson* is made woman, to that fantastic region where fancy dress is to those beings who inhabit it a necessary part of their existences; where one has an instinctive aversion for *le bas peuple*—who indeed are rarely permitted to intrude into the company of their betters. Most of Conder's men and women are as it were "languid with spent desire"; languid even when they listen to melancholy music; languid because the days are too short in duration for them and the nights too long. * * *

IV

This is Stella Conder's narrative that she told me in May, 1907. Before then I had seen Conder at the Private View of the New English Art School, vague and dejected, obviously very ill; he talked to me wearily of the need of rest. On Sunday night, while he was painting he suddenly said: "I feel as if I were going to faint," went and lay down, and as he tried to talk could not find the right words.

The dapper doctor enters, the saturnine Doctor Risien Russell,[11] who looking round the walls and seeing the pictures, says: "No wonder the man who has painted such things. . . !" He tells her that her husband cannot live six months: nothing to be done, humour him. Conder comes down, says he has told him that there is nothing the matter. The tragic supper, she knowing the danger. He begins to make plans for the summer. She bursts into tears. He asks what is the matter, and she says: "You know my aunt at Quebec whom I was so fond of: she is dead." He sympathises, suggests going to Canada to see the family.

Then doctor after doctor: the health cure in one seaside place after another, the nurses (thirteen doctors in all), every doctor discovers new symptoms. All disagree. They go to Brighton alone; he gets violent, begins to rave, raves for forty-eight hours, without food, till the blood drops from his mouth, he is reduced to a skeleton, turns almost green. All hope seems to be over. She borrows a friend's motor and takes him up to town, stretched unconscious, the local doctor holding his pulse. He reaches London, is put to bed, lies as if dead. The doctor who knows him shrieks out his name at him, and he opens his eyes; then the other, Woods, looks at him and says: "You have got to get well," and leaves him to sleep. Slowly he comes back to life, hypnotised by this doctor.

He quarrels with his nurses, attempts to get at knives and throws himself out of the window. Often he talks only in rhyme. He remembers, as if they were nightmares, and repeats what he has gone through. His language, "the bloody female nurse," and worse than that. He clings to his wife, begs her to send away the nurses. He is always worried by the thought that he was leaving his work unfinished. If he had had two years; at least, six months!

His sister comes over from India, and on the boat meets a Buddhist woman who tells her that her brother is dangerously ill, that he will be ill for two years, and then recover, and do his finest work; that he is the reincarnation of a great painter of the eighteenth century, and that he is to complete his work.

Now, when he goes into the garden he picks a flower from the conservatory as a button-hole, and takes his cane, jauntily, in his old manner. Note how once at lunch he looked out uneasily at some chimney pots, and at last said, that of course they were *not* people moving about but that he saw them so, and he must go into another room. When they were talking of engaging a new nurse he said: "I would like Constance Collier dressed as Cleopatra."[12]

He is sent to another rest-cure, and gets the idea that he will die; if he hears a noise, they are driving the nails into his coffin. Woods comes down again, put his hands on his stomach, and says: "You are not going to die, you are to live and finish your work." His whole mind is changed, and he is convinced that he will live and finish his work.

When he was talking for forty-eight hours he kept his arms upright most of the time, in remembrance of Pophnale, the hermit in *Thaïs*:[13] they had read the book in Paris and seen the mummies in the Louvre.

V

Mrs Conder showed a fan, which she used, in which a lovely border of red surrounds the outer edge. Rather than get up from the table—Conder was proverbially lazy—he took up a piece of red sealing-wax and melted it in some methylated spirits which happened to be on the table.

One of the masterpieces of Conder is the Spanish shawl, which he did in Seville in 1905. The shawl is one of those magnificent silken shawls with deep fringes that I found in Spain. Around that border are little squares and ovals and circles of silk, sewn in with silk, each as if enclosed in a little frame. The colours ravish, the designs enchant. Here is a single figure, nude or clothed in beautiful garments; here a scene, Watteau or Cervantes, a bull-fight with an impossible bull, the parody of the Lord in crimson garments; a garden of peacocks; little pictures as great in their small size as the larger compositions. The colour is, as always, what is rarest in Conder; but here there is not a single design, which seen without colour, is not perfect, a creation out of mist and magic.

And all that is fierce, gracious, coloured in Spain is in the Spanish shawl, created out of glittering nights and days and the heat, languors, and ardour of the land. Love is task-master, beauty a concession; the play is serious, as in the bull-fight, and the applause comes from cruel clapping hands indifferent to death. Ecstasy shudders through lace and trembles under cloaks, and draws its intoxication out of the sun. All Spain is there, gay and sombre, passionate and aloof, strange, austere, voluptuous, a dance of the senses, sword and lute, and all the lover's accoutrements.

There is an exquisite unreality in his fans—this new world which never existed except in dreams. Listen to the plain story of one. Overhead is a festoon of blue ribbons, miraculously suspended from a sky over which pink and purple and lavender clouds float vaguely. A solitary house with high walls stands up like a shadow against the sky. Touches of pale green and yellow deepening to the left into purple and a darker green indicate a vague plain; then trees, little clouds, stand up and shut in the scene of the background, where a lady delicately robed in shades of faint reds and yellows, with powdered hair, sits poised on nothing at all, leaning on one elbow; she is midway between the sky and the broken walls of an amphitheatre. A wind-blown lady with a large hat stands with a sinister gesture, one hand touching the face gracefully, the other holding lightly a basket of vague flowers. Beyond her and about her feet flowers grow faintly shaded and with hooped stalks woven into a pattern, with on the right the broken walls of a ruined castle, all in yellowing white marble to which a flight of steps leads up from a shimmering pool. Boughs of impossible trees float through the air like ribbons, and on the edge of a cliff a seated woman holds a black mask beside her fan; she wears a long silken dress of shot blue and a hat with plumes of a slightly darker colour. At her feet lies a naked baby, among the same flowers and woven stalks as the lady on the left hand sits with invisible feet. The three women and the child are aimless, permanently posed, like visions, modern, dainty, empty-headed, fashionable shadows, images of inert eloquence. They and the landscape and the visionary flowers and the hooped ribbons supporting the sky, and the marble steps and pillars and the trees like clouds, are all a world made out of the imagination of a painter who saw only beauty and strangeness and mazes of colours never seen before—a meaningless and mysterious world, permanent as a remembered dream, built out of nothing into a paradise of immortal shadows.

[Sarah Bernhardt]¹

It was in London in 1895 that by a curious accident I first met Sarah Bernhardt—the accident was that I met Leopold Wenzel, the Austrian conductor of the Empire, at a private view of Modern French Pictures in the Grafton Gallery in 1895. In less than five minutes I saw her enter; she began to talk to him; then went slowly on. "Wenzel?" I said, and Wenzel shouted after her: "Sarah! Sarah!" She turned with some surprise; I was introduced and left alone with her. Never have I forgotten the thrill that went all over me as she gave me her hand to kiss: which I did with all the fervour of my fiery youth. Her fingers were covered with rings, her long and slender fingers; the nails were dyed with red henna—which I saw afterwards in the East. She was then at the zenith of her fame and of her beauty. There was the "golden voice," with the Jewish drawl over the syllables—a voice that penetrated one's very heart, as the aching notes of the violins can penetrate one's heart and one's nerves. She seemed to me a vision, a heathen idol one ought to worship—to worship before the shrine of her genius. She had the evil eyes of a Thessalian witch; she could enchant with her slow, subtle and cruel spells men's souls out of their bodies. There was in this tall and thin actress such fire and passion as I have rarely seen in any woman; together with her luxuriousness, languor, indifference, haughtiness and hate. She seemed to me the Incarnation of the Orient. After she drifted away from me with her slow undulating steps, I, so as to keep her magic about me, went into the street, and finally myself back in Fountain Court. * * *

I never could enjoy *Cyrano de Bergerac,* because the verse was enormously clever, but not poetry; only, with Coquelin² and Sarah it received a splendid illumination. She had to play a secondary part as Roxane; she looked amazingly young and beautiful, she was condemned by her part to be ordinary. In a piece all charades and stage directions she had no chance to be any one of her finer selves, and to see her in *Cyrano,* immediately after seeing her in *Phèdre* was to realise the ability of the artist, and how much the artist is at the command of the actress. She gave one no creation; there was no creative material in the play; but all she did she did exquisitely. Still, when she acted with Coquelin in their greatest parts, both had an equal perfection; unlike her, his face was the face of his part, always a disguise, never a revelation.

On the night when I saw it, *L'Aiglon* went on till long after midnight, which was not altogether the fault of the play.[3] It was a fatiguing performance. Once more I admired Rostand's skill, as I saw how skilfully it was written to be acted; scrutinise the first act and you will see that was composed like a piece of music, to be played by one performer, Sarah Bernhardt. To her acting was a performance on a musical instrument. One seemed to see the expression marks: piano, pianissimo, allargando, and just when the tempo rubato comes in. She never forgot that art is not nature, and that, when one is speaking verse one is not talking prose. She spoke with a liquid articulation of every syllable, like one who loves the savour of words on the tongue, giving them a beauty and an expressiveness often not in themselves. The smile of the artist, a wonderful smile which never aged with her, pierced through the languor or the passion of the part. It was often accompanied with a suave voluptuous tossing of the head, and was like the smile of one who inhales some delicious perfume, with half-closed eyes. All through the level perfection of her acting there were sharp little snaps of the nerves; and these were but one indication of that perfect mechanism which her art really was. Coquelin, in his equal perfection, his mellow and ripe art, his touch of vehemence, his passion of humour, made himself seem less a divine machine, more a delightfully faulty person. His face was never a revelation, it was always the face of his part, never a disguise. His firm and sonorous and flexible voice, a harmonious and arresting and expressive voice, was not the elaborate musical instrument of Sarah, which seemed to go by itself, cooing, lamenting, raging, or in that wonderful swift chatter which she uses with such deliberate and instant appeal. Coquelin was not a temperament, nor a student, nor anything apart from the art of the actor; he was the actor, consummately master of his *métier*. I have always noticed how instructive and how amusing it is to see how much these French actors are the masters of themselves. Excitement, gesture, movement, are natural to them, and, so far from needing to be forced, which is the lamentable fault of most of our actors and actresses, can be temperately and vividly repressed. Unlike our actors, with most of them acting is a second nature, and a nature capable of training. With Coquelin and with Sarah, also, nature had been trained with infinite care; but then nature, with them, happened to be genius.

The front row of the stalls, on a first night, has a character of its own. On such a night the air is electrical. On such a night the air was always electrical to me when it was the first night of a ballet at the Alhambra or at the Empire; such nights, and such ballets, no longer exist. Still the air was electrical on the first night of the performance of Louis Verneuil's *Daniel,* where Sarah Bernhardt acted the part of a man who is destroying himself by opium.[4] The first two acts were intolerably tedious; the acting was certainly inadequate. The company ought to have worked with the effortless unanimity of a perfect piece of machinery—as they so often do in Paris; the machinery, such as it was, creaked. When the curtain rose on the third act, it disclosed the familiar figure seated. The smoke of some imaginary opium waved in the air before me; the vision was like the visions evoked by Haschisch. In any case, I can imagine Daniel seized by another just as insidious drug, and its having just the same morbid and disastrous effect on his senses. No sooner had Sarah begun to speak than I became aware that she had no more than the mere ghost of a voice; and at the same time that she said every word with that peculiar intonation that never left her. I have never seen more wonderful hands than hers. Still conscious of her genius, when she became almost pitiably emotional, I could not resist the almost cruel contagion of it. I saw a ravaged body and a ravaged face—the result of nerves and of opium, of imagination and of a lassitude that showed too much nervous excitement. To alleviate her pains she smoked her opium-scented cigarette; and, all the while, had almost the ghastly aspect of a living corpse, that writhes because it is alive, "chained by enchantment to her chair" in that intolerable unrest of a body condemned to endure infernal tortures. Her revelling and her rioting were over; the zest of her existence was no longer hers; there was only one way for her escape—the only one we all dread, the escape of death.

It goes without saying that she, Rachel, Mars, Déjazet, had their failures.[5] It was in Paris, in 1891, that I had the misfortune of seeing perhaps the worst failure she ever had. Haraucourt had written a drama in rhymed blank verse, *La Passion de Jésus Christ,* in which Sarah had to take the part of the Virgin Mary. The performance, oddly enough, was given in the Cirque d'Eté. I had heard beforehand of the scandal that was brewing in Paris; for two reasons, the supposed blasphemy of the play, and the fact that Sarah was a Jewess. It was not that the verses had any irreverence in them; it was the feeling there is in France against the Virgin Mary being associated with persons of her own race. I waited in great excitement; the beginning was long-drawn out and neither poetical nor dramatic. Suddenly Sarah appeared; gorgeous, covered with rich raiment, wearing all her jewels, painted and made up with her conscious art; wonderful, languid, languorous. She began; then, as always, her voice touched me, as if nerve thrilled nerve, and as if, as in Verlaine's superb phrase, *le contour subtil* of the voice were laid lingering on one's spinal chord. No sooner had she uttered thirteen lines of her speech than hisses began in the audience; she lifted her heavy eyelids in arrogant astonishment, raised her voice; the hisses grew louder and louder. The furious and angry glitter that I have seen gleam in her eyes as she felt bound to listen—against her will—to the utter turpitudes of people who misunderstood her—shone in them, like the cold steel of a poisoned blade. There was a long pause; she resumed the broken thread of her speech. Then began a din of tongues—in opposition, naturally—which I am certain affected her as it affected me and at least half of her audience; in the same sense as Lamb was affected when his comedy in Drury Lane was damned. "It was not a hiss neither, but a sort of a frantic yell, like a congregation of mad geese, with roaring something like bears, mows and mops like apes, sometimes snakes, that hissed one into madness."[6] An effect not altogether unlike this—momentary as it was—was made on the infuriated author, who rushed forward, in evening dress, waved his hands, gesticulated wildly, made effort after vain effort to stem the tide of these roaring tongues. The lamentable and, to me, absurd end of it was that Sarah had to retire, like a furious tigress. * * *

[Edouard de Max]¹

De Max—I met him in the house of Marcel Schwob, 41 rue de Valois—
has lately been interviewed by a friend of mine in Paris—Lugné-Poe.²
The test of the artist, the test which decides how far the artist is still
living as more than a force of memory, lies in the power to create a new
part, to bring new material to life. In the case of de Max, on the stage
and off the stage, he inevitably contrived to create an illusion—which
means the living on of a mastery once absolutely achieved, without so
much as the need of a new effort: and, besides this, by sheer instinct and
sheer imagination, and with perfect technique, he thrilled me by the way
in which he touched every nerve and indicated every vein in the characters he represented. His acting, of course, is almost a science, a science
founded on tradition. Yet, in one of those terrible parts which he adored,
he reminded me of Irving in *Louis XI:*³ that is to say, in representing the
shrivelled carcase, from which age, disease, and fear have picked all the
flesh, leaving the bare framework of bone and the drawn and cracked
covering of yellow skin; for, as in the original—one of the most cruel
and sinister of kings, whose fears were monstrous, who trembled at the
shadow of a leaf tossed in the wind—it is the picture that magnetises us.
Every wrinkle seems to have been studied in movement; the hands act
almost by themselves, as if every finger were a separate actor: one saw, in
a face whose expressions were infinite, the instinct of craft, the malady of
suspicion. De Max can give one the sense of some vague spiritual fear,
a mist, a mere delusion of the senses, that escapes, snake-like, across
some poisonous valley, covered with wicked weeds, a haunt of demons
that beat at some unseen, at some terrifying door the opening of which
they dread.

Imagine him as Orestes or as Hamlet. He incarnates in them their
sense of spiritual pride: their tragedies are the shock of matter against
spirit, the invasion of spirit by matter, the temptation of evil by spiritual
evil. It is part of his curiosity in souls to prefer the complex to the simple,
the perverse to the passionate, the ambiguous to either; with, I imagine,
some of that overwhelming and insatiable curiosity which obsessed Villiers de l'Isle-Adam, whom de Max had met. When de Max acts Hamlet,
Hamlet seeks the absolute, the world's mystery, the miracle of death's
mystery; only, when all Hamlet's plots of revenge have been executed,
with the one exception of his unnecessary death, before he utters his last

immortal words, "The rest is silence," the thought of death to him is as if a veil had been withdrawn for an instant, the veil which renders life possible, and, for that instant, he has seen. De Max showed that Hamlet's pretence of madness—which is not the result of his passion for living, for he loves no one—is almost transparent, used maliciously for the confusion of fools, not excluding Polonius, a curious mixture of wisdom and folly, whose life Hamlet, cursed with the veritable genius of inaction, is fated to cast out of its intruding carcase. When de Max acts Orestes, Orestes pants with the shameful sensation of blood he has spilt, with the horror of the crime he has committed; who, after having in vain evoked phantoms, finds in himself nothing less than a phantom. When he acted with Sarah Bernhardt in a melodrama named *Francesca da Rimini*,[4] which degrades the story we owe to Dante and not to history (for, in itself, the story is a quite ordinary story of adultery: Dante and the flames of hell purged it), I found that Sarah was lifeless, a failure, and no more than a melodious image, whereas de Max made hardly less than a creation out of the part of Giovanni, filling it with his own nervous force and passionately restrained art.

La Sorcière seems to me Sardou's greatest creation; it is filled with suspense—the suspense of witchcraft, of the Demons of the night, of the Sabbats; it reveals the intense hatred that existed between the Spaniards and those of pure Moorish race; it gives us in Ximenes a kind of less magnificent Torquemada than Hugo's. I was present at its first performance, on the 15th of December, 1903, at the Théâtre Sarah Bernhardt. As Zoraya, the sorceress, who has the perfection and the sweet poison and the diabolical malice of her race; whose body's heat is contagious, whose beauty is unsurpassable, whose passion is primitive, Sarah was wonderful: she was literally Zoraya. Jewish, she was Moorish in her furies, her exultations, her sultry heats of sombre passion. She bewitches Enrique de Salacios as she tells his fortune. "Elle s'est penché de plus en plus, troublé pas le rapprochement de leurs corps, par les parfumes arabes qui se dégagent de la chevelure de Zoraya, par la chaleur de sa main." During her examination, which is to lead to her death at the stake, she defends herself with vehemence; but, as her flesh begins to quiver at the sensation of so ignominious a death, her mouth pours out the hatred of her race against her accusers. She speaks to the Christ on the Crucifix. "They have nailed your feet and your hands, lest you should have mercy on us the miserable. But, if you could tear yourself off from your cross, you would cry to these infamous judges not to seek otherwise Hell and the Sabbats. Here is Hell, where they sacrifice to you living beings, where they offer you by way of chants the groans of the tortured, and for incense the odour of their burnt flesh. Here is Hell, Hell with its furnaces, the Hell of the damned. Hell! Hell! with its demons!"

Ximenes, de Max created with magnificence and with passion: the sublime and cruel figure, prodigious, sacrilegious, loomed before us; in fact, I saw almost a revelation of Alexander, the Spanish Pope who filled the Vatican and the world with his contagious clouds, who contained in himself the most ignobly splendid vices that have swayed the world: a strangling serpent, whose immense coils have the blood-red colour of rich jewels, the green of jade. Ximenes' last words are: "Nous la brûlerons après vêpres!"—burning words that literally froze my blood.

The premature death of Marcel Schwob was certainly a loss to French literature. Living as he did with Marguerite Moreno,[5] he had in his service an amazing Chinese, who always startled one when he opened the door, garbed in curious vestments, with his oblique eyes and olive skin. One afternoon, among the many guests, was de Max, the perverse, somewhat painted actor, whose sinister genius always appealed to me—most of all when he acted with Sarah Bernhardt; chiefly, indeed, in *Phèdre,* where his creation of Hippolytus, which he filled with his own nervous force and passionately restrained art, thrilled me. * * *

We were discussing certain questions in regard to Racine's tragedies; and after de Max had spoken violently in favour of the part he had been playing, Moreno began to tease him mockingly on one fault he made when he spoke French: that he always said *père* with a Roumanian accent. * * *

* * * Trick or instinct, there it is, the power to make you feel intensely; and that is precisely the final test of a great dramatic artist. Only you can never fathom his secret: indeed, has any great actor ever fathomed his own secret? *Macabre* and brutal, evil, exquisite and menacing, dealing when he chooses with sordid material, where people are vicious and miserable, a sordid and barren land, under the sway of the *Eros vanné* of Verlaine, a world weary of itself, having no means of escape from the serpent's coils that are twined around it, de Max fixes you, magnetises you, bewilders you: has, in fact, in one of his most horrible creations, done what Réjane did in *Sappho* or in *Zaza,*[6] showed you—showed me, for instance—with all the actor's or actress's muscles and nerves, a gross, pitiable, horribly human thing, whose direct appeal, like that of a sick animal, seizes you by the throat at the instant in which it reaches your eyes and ears.[7]

The genius of de Max is essentially, fundamentally, sexual; and his appeal to me has often been the appeal of Réjane, because it is sex and not instinct. I have said: "Sex in her calculates and is cunning. It has none of the vulgar warmth of mere passion, none of its health or simplicity. It leaves a little red sting where it has kissed. And it intoxicates us by its appeal to so many sides of our nature at once. We are thrilled, and we admire, and are almost coldly appreciative, and yet aglow with the response of the blood."[8] * * *

Morbid as ever, he shows that tragic mask of his and his Asiatic luxury, surrounded with treasures of his own choice, at the very end of the room, which is painted with shadows of pale gold: the actor with his strange silhouette, whose voice is monstrous, on account of its beauty, who has dead black eyes, dead black hair, who smokes incessantly, creates a sudden hallucination, together with the scent of some strange perfume, which might be thick, stupefying incense-smoke. * * *

* * * A play is said to be well acted in proportion to the scenical illusion produced: whether or not such illusions can in any case be perfect, is not the question. The nearest approach to it is when the actor appears wholly unconscious of the presence of spectators. I have referred to the fixity of the eyes of actors, which is more essential than most of us suppose. So did de Max, when he felt inclined to, assume a kind of evil mask which only half concealed his creations. In this he reminds me of Irving in his impersonation of the weary spirit, an image of unhappy pride, for in such a part no mannerism can seem unnatural, and the image with its solemn mask lives in a kind of volcanic life of its own, seductively, with some mocking suggestion of his "cousin the snake."

[Alfred Jarry]¹

I

* * * I met [Jarry] in Remy de Gourmont's rooms in la rue du Bac, one afternoon, when, in the middle of our conversation, someone knocked. Gourmont went out and returned with Alfred Jarry, a small, nervous, sad youth, with a square face, and black savage eyes, and, as he spoke, we noticed a kind of pose in the way he weighed his words: for he was face to face, for the first time in his life, with two writers, before whom he assumed a surprising humility. He laid on the table with hieratic gestures a huge portfolio, which contained some of his prose and some of his amazing designs. Nor did we wonder at his air of grotesque absurdity when he mentioned the fact that he lived in a garret in the company of Owls. He admitted that he lived in great starvation: he always surrounded himself with an air of solemn mystery.

After he had gone Gourmont and I began by laughing at his meagre appearance and at some of his prose; but the prose turned out much better than we had imagined. Gourmont, one of the kindest men I have known, besides his mastery of style and his imaginative prose, took up Jarry, got him to collaborate with him, introducing him to Huysmans and Vallette and Rachilde.²

Jarry was poor, horribly poor, and sensitive and proud and quick to take offence; that is the chief cause, or at least one of the causes of his eccentricities, which in turn made it difficult to help him. At times he was literally in rags, and Dr. Saltas records how Jarry came to work with him during one severe winter with shoes that leaked badly.³ Apollinaire says that Jarry rented in Paris one room, which was numbered 3½, because the owner of the house had divided each storey into two for the purpose of letting out more "rooms."⁴ This wretched place was too low for Apollinaire to stand erect; its furniture consisted of a pallet bed, a cheap edition of Rabelais, two or three pamphlets, and a large Japanese emblem presented to Jarry by Félicien Rops. Jarry had a country as well as a town house: this was an old railway carriage on a bit of waste ground (which the novelist surrounded with barbed wire) situated just outside Paris.

II

A Symbolist Farce[5]

The performance of *Ubu Roi: comédie guignolesque* by Alfred Jarry, at the Théâtre de l'Oeuvre, in 1896, when Gemier[6] played the part of Père Ubu, of little importance in itself, is of considerable importance as a symptom of tendencies agitating the minds of the younger generation in France. The play is the first Symbolist farce: it has the crudity of the schoolboy or a savage: what is, after all, most remarkable about it is the insolence with which a young writer mocks at civilization itself, sweeping all art, along with all humanity, into the same inglorious slop-pail. That it should ever have been written is sufficiently surprising: but it has been praised by Catulle Mendès,[7] by Anatole France; the book has gone through several editions, and now the play has been mounted by Lugné-Poe (whose mainly Symbolist Théâtre de l'Oeuvre has so significantly taken the place of the mainly Naturalist Théâtre Libre) and it has been given twice over, before a crowded house, howling but dominated, a house buffeted into sheer bewilderment by the wooden lath of a gross undiscriminating, infantile Philosopher-Pantaloon.

Jarry's idea in this symbolical buffoonery, was to satirise humanity by setting human beings to play the part of marionettes, hiding their faces behind cardboard masks, tuning their voices to the howl and squeak which tradition has considerably assigned to the voices of that wooden world, and mimicking the rigid inflexibility and spasmodic life of puppets by a hopping and reeling gait. The author, who has written an essay, "De l'Inutilité du Théâtre au Théâtre,"[8] has explained that a performance of marionettes can only suitably be accompanied by the marionette music of fairs; and therefore the motions of these puppet-people were accompanied from time to time, by an orchestra of piano, cymbals, and drums, played behind the scenes, and reproducing the note of just such a band as one might find on the wooden platform outside a canvas booth in a fair. The action is supposed to take place "in Poland, that is to say, in the land of Nowhere"; and the scenery was painted to represent, by a child's conventions, indoors and out of doors, and even the torrid, temperate, and arctic zones at once. Opposite to you, at the back of the stage, you saw apple trees in bloom, under a blue sky, and against the sky a small closed window and a fireplace, containing an alchemist's crucible, through the very midst of which (with what refining intention, who knows?) trooped in and out these clamorous and sanguinary persons

of the drama. On the left was painted a bed, and at the foot of the bed a
bare tree, and snow falling. On the right were palm trees, about one of
which coiled a boa-constrictor; a door opened against the sky, and beside
the door a skeleton dangled from a gallows. Changes of scene were announced by the simple Elizabethan method of a placard, roughly scrawled
with such stage directions as this: "La scène représente la province de
Livonie couverte de neige." A venerable gentleman in evening-dress,
Father Time, as we see him on Christmas-trees, trotted across the stage on
the points of his toes between every scene, and hung the new placard on
its nail. And before the curtain rose, in what was after all but a local
mockery of a local absurdity, two workmen backed upon the stage carrying a cane-bottomed chair and a little wooden table covered with a sack,
and Jarry (a small, very young man, with a hard, clever face) seated
himself at the table and read his own "conférence" on his own play.

In explaining his intentions, Jarry seemed to me rather to be explaining the intentions which he ought to have had, or which he had singularly failed to carry out. To be a sort of comic antithesis to Maeterlinck, as
the ancient satiric play was at once a pendant and an antithesis to the
tragedy of its time: that, certainly, though he did not say it, might be
taken to have been one of the legitimate ambitions of the writer of *Ubu
Roi*. "C'est l'instauration du Guignol Littéraire," as he affirms, and a
generation which has exhausted every intoxicant, every soluble prepara-
tion of the artificial, may well seek a last sensation in the wire-pulled
passions, the wooden faces of marionettes, and, by a further illusion, of
marionettes who are living people; living people pretending to be those
wooden images of life which pretend to be living people. There one
sees truly, the excuse, the occasion, for an immense satire, a Swiftian
or Rabelaisian parody of the world. But at present Jarry has not the
intellectual grasp nor the mastery of a new technique needful to carry
out so vast a programme. Swift, Rabelais, is above all the satirist with
intention, and the satirist who writes. Jarry has somehow forgotten his
intention before writing, and his writing when he takes pen in hand.
Ubu Roi is the gesticulation of a young savage of the woods, and it is
his manner of expressing his disapproval of civilisation. Satire which is
without distinctions becomes obvious, and Jarry's present conception of
satire is very much that of the schoolboy to whom a practical joke is the
most efficacious form of humour, and bad words scrawled on a slate
the most salient kind of wit.

These jerking and hopping, these filthy, fighting, swearing "gamins"
of wood bring us back, let us admit, and may legitimately bring us back,
to what is primitively animal in humanity. Ubu may be indeed "un sac à
vices, un outre à vins, une poche à bile, un empereur romain de la
décadence, idoine à toutes cacades, pillard, paillard, braillard, un

goulaphre," as the author describes him; but he is not sufficiently that, he is not invented with sufficient profundity, nor set in motion with a sufficiently comic invention. He does not quite attain to the true dignity of the marionette. He remains a monkey on a stick.

Yet, after all, Ubu has his interest, his value; and that strange experiment of the Rue Blanche its importance as a step in the movement of minds. For it shows us that the artificial, when it has gone the full circle, comes back to the primitive; des Esseintes[9] relapses into the Red Indian. Jarry is logical, with that frightful irresistible logic of the French. In our search for sensation we have exhausted sensation; and now, before a people who have perfected the fine shades to their vanishing point, who have subtilised delicacy of perception into the annihilation of the very senses through which we take in ecstasy, a literary Sansculotte has shrieked for hours that unspeakable word of the gutter[10] which was the refrain, the "Leitmotiv" of this comedy of masks. Just as the seeker after pleasure whom pleasure has exhausted, so the seeker after the material illusions of literary artifice turns finally to that first, subjugated never quite exterminated, element of cruelty which is one of the links which bind us to the earth. *Ubu Roi* is the brutality out of which we have achieved civilisation, and those painted, massacring puppets the destroying elements which are as old as the world, and which we can never chase out of the system of natural things.

André Gide[1]

I met André Gide in 1896 at a dinner given by Jacques Blanche; he had long hair and a long beard; and at first sight struck me as being a singularly original man. His personality has always been bizarre; I saw something in the whole man quite unlike other men of letters: a mixture of kindness and of irony, of refined culture and of strange tastes.[2]

And like myself, for instance, he has learned much from his travels; for, without travelling, living in foreign countries, one's blood stagnates; and, indeed, what can be imagined for such men as Gide and myself, with mixed blood in our veins, whose most exciting form of existence is to find ourselves in cities and on seashores, seeking adventures that come by hazard and sensations that come by chance?[3]

I have been reading his book, *Les Caves du Vatican*, which is certainly the finest book he has written since *L'Immoraliste* of 1902. It is ironical, malign, sardonical, Catholic and anti-Catholic; full of grim humour, of much too refined cruelty; giving sudden aspects of his characters, then leaving them to weave their way across an intricate plot. He hates all the characters he has created, with a few exceptions. As, for instance, in the criminal Protos—a parody of Balzac's Vautrin—who has the devil's cunning; and Lafcadio, the bastard of the famous family of the Baraglioul, originally Italians, who has the insolence of youth and beauty, the pride of his race, and a certain obscure criminality which drives him, in a kind of stupor, to hurl one of the Baragliouls out of the train near Capua. His crime, once committed, has to him simply one motive: hatred of this hideous creature. "Un crime immotivé, continuait Lafcadio: quel embarras pour la police!"

But, as Gide has no sinister intentions against him; he lets his escape, remain unpunished; makes him marry, after an amorous night-scene, the lovely Geneviève de Baraglioul; and, at the same time, as Protos has strangled a certain Carlotte Vanilegua, who had betrayed him to the Roman police, he is properly condemned for his actual crime, and also on the supposition that he had committed Lafcadio's.

As a writer's opinion of his own prose is always interesting to know, I quote the first sentence from a letter Gide sent to me in answer to one of mine. "Vous êtes exquis de m'écrire ainsi, mon cher Symons, et votre louange m'est d'autant plus précieuse, que mes *Caves* ont été jusqu'à présent peu appreciées et que peu des très rares esprits—mais je *sais* que ce livre est d'une importance." * * *

Now Gide, who is the finest master of prose we have in France, has not only an unbounded devotion to form, but has, on the whole, nothing but original ideas; and, as to his style, which has never essentially changed, it is always exquisite, always original, always surprising. * * *

L'Immoraliste is simply a detailed study—"l'exposé d'un cas bizarre"—of a sick man who gets cured in Biskra and whose wife, after their return to Paris, catches his disease and dies of it. In Michel, who relates the story, there is certainly something of Gide, who, as the writer states, has put in this book "toute sa passion, toutes ses larmes et tout son soin." And this effect of the whole narrative on me is that it gives me an intense sense of the East, of heat, of atmosphere, of the changes of light and shade; almost to the point of having actually been there.

In Biskra, Michel's whole concern is with his body, leaving aside "la part de l'esprit." At a certain moment he is invaded by the tragic sentiment of his life, so violent, so sorrowful, that he cries aloud like a beast. In Paris, enters again into his existence his sinister friend Ménalgue, who has tracked him in his wanderings in the East and who reveals, nakedly, to Michel his most secret thoughts. That night his wife, Marceline, gives birth to a still-born child. "The earth gave way under my feet; before me was no more than an empty void into which I stumbled."

In his vain attempt to save her life they return to Biskra; the night before she dies he sleeps with an Arab woman in a Moorish café. And it seems to me that Gide shows in Marceline's death the hideous revenge of nature on two creatures who may have loved too little or too much.

Algernon Charles Swinburne[1]

I

It was on January 28th, 1898, that Swinburne said to me, as he showed me his copy of Baudelaire's *Richard Wagner et Tannhäuser à Paris* (1861)—a pamphlet of seventy pages, on which was written "à Mr. Algernon C. Swinburne, Bon Souvenir et mille Remerciements. C.B.," in pencil—"that Baudelaire was always a boy; he liked to contradict people." He spoke with the greatest admiration of *Les Fleurs du Mal* and of most of his prose, but pointed out his critical failures in his worship of Poe and of "a popular draughtsman in the *Illustrated London News*"—that is, Constantin Guys. "Poe," he went on, "had the luck to be born on the right side of the Atlantic. Now Tupper, had he done the same, would have combined Walt Whitman and Longfellow in one: half would have been Martin and half Tupper."[2]

After these splendid paradoxes one has simply to say that Swinburne was the first English writer who ever praised *Les Fleurs du Mal*. His review was printed in *The Spectator,* September 6th, 1862. * * *

Swinburne was a great praiser of great work, as he himself admits in his *Notes on Poems and Ballads* (1868): "I have never been able to see what should attract men to the profession of criticism but the mere pleasure of praising." He was the only critic of our time who never, by design or by accident, praised the wrong things. The main quality in his criticism was its exultation. "There is a joy in praising" (words written by Landor) might have been written for him (they were written for Browning). The motto from Baudelaire that Swinburne gave at the head of his *William Blake,* that "it would be prodigious for a critic to become a poet, and it is impossible for a poet not to contain a critic," is equally true of that prose-poet whose genius was not unsimilar with Baudelaire. In certain pages even the paradoxes make one realise how much of this solemn jocoseness went to the making of these unwounding darts: so curiously exhilarating are these criticisms which quicken the blood rather than stir the intelligence. And for these reasons Swinburne's place is eternally among the greatest of creative writers, with Lamb and with Coleridge and with Baudelaire.

He had a sovereign disdain, an infinite contempt, for the mediocrities, the pedants, that, as they seemed to crawl in his way, he crushed under his heels. He had a kind of instinct in the art, not of making mischief, but of mischief-making, which came and went in innumerable nick-names, in sly insinuations, in shouts of ironical laughter; in a word, he inherited Blake's "subtle humour of scandalising."

I shall never forget a certain morning at The Pines, as I waited in Watts-Dunton's study for Swinburne's appearance before luncheon.[3] He floated in, entirely unconscious of my being there; went up to his friend with a newspaper in his hand; from one of the pages he read, with a smile of calm contempt, in his usual voice—yet with mocking accents in it—a scrap of a kind of advertisement taken from the review of a mediocre verse-writer, where the insolent critic had dared to contrast *his début* with this poetaster's. I was aware of the comedy of this pro-ceeding before Swinburne was aware of my presence. Without a word more he came up to me and shook hands in his cordial way of welcoming one who was not quite a stranger in the house.

I remember also our entire agreement in regard to Tennyson: that he had an imperfectness of the ear, which even after much cultivation was never entirely out of his verse. I find, in reference to this, in his essay on Morris's verses,[4] when, after quoting from memory those un-forgettable lines:

> O sickle cutting harvest all day long,
> That the husbandman across his shoulder hangs,
> And going homeward about evensong,
> Dies the next morning, struck through by the fangs,

he says: "They are not indeed—as are *The Idylls of the King*—the work of a dexterous craftsman in full practice. Little beyond dexterity, a rare eloquence, and a laborious patience of hand has been given to the one and denied to the other. These are good gifts and great; but it is better to want clothes than limbs." There, to a certainty, is "the sting in the tail of the honey."

As for Swinburne's persiflage, I have an amusing story to relate. One afternoon he came up to me in his study and, with a curious smile, said: "Mr. Symons, shall I quote for your edification the most indecent line in the Elizabethan drama?" This is the line, which he had only recently discovered—of course, a question of sex:

> On this soft anvil all the world was made.[5]

* * *

III

There was something ceremonial in the lunches at The Pines; in that immense room, study and dining-room, glorified by some of Rossetti's finest pictures in oils. In the centre was the long table; Watts-Dunton sat at the top, Swinburne on his right, I at the end. There was generally near me a small bottle of sherry, which no one ever tasted; Watts-Dunton and I drank water, Swinburne stout. He drank it with a certain air of satisfaction, holding up the glass to see how much was left in it. I thought then of his earlier years, when it pleased him to drink wine; when only a few glasses of wine inspired him in his unsurpassable conversations. He felt as one feels that actual luxury when one's tongue is loosened and one forgets half of what one is saying. It is certainly a Bacchic luxury that the Bacchanals in ancient ages exulted in; it gives one the sublime qualities of a liar; it "loses count in the hours"; it stirs one's blood till one is rapt into the exquisite life-in-death of Circe's sorcerous wine.

I had a certain difficulty in raising my voice high enough to be heard by Swinburne, as we were seated at a certain distance from one another. Generally my voice reached him, and his answers were prompt, spontaneous, wonderful. At times when he failed to hear my voice he said resignedly, "I don't quite hear," and relapsed into silence.

Rarely did I hear him talk with more eloquence than of Mazzini and Sir Richard Burton—Mazzini, who had inspired in him a breath of lyrical song unsung by him until his *Songs before Sunrise;* Burton, who had saved him from a certain sickness that came on him on the French coast,[6] to whom he dedicated *Poems and Ballads* of 1878, in these words: "Inscribed to Richard L. Burton in redemption of an old pledge and in recognition of a friendship which I must always count among the highest honours of my life."

Swinburne continually spoke to me of Rossetti; for his reverence for the man himself and for the man's genius was quite wonderful. Nor is it questionable that Rossetti was the inspiring spirit of his *Cénacle;* for in every one of them one finds his influence, in the lesser as in the greater; and this one man alone possessed the double gift of the poet and the painter. And in the intensity of his imagination, in the fire and glory of his genius, there was, I think, in him alone that "sweep from left to right, fiery and final," which he applied to the work of Dante and of Michelangelo. * * *

One thing I have never forgotten in regard to his conversation was that he talked to me as man to man, with a simplicity of manner all his own; so much so that all this left on me a kind of entrancement, of enchantment. Living, as he did, at a height higher than an eagle's flight, he showed it as often in his silences as in his words. And it was always there—in the strange green eyes that gazed in yours in a kind of abstract passion; in the face, that suggested the sense of flight, with its aquiline features. And one saw in his whole aspect his French subtlety, ardour, susceptibility, with his sensual and sensuous temperament; and in his northern blood the wildness of his imagination, the strength that vibrated in every movement, slender in body though he was. Nor was there ever, I think, a more perfect mixture of foreign blood than in Swinburne. I saw in him that inordinate nervous energy that rose to a point of excitability, that dropped to the level of courteous resignation, as if he had never flagged in life's endeavour, had never been over-weary of life's worst evils. Nor was any man more certain of his own existence than Swinburne. There shone, shook, surged before me his race, his genius, as inevitably as if his own destiny had shown itself, star-like, in his words:

Save his own soul man has no star.

His voice, when he read his verse, was high-pitched; it was an ecstatic, a rapturous voice; it never went deep, but often up and up as he emphasised every word that had a special significance; he stressed them, he cadenced them, as when he uttered his favourite words, "fire," "sea," "wind," "spirit and sense," "scent and shade"—

The very soul in all my senses aches.

as if such words as these had never before been said with so intense a sense of their inner meaning. His voice was not musical yet it was a beautiful voice; it did not ring many changes on the variations of the notes, but it was an inspired voice—a voice that went on and on as he lifted his eyes from his MS. and raised them to the ceiling or fixed them on mine. I have heard many poets read their verse, but (save with the sole exception of Verlaine) never have I been so thrilled, so rooted in my chair, nor drawn in my breath as I did when Swinburne read me his verses.

IV

One afternoon, as I arrived rather late, I was shown into Swinburne's study when he was in the act of reading some of his MS. prose to Sir

Frederick Pollock.[7] He went on with it; it was one of his tremendously denunciatory invectives against some tamperers with the texts of Elizabethan dramas; underlying which I saw, for the first time, that natural sense of humour (never wit) but often fine satire, and that kind of quaint jesting that was more in the man when he spoke than in the writer when he wrote. He relished this sort of prose as he relished his malevolent and magnificent sonnets "Diræ";[8] certainly the most stupendous things he ever wrote: they have that eternal ring of just anger, that infinite hatred of all the spawned forces of evil that have besmeared the surface of the world, shown in that incredible King-Idol named (wrongly) the Saviour of Society.

The sense of Fate's implacable laws, of Destiny's inexorable following on men's steps, both primeval conceptions, fashioned for eternity by the genius of Æschylus, passed, I think, into the life-blood of Swinburne. And he believed, as all great artists have believed: "In art all that ever had life in it has life for ever." He said also: "No man can prove or disprove his own worth except by his own work; and is it, after all, so grave a question to determine whether the merit of that be more or less?" This also he wrote: "No work of art has any worth of life in it that is not done on the absolute terms of art. [. . .] It is equally futile to bid an artist forego the natural bent of his genius or to bid him assume the natural office of another."[9] And if ever poet left his *Credo* to the world, he, I think, does in those sentences.

"To the question, 'Can these bones live?' there is but one answer; if the spirit and breath of art be breathed upon them indeed, and the voice prophesying upon them be indeed the voice of a prophet, then assuredly will the bones 'come together, bone to his bone,' and the sinews and the flesh will come up upon them, and the skin cover them above, and the breath come into them, and they live."[10]

V

Swinburne said to me, at the beginning of 1907: "My *magnum opus* will be my book on the Elizabethan Dramatists. I have put so much of my life, of my thoughts, of my reading, of my research, of even my painstaking in minute details, into the production of this volume that I don't mind if it chances to be my last book of prose." It was so: *The Age of Shakespeare* (1908). I think, on the whole, that he was right; for it began with his "John Ford" in 1871, and ended with "Cyril Tourneur." In so absolute an achievement of so fixed a purpose there is the passion and enthusiasm of his youth, his maturer judgments, his last refinements. Yet it has neither the glory of his *Blake* (1868) nor the absolute perfection of his *Study of Shakespeare* (1886); for in this there is an adoration, purer perhaps in essence than in his adoration of Blake, for Shakespeare; it is written in his most imaginative prose style; it is faultless.

I saw Swinburne for the last time in the winter of 1907. After some general conversation he told me of his intention of writing a five-act play on the Borgias; he showed me his Yriarte, with his scraps of paper neatly inserted between the pages, by way of reference. Then he lighted his three small candlesticks, arranged them before him on his desk with an infinite sense of order; then turned to the small cupboard behind his chair where he kept all his manuscripts. Those he took out were written on blue paper, a kind of paper that he invariably used for writing either prose or verse. I saw, as he turned the leaves over, certain traces, not many, of his revisions. What he read was the crisis of what was finally his *Duke of Gandia,* from the beginning of Scene III to the end of Scene IV—that is, to the final *exeunt*.[11]

I never imagined that Swinburne could have conceived this one-act drama so subtly, so supremely, out of such sorcerous material as lies in the loves and hates and deaths of the Borgias, and carried it to so consummate an end. For the story is the most shameful, the most shameless, the most fascinating of all such relations of actual lives. In those scenes he evokes the spirit, the flesh, the bodies of these sinister creatures: from the exquisite Lucrezia, famed for her surpassing beauty, to Vanozza, the Pope's concubine, whose fair loveliness had snared him to the begetting with her of this minute world of sinners. And in these two scenes I found, as I heard them (I feel them now as I write), that salt and sense of pity and wonder—not quite as in Aristotle's definition, but in their elemental grandeur, severity, and implacability, that have a spiritual kinship with the great dead and alive spirits, from Aeschylus to Shakespeare.

Whistler[1]

I

* * * Unlike most artists, [Whistler] was to be seen everywhere, and he was heard wherever he was seen. He was incapable of rest, and incapable of existing without production. When he was not working at his own art, he was elaborating a fine art of conversation. In both he was profoundly serious, and in both he aimed at seeming to be the irresponsible butterfly of his famous signature. He deceived the public for many years; he probably deceived many of his acquaintances till the day of his death. Yet his whole life was a devotion to art, and everything that he said or wrote proclaimed that devotion, however fantastically. I wish I could remember half the things he said to me, at any one of those few long talks which I had with him in his quiet, serious moments. I remember the dinner party at which I first met him, not many years ago,[2] and my first impression of his fierce and impertinent chivalry on behalf of art. Some person officially connected with art was there, an urbane sentimentalist; and after every official platitude there was a sharp crackle from Whistler's corner, and it was as if a rattlesnake had leapt suddenly out. The person did not know when he was dead, and Whistler transfixed him mortally, I know not how many times; and still he smiled and talked. I had said something that pleased Whistler, and he peered at me with his old bright eyes from far down the room; and after dinner he took me aside and talked to me for a full hour. He was not brilliant, or consciously clever, or one talking for effect; he talked of art, certainly for art's sake, with the passionate reverence of the lover, and with the joyous certainty of one who knows himself beloved. In what he said, of his own work and of others, there was neither vanity nor humility; he knew quite well what in his art he had mastered and what others had failed to master. But it was chiefly of art in the abstract that he talked, and of the artist's attitude towards nature and towards his materials. He only said to me, I suppose, what he had been saying and writing for fifty years; it was his gospel, which he had preached mockingly, that he might disconcert the mockers; but he said it all like one possessed of a conviction, and as if he were stating that conviction with his first ardour.

And the man, whom I had only before seen casually and at a distance, seemed to me almost preposterously the man of his work. At dinner he had been the controversialist, the acrobat of words; I understood how this little, spasmodically alert, irritably sensitive creature of brains and nerves could never have gone calmly through life, as Rodin, for instance, goes calmly through life, a solid labourer at his task, turning neither to the right nor to the left, attending only to his own business. He was a great wit, and his wit was a personal expression. Stupidity hurt him, and he avenged himself for the pain. All his laughter was a crackling of thorns under the pot, but of flaming thorns, setting the pot in a fury of boiling. I never saw any one so feverishly alive as this little, old man, with his bright, withered cheeks, over which the skin was drawn tightly, his darting eyes, under their prickly bushes of eyebrow, his fantastically-creased black and white curls of hair, his bitter and subtle mouth, and, above all, his exquisite hands, never at rest. He had the most sensitive fingers I have ever seen, long, thin, bony, wrinkled, every finger alive to the tips, like the fingers of a mesmerist. He was proud of his hands, and they were never out of sight; they travelled to his moustache, crawled over the table, grimaced in little gestures. If ever a painter had painter's hands it was Whistler. And his voice, with its strange accent, part American, part deliberately French, part tuned to the key of his wit, was not less personal or significant. There was scarcely a mannerism which he did not at one time or another adopt, always at least half in caricature of itself. He had a whole language of pauses, in the middle of a word or of a sentence, with all sorts of whimsical quotation-marks, setting a mocking emphasis on solemn follies. He had cultivated a manner of filling up gaps which did not exist; "and so forth and so on," thrown in purely for effect, and to prepare for what was coming. A laugh, deliberately artificial, came when it was wanted; it was meant to annoy, and annoyed, but needlessly.

He was a great wit, really spontaneous, so far as what is intellectual can ever be spontaneous. His wit was not, as with Oscar Wilde, a brilliant sudden gymnastic, with words in which the phrase itself was always worth more than what it said; it was a wit of ideas, in which the thing said was at least on the level of the way of saying it. And, with him, it was really a weapon, used as seriously as any rapier in an eternal duel with the eternal enemy. He fought for himself, but in fighting for himself he fought for every sincere artist. He spared no form of stupidity, neither the unintelligent stupidity of the general public, and of the critics who represent the public, nor the much more dangerous stupidity of intelligences misguided, as in the "leading case" of Ruskin.[3] No man made more enemies, or deserved better friends.

He never cared, or was able, to distinguish between them. They changed places at an opinion or for an idea.

He was a great master of the grotesque in conversation, and the portrait which he made of Mr. Leyland[4] as a many-tentacled devil at a piano, a thing of horror and beauty, is for once a verbal image put into paint, with that whole-hearted delight in exuberant extravagance which made his talk wildly heroic. That painting is his one joke in paint, his one expression of a personal feeling so violent that it overcame his scruples as an artist. And yet even that is not really an exception; for out of a malicious joke, begun, certainly, in anger, beauty exudes like the scent of a poisonous flower.

Many of his sayings are preserved, in which he seems to scoff at great artists and at great artistic qualities.[5] They are to be interpreted, not swallowed. His irreverence, as it was called, was only one, not easily recognisable, sign of a delicate sensitiveness in choice. And it had come to be one of the parts that he played in public, one of the things expected of him, to which he lent himself, after all, satirically. And he could be silent on occasion, very effectively. I happened to meet him one day in front of the Chigi Botticelli,[6] when it was on view at Colnaghi's. He walked to and fro, peered into the picture, turned his head sideways, studied it with the approved air of one studying it, and then said nothing. "Why drag in Botticelli?" was, I suppose, what he thought.

II

Taste in Whistler was carried to the point of genius, and became creative. He touched nothing, possessed nothing, that he did not remake or assimilate in some faultless and always personal way: the frames of his pictures, the forms of the books which were printed for him, the shapes of the old silver which he collected, the arrangement of that silver when it was exhibited among other collections. The monogram which he designed for a friend who was a publisher is the simplest and the most decorative monogram that I can remember. He drew the lettering for the books of another friend, and this lettering, which seems the most obvious thing in the world, makes the lettering on every other modern book look clumsy or far-fetched. And in none of these things does he try to follow a fine model or try to avoid following a model. He sees each thing in its own way, within its own limits.

No one ever had a more exact and reverent sense of limits, a narrower and more variable standard of perfection. He mastered, in his own art, medium after medium, and his work, in each medium, is conspicuous for its natural sense of the canvas or the paper, for its precise knowledge of exactly what can be done with all the substances and materials of art. He never sought novelty by confusing two methods, but made the most of each with a tender and rigid economy. When he paints, you distinguish the thread of his canvas; in his etchings and lithographs the meaning of the design extends to the rim of the margin.

And of all modern painters he is the only one who completely realised that a picture is part of the decoration of a wall, and of the wall of a modern room. When pictures ceased to be painted on the walls of churches and palaces, or for a given space above altars, there came into the world that abnormal thing, the easel-picture. At the present day there is only one country in which the sense of decoration exists, or is allowed to have its way; and it was from the artists of Japan that Whistler learnt the alphabet of decorative painting. His pictures and his black and white work are first of all pieces of decoration, and there is not one which might not make, in the Japanese way, the only decoration of a room.

Once, indeed, he was allowed, as no other great artist of our time has been allowed, to decorate a room for one of his own pictures. The Peacock Room[7] was made out of a gradual transformation, and it was made as a sort of shrine for the lovely picture, *La Princesse du Pays de la Porcelaine*. Every inch of the wall, ceiling, and wainscoting, the doors, the frames of the shutters, was worked into the scheme of the blues and golds, and Mr. Leyland's china had its part, no doubt, in the scheme. But I do not think Whistler can be held responsible for the gilded cages (though, indeed, making the best of a bad bargain, he gilded them) which prop up the china round so much of the walls. These, I gather, he found already made, and with them he had to struggle: he accepted them frankly, and their glitter is a pretence on his part that he liked a room hung with bird-cages and plate-racks. But the gold peacocks on the shutters, with their solid and glowing fantasy of design, the gold peacocks on the blue leather of the wall facing the picture, with their dainty and sparkling fantasy of design, the sombre fantasy of the peacocks' feathers, untouched by gold, their colours repressed and withdrawn into shadow, above the lamps on the ceiling: all these, into which he put his very soul, which are so many signatures of his creed and science of beauty, are woven together into a web or network of almost alarming loveliness, to make a room into which nature, sunlight, or any mortal compromise could never enter, a wizard's chapel of art. Here, where he is least human, he joins with that other part of himself in which all this sense of what goes to make decoration mingled with another sense, completing it. When he is greatest, in the portrait of his mother,[8] for instance, he is only more, and not less, decorative, as he gives you so infinitely much more than mere decoration. There is no compromise with taste in the abandonment to a great inspiration. Inspiration, with him, includes taste, on its way to its own form of perfection.

It was characteristic of Whistler that he should go to music for the titles of his pictures. A picture may indeed be termed a *Nocturne,* even more justly than a piece of music, but it was quite as it should be if Chopin really was in Whistler's mind when he used the word. Gautier had written his "Symphonie en Blanc Majeur"[9] before Whistler painted his *Symphonies in White, Harmony in Grey and Green, Arrangement in Black and Brown, Caprice in Purple and Gold:* all are terms perfectly appropriate to painting, yet all suggest music. And to the painter of Sarasate, music could hardly have failed to represent the type of all that his own art was aiming at, in its not always fully understood or recognised way. In music, too, he had his significant choice. I remember once his impatience with my praise of Ysaÿe, whom he had never heard, because the praise seemed like a poor compliment to Sarasate, whose marvellous purity of tone he recalled with an intolerant and jealous delight.[10] He thought, and was perhaps right in thinking, that there never could have been a purer tone than Sarasate's, and the rest mattered, at all events, much less.

And so, in speaking of Whistler's pictures, though nothing so merely and so wholly pictorial was ever done, it is musical terms that come first to one's mind. Every picture has a purity of tone like that of the finest violin playing. Sometimes a Giorgione, sometimes a Watteau, comes to one as if in exchange for music; Whistler always.

"Art should be independent of all claptrap," he wrote, in one of the most valuable of his pastoral letters, "should stand alone, and appeal to the artistic sense of eye or ear, without confounding this with emotions entirely foreign to it, as devotion, pity, love, patriotism, and the like. All these have no kind of concern with it; and that is why I insist on calling my works 'arrangements' and 'harmonies.' Take the picture of my mother, exhibited at the Royal Academy, as an *Arrangement in Grey and Black.* Now that is what it is. To me it is interesting as a picture of my mother; but what can or ought the public to care about the identity of the portrait?"[11]

There, finally stated, is one of the great, continually forgotten, truths of art; and, in the paragraph which follows, the lesson is completed. "The imitator is a poor kind of creature. If the man who paints only the tree, or flower, or other surface he sees before him were an artist, the king of artists would be the photographer. It is for the artist to do something beyond this: in portrait painting to put on canvas something more than the face the model wears for that one day; to paint the man, in short, as well as his features; in arrangement of colours to treat a flower as his key, not as his model."

In "Mr. Whistler's Ten o'Clock,"[12] he tells us: "Nature contains the elements, in colour and form, of all pictures, as the keyboard contains the notes of all music. But the artist is born to pick and choose, and group with science, those elements, that the result may be beautiful— as the musician gathers his notes, and forms his chords, until he brings forth from chaos, glorious harmony. To say to the painter that Nature is to be taken as she is, is to say to the player, that he may sit on the piano." Now, in all this, which was once supposed to be so revolutionary, so impertinent even, there is just so much exaggeration as wit lends to any single aspect of truth. But it is truth, and that aspect of truth which, in our time, most needs emphasis.

In our time, art is on its defence. All the devouring mouths of the common virtues and approved habits are open against it, and for the most part it exists on sufferance, by pretending to be something else than what it is, by some form of appeal to public charity or public misapprehension; rarely by professing to be concerned only with itself, and bound only by its own laws. Great critics like Ruskin and great artists like Watts have done infinite harm by taking the side of the sentimentalists, by attaching moral values to lines and colours, by allowing themselves to confirm the public in some of its worst confusions of mind. When Whistler said of one of his "harmonies in grey and gold," in which a black figure is seen outside a tavern in the snow, "I care nothing for the past, present, or future of the black figure placed there, because the black was wanted at that spot," he was challenging, in that statement so simple as to be self-evident, a whole æsthetics, the æsthetics of the crowd and its critics. Only Mallarmé, in our time, has rendered so signal a service to art.

III

"A picture is finished," wrote Whistler, "when all trace of the means used to bring about the end has disappeared. To say of a picture, as is often said in its praise, that it shows great and earnest labour, is to say that it is incomplete and unfit for view. . . . The work of the Master reeks not of the sweat of the brow—suggests no effort—and is finished from the beginning."[13] In that last phrase, it seems to me, Whistler has said the essential thing, the thing which distinguishes the masterpiece from the experiment. People have said, people still sometimes say, that

Whistler's work is slight, and they intimate, because it is slight, it is of little value. The question is, is it finished from the beginning, and has all trace of labour disappeared at the end?

There is a lithograph of Mallarmé, reproduced in the *Vers et Prose*, which, to those who knew him, recalls the actual man as no other portrait does. It is faint, evasive, a mist of lines and spaces that seem like some result of happy accident: "subtiles, éveillées comme l'improvisation et l'inspiration," as Baudelaire said of the Thames etchings.[14] Yet it cost Whistler forty sittings to get this last touch of improvisation into his portrait. He succeeded, but at the cost of what pains? "All trace of the means used to bring about the end has disappeared," after how formidable, how unrelaxing a labour!

It is the aim of Whistler, as of so much modern art, to be taken at a hint, divined at a gesture, or by telepathy. Mallarmé, suppressing syntax and punctuation, the essential links of things, sometimes fails in his incantation, and brings before us things homeless and unattached in middle air. Verlaine subtilises words in a song to a mere breathing of music. And so in Whistler there are problems to be guessed, as well as things to be seen. But that is because these exceptional difficult moments of nature, these twilight aspects, these glimpses in which one sees hardly more than a colour, no shape at all, or shapes covered by mist or night, or confused by sunlight, have come to seem to him the only aspects worth caring about. Without "strangeness in its proportion," he can no longer see beauty, but it is the rarity of beauty, always, that he seeks, never a strange thing for the sake of strangeness; so that there is no eccentricity, as there is no display, in his just and reticent records. If he paints artificial light, it is to add a new, strange beauty to natural objects, as night and changing lights really add to them; and he finds astonishing beauties in the fireworks at Cremorne Gardens, in the rockets that fall into the blue waters under Battersea Bridge. They are things beautiful in themselves, or made beautiful by the companionship and co-operation of the night; in a picture they can certainly be as beautiful as stars and sunsets.

Or, take some tiny, scarcely visible sketch in water-colour on tinted paper; it is nothing, and it is enough, for it is a moment of faint colour as satisfying in itself as one of those moments of faint colour which we see come and go in the sky after sunset. No one but Whistler has ever done these things in painting; Verlaine has done the equivalent thing in poetry. They have their brief coloured life like butterflies, and with the same momentary perfection. No one had ever cared to preserve just these aspects, as no one before Verlaine had ever cared to sing certain bird notes. Each was satisfied when he had achieved the particular, delicate beauty at which he had aimed; neither cared or needed to go on, add the footnote to the text, enclose the commentary within the frame, as most poets and painters are considerate enough to do.

* * * [L]ike Poe, it was a combination of beauty and strangeness which Whistler sought in art: 'l'étrangeté, qui est comme le condiment indispensable de toute beauté.''[15] There is something mysterious in most of his pictures, and the mystery is for the most part indefinable. These fashionable women, drawing on their gloves in the simplest of daily attitudes, these children, standing in the middle of the floor as a child stands to be looked at, these men in black coats, are all thinking thoughts which they hide from us, or repressing sensations which they do not wish us to share. * * * He is the visionary of reality, which he sees with all the vividness of hallucination. And it was alike this characteristic of his temperament and a definite artistic theory of the means to an end, in portrait-painting, which led to the production of perhaps his greatest pictures.

It was one of Whistler's aims in portrait-painting to establish a reasonable balance between the man as he sits in the chair and the image of the man reflected back to you from the canvas. "The one aim," he wrote, "of the unsuspecting painter is to make his man 'stand out' from the frame—never doubting that, on the contrary, he should, and in truth absolutely does, stand *within* the frame—and at a depth behind it equal to the distance at which the painter sees his model. The frame is, indeed, the window through which the painter looks at his model, and nothing could be more offensively inartistic than this brutal attempt to thrust the model on the hither-side of this window!"[16] Here, as always, it was the just limit of things which Whistler perceived and respected. He never proposed, in a picture, to give you something which you could mistake for reality; but, frankly, a picture, a thing which was emphatically not nature, because it was art.

In Whistler's portraits the pose itself is as much a part of the interpretation as the painting; and the quality of a portrait such as the Sarasate is not to be judged, as it commonly is, by the apparent lack of seriousness in it. M. Boldini's startling portrait of Whistler himself was an example of the art which tries for this common kind of success;[17] there was the likeness, and the shining hat, and as much real artistic sense as is contained in a flash-light. Even in Whistler's portrait of the Comte de Montesquiou,[18] a harlequin of letters, there was no actual harlequinade on the part of the painter, though he may have seemed indulgent to it in his model. How much less is there in the Sarasate,[19] where a genuine artist, but not a profound artist, is seen making his astonishing appearance, violin in hand, out of darkness upon a stage, where he is to be the virtuoso. Sarasate's tone is a miracle, like Melba's, and he added to this miracle of technique a southern fire, which used to go electrically through his audience. He has his temperament and his technique, nothing else. The man who holds the violin in his hands is a child, pleased to please; not a student or a diviner. And Whistler has rendered all this, as truthfully as Watts has rendered the very different problem of Joachim, in perhaps the greatest of his portraits. Joachim is in the act of playing; he bends his brows over the music which he is studying, not reading; if there is any platform or any audience, he is unconscious of them; he is conscious only of Beethoven. Note how Sarasate dandles the violin. It is a child, a jewel. He is already thinking of the sound, the flawless tone, not of Beethoven. Whistler has caught him, poised him, posed him, another butterfly, and alive. Imagine Sarasate painted by Watts, or indeed in any way but Whistler's! There might have been other great pictures, but no other such interpretation.

To Whistler, unlike Manet, there are many things in the world besides good painting, and the mind which sees through his eyes is not, like Manet's, either "joyful" or "heedless." Unlike most modern painters, Whistler does not fling the truth at you stark naked; he wishes you to know that you are looking at a picture, a work of art, and not at yourself or your neighbour in a mirror. He would feel, I think, that he had failed with you if you did not say: "How beautiful!" before saying "How true!" Nature can take good care of herself, and will give you all the reality you want, whenever you want it; but the way of looking at nature, which is what art has to teach you, or to do in your place, can come only from the artist. Look at this corner of the sea and sand, and then at Whistler's picture of it. How roughly, crudely, imperfectly, uninterestingly, you had seen the thing itself, until the picture taught you how to look. The exact shape of the wave, the exact tints of its colouring: had you found them out for yourself? Above all, had you felt them as you feel these lines and colours in the picture? And yet the picture is only a suggestion, a moment out of an unending series of moments; but the moment has been detached by art from that unending and unnoted series, and it gives you the soul of visible things in that miraculous retention of a moment.

Whistler gives you the picture, then, frankly as a picture. He gives it to you for its lines, its colours, as at all events its primary meaning for him; a meaning in itself almost or quite sufficient, if need be, but capable of an indefinite extension or deepening. Unlike most men, he sees, sees really, with a complete indifference to what other significance things may have, besides their visible aspect.

Only, for him, the visible aspect of things is the aspect of a continual miracle, and it is from this fresh sense of wonder that there comes that mystery in which he envelops mere flesh and blood, in which there is no inherent strangeness. Some aspect of a thing dreamed or seen in passing, and then remembered in the transfiguring memory of the brain, comes hauntingly into all his faces. The look they show you is not the look which their mirror sees every morning and every evening. It has come to them out of the eye that sees them, as it were, for the first time. Until Whistler looked at this young girl's face, it was but a young girl's face; now it is something besides, it means all that the brush has thought into it, it has the weight and meaning and mysterious questioning of a work of art. Every work of art is an interrogation; these faces exist softly, like flowers, delicately on a canvas; they challenge us idly, offering their most secret perfumes if we will but drink them in. They await time in an uneager patience, content to be themselves. They have the flower's assurance, the flower's humility.

Look round a picture gallery, and you will recognize a Whistler at once, and for this reason first, that it does not come to meet you. Most of the other pictures seem to cry across the floor: "Come and look at us, see how like something we are!" Their voices cross and jangle like the voices of rival sellers in a street fair. Each out-bids his neighbour, promising you more than your money's worth. The Whistlers smile secretly in their corner, and say nothing. They are not really indifferent; they watch and wait, and when you come near them they seem to efface themselves, as if they would not have you even see them too closely. That is all part of the subtle malice with which they win you. They choose you, you do not choose them.

One of the first truths of art has needed to be rediscovered in these times, though it has been put into practice by every great artist, and has only been seriously denied by scientific persons and the inept. It has taken new names, and calls itself now "Symbolism," now "Impressionism"; but it has a single thing to say, under many forms: that art must never be a statement, always an evocation. In the art of Whistler there is not so much as a momentary forgetfulness of this truth, and that is why, among many works of greater or less relative merit, he has done nothing, however literally slight, which is not, so far as it goes, done rightly. No picture aims at anything else than being the evocation of a person, a landscape, some colour or contour divined in nature, and interpreted upon canvas or paper. And the real secret of Whistler, I think, is this: that he does not try to catch the accident when an aspect becomes effective, but the instant when it becomes characteristically beautiful.

It is significant of a certain simplicity in his attitude towards his own work, that Whistler, in all his fighting on behalf of principles, has never tried to do more than establish (shall I say?) the correctness of his grammar. He has never asked for more praise than should be the reward of every craftsman who is not a bungler. He has claimed that, setting out to do certain things, legitimate in themselves, he has done them in a way legitimate in itself. All the rest he is content to leave out of the question: that is to say, everything but a few primary qualities, without which no one can, properly speaking, be a painter at all. And, during much of his lifetime, not even this was conceded to him. He wasted a little of his leisure in drawing up a catalogue of some of the blunders of his critics, saying, "Out of their own mouths shall ye judge them." Being without mercy, he called it "The Voice of a People."[20]

Eleonora Duse[1]

I

Eleonora Duse is a great artist, the type of the artist, and it is only by accident that she is an actress. Circumstances having made her an actress, she is the greatest of living actresses; she would have been equally great in any other art. She is an actress through being the antithesis of the actress; not, indeed, by mere reliance upon nature, but by controlling nature into the forms of her desire, as the sculptor controls the clay under his fingers. She is the artist of her own soul, and it is her force of will, her mastery of herself, not her abandonment to it, which make her what she is.

A great, impersonal force, rushing towards the light, looking to every form of art for help, for sustenance, for inspiration; a soul which lives on the passionate contemplation of beauty, of all the forms of beauty, without preference for Monteverde or Rodin, for Dante or Leonardo; an intelligence alert to arrest every wandering idea that can serve it; Duse seems to live in every nerve and brain-cell with a life which is sleepless and unslackening. She loves art so devotedly that she hates the mockery of her own art, in which disdain forces her to be faultless; hating the stage, wondering why some one in the audience does not rise from his seat, and leap upon the stage, and cry, "Enough of this!" she acts half mechanically, with herself, pulling up all the rags of her own soul, as she says, and flinging them in the face of the people, in a contemptuous rage. When she is not on the stage she forgets the stage; if, in the street, some words of one of her parts come to her with a shiver, it is some passage of poetry, some vivid speech in which a soul speaks. Why she acts as she does, and how she succeeds in being so great an artist while hating her art, is her secret, she tells us; hinting that it is sorrow, discontent, thwarted desires, that have tortured and exalted her into a kind of martyrdom of artistic mastery, on the other side of which the serenity of a pained but indomitable soul triumphs.

To those who have seen Duse only across the footlights, Duse must be impenetrable, almost the contradiction of herself. As one talks with her one begins to realise the artist through the woman. There is in her a sombre and hypnotic quietude, as she broods in meditation, her beautiful, firm hand grasping the arm of the chair without movement, but so tightly that the knuckles grow rigid; her body droops sideways in the chair, her head rests on her other hand, the eyes are like a drowsy flame; the whole body thinks. Her face is sad with thought, with the passing over it of all the emotions of the world, which she has felt twice over, in her own flesh, and in the creative energy of her spirit. Her stillness is the stillness of one in the act to spring. There is no transition from the energy of speech to the energy of silence. When she speaks, the words leap from her lips one after another, hurrying, but always in coloured clothes, and with beautiful movements. As she listens silently to music, she seems to remember, and to drink in nourishment for her soul, as she drinks in perfume, greedily, from flowers, as she possesses a book or a picture, almost with violence. I have never seen a woman so passionate after beauty. I have never seen a woman so devoured by the life of the soul, by the life of the mind, by the life of the body.

When she talks intently with some one whose ideas interest her, she leaves her chair, comes and sits down quite close, leans over till her face almost touches one's face, the eyes opening wider and wider until one sees an entire rim of white about the great brown pupils; but, though she occasionally makes a gesture, she never touches one, never lays her hand on one's sleeve; remains impersonal, though so close. Her intent eyes see nothing but the ideas behind one's forehead; she has no sense of the human nearness of body to body, only of the intellectual closeness of soul to soul. She is a woman always, but she is a women almost in the abstract; the senses are asleep, or awake only to give passion and substance to the disembodied energy of the intellect. When she speaks of beautiful things her face takes light as from an inner source; the dark and pallid cheeks curve into sensitive folds, the small, thin-lipped mouth, scarcely touched with colour, grows half tender, half ironical, as if smiling at its own abandonment to delight; an exquisite tremor awakens in it, as if it brushed against the petal of a flower, and thrilled at the contact; then the mouth opens, freely, and the strong white teeth glitter in a vehement smile.

I have seen her before a Rodin, a Whistler, and a Turner. As she handled the little piece of clay, in which two figures, suggested, not expressed, embrace passionately, in a tightening quiver of the whole body, which seems to thrill under one's eyesight, it seemed as if force drank in force until the soul of the woman passed into the clay, and the soul of the clay passed into the woman. As she stood before the portrait of Carlyle, which she had never seen, though a photograph of it goes with her wherever she goes, there was the quietude of content, perfect satisfaction, before a piece of ardent and yet chastened perfection. As she moved about the room of the Turners, in the National Gallery, it was with little cries, with a sort of unquiet joy. "The dear madman!" she repeated, before picture after picture, in which a Venice, so false to the Venice which she knew, so true to a Venice which had been actually thus seen, rose up like a mist of opals, all soft flame and rushing light. And, her eyes full of that intoxication, she almost ran out of the gallery, refusing to look to right or left, that she might shut down her eyelids upon their vision.

II

Here are a few of her words, written down from memory, as nearly as I can in the way she said them; but how empty, as I see them written down, of the colour and life of the words themselves!

> To save the theatre, the theatre must be destroyed, the actors and actresses must all die of the plague. They poison the air, they make art impossible. It is not drama that they play, but pieces for the theatre. We should return to the Greeks, play in the open air; the drama dies of stalls and boxes and evening dress, and people who come to digest their dinner.

> The one happiness is to shut one's door upon a little room, with a table before one, and to create; to create life in that isolation from life.

> We must bow before the poet, even when it seems to us that he does wrong. He is a poet, he has seen something, he has seen it in that way; we must accept his vision, because it is vision.

> Since Shakespeare and the Greeks there has been no great dramatist, and these gathered up into themselves the whole life of the people and the whole work of their contemporaries. When we say Shakespeare we mean all the Elizabethan drama. Ibsen? Ibsen is like this room where we are sitting, with all the tables and chairs. Do I care whether you have twenty or twenty-five links on your chain? Hedda Gabler, Nora and the rest: it is not that I want! I want Rome and the Coliseum, the Acropolis,

Athens; I want beauty, and the flame of life. Maeterlinck? I
adore Maeterlinck. Maeterlinck is a flower. But he only gives me
figures in a mist. Yes, as you say, children and spirits.

I have tried, I have failed, I am condemned to play Sardou and
Pinero. Some day another woman will come, young, beautiful, a
being all of fire and flame, and will do what I have dreamed;
yes, I am sure of it, it will come; but I am tired, at my age I
cannot begin over again. Ah, my dear friend (to Dolmetsch)
how happy you are here. What are those boards up there? You
have had them for twelve years, you say, and they are ripening
to be made into instruments; they are only boards now, one day
they will sing. My head is full of old boards like that.

Rossetti is like a perverse young man who has been nicely
brought up: he does not give himself up to it, he is only half
himself. Look at Watts's portrait: the fine, mad eyes, and then
the weak and heavy chin. The eyes desire some feverish thing,
but the mouth and chin hesitate in pursuit. All Rossetti is in that
story of the MS. buried in his wife's coffin.[2] He could do it, he
could repent of it; but he should have gone and taken it back
himself: he sent his friends!

Rossetti's Italian verse, how can I give you an idea of it? Suppose
a blind man, and one puts before him a bouquet of flowers, and
he smells it, and says: "This is jasmine, and this is a rose," but
he says it like one who does not know flowers.

At Athens, in the Museum, there is the mask of a tragic actress;
the passion of sorrow, seen for a moment on the face of a woman
on the stage, is engraved into it, like a seal. In Rome, quite lately,
they have found a bronze head, which has lain under water for
centuries; the features are almost effaced, but it is beautiful, as if
veiled; the water has passed over it like a caress.

I have known Wagner in Venice, I have been in Bayreuth, and I
saw in Wagner what I feel in his music, a touch of something a
little conscious in his supremacy. Wagner said to himself: "I will
do what I want to do, I will force the world to accept me"; and
he succeeded, but not in making us forget his intention. The
music, after all, never quite abandons itself, is never quite without
self-consciousness, it is a tremendous sensuality, not the uncon-

sciousness of passion. When Beethoven writes music he forgets both himself and the world, is conscious only of joy, or sorrow, or the mood which has taken him for its voice.

Do you remember what Flaubert, that little priest, said of Shakespeare? "If I had met Shakespeare on the stairs, I should have fainted." The people I would like to have met are Shakespeare and Velasquez.

Could I live without the stage? You should not have said that. I have passed three years without acting. I act because I would rather do other things. If I had my will I would live in a ship on the sea, and never come nearer to humanity than that.

III

The face of Duse is a mask for the tragic passions, a mask which changes from moment to moment, as the soul models the clay of the body after its own changing image. Imagine Rodin at work on a lump of clay. The shapeless thing awakens under his fingers, a vague life creeps into it, hesitating among the forms of life; it is desire, waiting to be born, and it may be born as pity or anguish, love or pride; so fluid is it to the touch, so humbly does it await the accident of choice. The face of Duse is like the clay under the fingers of Rodin. But with her there can be no choice, no arresting moment of repose; but an endless flowing onward of emotion, like tide flowing after tide, moulding and effacing continually. Watch her in that scene of *La Dame aux Camélias,* where Armand's father pleads with Marguerite to give up her lover for the sake of her love. She sits there quietly beside the table, listening and saying nothing, thinking mournfully, debating with herself, conquering herself, making the great decision. The outline of the face is motionless, set hard, clenched into immobility; but within that motionless outline every nerve seems awake, expression after expression sweeps over it, each complete for its instant, each distinct, each like the finished expression of the sculptor, rather than the uncertain forms of life, as they appear to us in passing. The art of the actor, it is supposed, is to give, above all things, this sense of the passing moment, and to give it by a vivacity in expression which shall more than compete with life itself. That is the effective thing; but what Duse does is, after all, the right thing. We have rarely, in real life, the leisure to watch an emotion in which we are the sharers. But there are moments, in any great crisis, when the soul seems to stand back and look out of impersonal eyes, seeing things as they are. At such moments it is possible to become aware of the beauty, the actual plastic beauty, of passionate or sorrowful emotion, as it interprets itself, in all its succession of moods, upon the face. At such moments, as at the supreme moment of death, all the nobility of which a soul is capable comes transformingly into the body; which is then, indeed, neither the handmaid, nor the accomplice, nor the impediment of the soul, but the soul's visible identity. The art of Duse is to do over again, consciously, this sculpture of the soul upon the body.

The reason why Duse is the greatest actress in the world is that she has a more subtle nature than any other actress, and that she expresses her nature more simply. All her acting seems to come from a great depth, and to be only half telling profound secrets. No play has ever been profound enough, and simple enough, for this woman to say everything she has to say in it. When she has thrilled one, or made one weep, or exalted one with beauty, she seems to be always holding back something else. Her supreme distinction comes from the kind of melancholy wisdom which remains in her face after the passions have swept over it. Other actresses seem to have heaped up into one great, fictitious moment all the scattered energies of their lives, the passions that have come to nothing, the sensations that have withered before they flowered, the thoughts that have never quite been born. The stage is their life; they live only for those three hours of the night; before and after are the intervals between the acts. But to Duse those three hours are the interval in an intense, consistent, strictly personal life; and, the interval over, she returns to herself, as after an interruption.

And this unique fact makes for her the particular quality of her genius. When she is on the stage she does not appeal to us with the conscious rhetoric of the actress; she lets us overlook her, with an unconsciousness which study has formed into a second nature. When she is on the stage she is always thinking; at times, when the playing of her part is to her a mere piece of contemptuous mechanism, she thinks of other things, and her acting suddenly becomes acting, as in *Fedora* and all but the end of *The Second Mrs. Tanqueray*.[3] At every moment of a play in which emotion becomes sincere, intelligent, or in which it is possible to transform an artificial thing into reality, she is profoundly true to the character she is representing, by being more and more profoundly herself. Then it is Magda, or Gioconda, or Marguerite Gautier[4] who thinks, feels, lives, endures love and anguish and shame and happiness before us; and it is Magda, or Gioconda, or Marguerite Gautier because it is the primary emotion, the passion itself, everything in it which is most personal because it is most universal.

To act as Duse acts, with an art which is properly the antithesis of what we call acting, is, no doubt, to fail in a lesser thing in order to triumph in a greater. Her greatest moments are the moments of most intense quietness; she does not send a shudder through the whole house, as Sarah Bernhardt does, playing on one's nerves as on a violin. "Action," with her as with Rimbaud, "is a way of spoiling something," when once action has mastered thought, and got loose to work its own way in the world. It is a disturbance, not an end in itself; and the very expression of emotion, with her, is all a restraint, the quieting down of a tumult until only the pained reflection of it glimmers out of her eyes, and trembles among the hollows of her cheeks. Contrast her art with the art of Irving, to whom acting is at once a science and a tradition. To Irving acting is all that the word literally means; it is an art of sharp, detached, yet always delicate movement; he crosses the stage with intention, as he intentionally adopts a fine, crabbed, personal, highly conventional elocution of his own; he is an actor, and he acts, keeping nature, or the too close semblance of nature, carefully out of his composition. He has not gone to himself to invent an art wholly personal, wholly new; his acting is no interruption of an intense inner life, but a craftsmanship into which he has put all he has to give. It is an art wholly rhetoric, that is to say wholly external; his emotion moves to slow music, crystallises into an attitude, dies upon a long-drawn-out word. And it is this external, rhetorical art, this dramatised oratory, that we have always understood as acting, until Duse came upon the stage with new ideas and a new method. At once rhetoric disappeared, with all that is obvious in its loss, as well as what is somewhat less obviously gained by it. Duse's art, in this, is like the art of Verlaine in French poetry; always suggestion, never statement, always a renunciation. It comes into the movement of all the arts, as they seek to escape from the bondage of form, by a new, finer mastery of form, wrought outwards from within, not from without inwards. And it conquers almost the last obstacle, as it turns the one wholly external art, based upon mere imitation, existing upon the commonest terms of illusion, triumphing by exaggeration, into an art wholly subtle, almost spiritual, a suggestion, an evasion, a secrecy.

[Duse and D'Annunzio]¹

Duse would find in d'Annunzio genius, imagination, creative power, intense sensitiveness, animalism, bestiality, and a wild beast's implacable passions. Between the abyss of Wagner's music, out of which the world rises with all its voices, in which the scenery carries us onward to the last horizon of the world, gods and men act out the brief human tragedy as if on a narrow island in the midst of a great sea. A few steps this way or that will plunge them into darkness; but the darkness awaits them, however they succeed or fail, whether they live nobly or ignobly, in the interval; but the interval absorbs them, as if it were to be eternity, and we see them rejoicing and suffering with an abandonment to the moment which intensifies the pathos of what we know is futile. There was nothing futile between these Italian lovers. They were not even tragic comedians. * * *

Duse's love for d'Annunzio was a consuming, but not a devouring passion. She was inevitably aware of his infidelities and of his unfaithfulness to her; she was aware that he was insatiable, that women's flesh attracted and fascinated him, and enthralled him. Inwardly, in her burning spirit, she suffered intense tortures, intense agonies, bitter despairs. Outwardly she appears to have taken such things for granted. Apparently she never even condescended to be jealous. She had lived her life, she had had lovers, she had had two children, one of whom had died. When she was acting with Giacinta Pezzana in Naples, in 1879, she made the acquaintance of Martino Cafiero, a man of letters, a distinguished poet and a dandy; he had on his side, as she had on hers, youth and fascination. She was then twenty; she fell madly in love with him. He had free access to the theatre; they gazed on one another across the footlights; she attracted him immensely, he was wild and wanton and light-hearted. He was sought after by women; he haunted Duse's nights, he made her restless by day. At last he seduced her. Evidently the mad passion he evoked in the young girl's unawakened heart aided her immensely in her nervous representation of Thérèse Raquin.² * * *

Duse left d'Annunzio some time after the publication of *Il Fuoco* in 1900.³ She finally forgave him; she never forgot the injury he had inflicted upon her, which wounded her to the quick. The book, so far as he had read it to her, seemed a kind of spiritual infidelity. It is a well-known fact that the novelist read her the majority of his chapters soon after they were written, and that he never dared read her, or to let her read, those chapters in which he treats her infamously, shamelessly. D'Annunzio, who always wrote from the purely artistic point of view, was obviously in need of money, and obviously he had other reasons besides this for having the book published on March 5th, 1900, at Milan. For it has been conjectured—and the conjecture might be legitimate—that he began his novel some time before he had become Duse's lover, that he invented some real or imaginary actress as the heroine before he had developed the main intrigue, and that he inserted certain pages from *La Città Morta,* which in the novel cover pp. 198–228; that after he had reached that point he left the manuscript as it was; that he wove it together and finished the book during these years when he lived at the Villa Capponcina and Duse at the Porziuncula, and that there is evidently something uneven in the composition of the novel itself * * *

He may be imaged as a kind of rare, cultured, exotic aftergrowth of the Renaissance, flowering again in modern soil; a creature of complex sensations, of capricious senses, of angry passions, of distressed sentiments, of nervous susceptibility, elaborately and utterly himself, as he weaves his fictions, never out of human entrails, but out of the bare physical facts—life, death, desire, one's fate, one's misfortune—as a subtle spider turned animally human. He is immoral as sex is. His characters are soulless. They show their nerves in gestures, cries, caresses. They are of the world, worldly; and have no relation with the age they live in, so unreal are they in their reality. He generally makes them beautiful, strange, bizarre; rarely ugly; a question of visual preference. We see his women living on their sensations, for their sensations' sake; catching eagerly at every instant as it passes; hating the past, fearing the future, so infinite to them is the lure of life. And they sin for the mere luxury of it, from their incapability of avoiding it.

So this writer, whose faculty of imagination is unquestionable (as original as the man himself) has gone on creating one thing after another; using all his wizardry in evoking mediæval deliriums, sterile Pagan ecstasies, sensual raptures, with evocations of scented enchantments, with rare magical touches. And, without one atom of wit, of humour, of comedy, his imagination has created the tragic, often to an almost supreme height. For to him the whole of life is, in a sense, one tragedy; unvisited by the Comic Spirits; a tragedy of the senses.

I never realised the full charm of the Italian language until I heard the *Parable of the Wise and Foolish Virgins* read by Gabriele d'Annunzio at Count Primoli's,[4] and d'Annunzio reads Italian more beautifully than any one I ever heard. Delicately articulated, all those triple endings, *avano, arano, ovono,* ringing like bells, fatigued the ear as the blue of the Mediterranean fatigues the eye; there were no grey shades, and there was also no brief, emphatic pause in the music. I realised then that it is a language of beautiful exteriorities, and that its beauty is without subtlety; the typical feminine language. But the day when I made this discovery is worth remembering for other reasons as well; for the ceremony of the reading, in that interesting house, and before the choice of Roman society was like one of those readings in the days of powder and peruke, when poets were still elegant, and a part of society's amusement. D'Annunzio, small, blond, at once eager and discreet, with the air of a perfectly charming bird of prey, his eyes full of bland smiles, his mouth, with its uplifted moustache, poised in a keen, expectant smile, had indeed the air of a court poet as he stood in the ante-room greeting his friends as they entered, before he made his way to the dais, draped at the back with crimson cloth, where he sat down at the table on which were his MS. and a Bible. Once seated, the reading once begun, you saw that other side to what you might have thought the merely mundane young man; you saw the artist, who, as he told me, was well content if twelve hours' work had given him two pages; for his own words visibly absorbed, possessed him; he never lifted his eyes from the paper, he read all that chanting prose as if he were reading it, not to the duchesses, but to the unseen company of the immortal judges of art. It had been announced that the conference was to be by some one else; and one careful mother went to the host and asked if he thought her daughter might remain. A French abbé, who had come to hear the unexceptionable Costa, seeing d'Annunzio, quietly disappeared. Neither the abbé nor the mother need have been alarmed. D'Annunzio first read the parable out of the Bible, then his gloss upon it. The gloss was full of colour and music. Then he read one of the most delicate of his poems, "Villa Chigi."[5] Every one was charmed, d'Annunzio and all his hearers and the duchesses went. * * *

There is a certain thing called the suicide of one's genius. The question I ask myself is: "Has Gabriele d'Annunzio committed the same kind of suicide?" Is one of the innumerable problems of this problematical man the problem of one who has lost the whole world and gained his own soul; or of one who desired to lose his own soul—as Faustus, who sold his soul to the Devil—so as to gain the whole world? I think that he is one who has gazed at light till it has blinded him—not indeed to his heroic sense of his duty to Italy, but that he has seen something, and that his eyesight has been too weak to endure the presence of light over-flowing the world from beyond the world.

His genius, on which a kind of insanely egoistical madness has finally seized hold, might have shown him, as if by lightning flashes, the hidden links of divergent and distant things; perhaps in somewhat the same manner as that in which a similarly new, startling, perhaps over-true sight of things is gained by the artificial stimulation of haschish, opium, and those other drugs by which vision is produced deliberately, and the soul, sitting safe within the perilous circle of its own magic, looks out on the panorama which either rises out of the darkness before it or drifts from itself into the darkness. In a different sense from Villiers de l'Isle-Adam, for d'Annunzio, when he sought the absolute beauty, it was beyond the world that he found it; when he sought horror, it was a breath blowing from the invisible darkness which brought it to his nerves. Love and regret he has sung of; and he could have sung of them at much less "expense of spirit in the waste of shame." It requires a strong man to "sin strongly"; he has sinned with a more animal, a more calculated, a more deliberate, a more malicious insatiability than any man I have known. To him, in that "seemingly creative predominance in his interests, of beautiful physical things, a kind of tyranny over the senses" (that phrase of Pater's seems to have been made for his definition), things seen are already felt; the lust of the eye, in him, is a kind of intellectual energy. So his feeling narrows itself down to what can be hurt or gratified in himself, or in some one imagined after the pattern of himself. He gets sheer away from civilisation in his bodily consciousness of things, which he apprehends as directly, with however much added subtlety, as a peasant of his own Abruzzi. * * *

I saw d'Annunzio fairly often in Rome, sometimes in a circular room at the top of the Palazzo Borghese, sometimes in cafés. One afternoon when we were seated in a café in the Corso he began to tell me of a certain Italian woman, who had written verses; he said vivid things about her; he gave me a tiny book written by her, *Novissima*.[6] Some of the verse struck me as very immature, very feverish, written in very peculiar English, with a curious absence of technique, and of the manner of using rhymes. Many of these were certainly written about the poet who gave me her book. As, for instance, in this stanza:

> His gaze, as I felt, called me back when I sauntered away,
>   No longer so sure of itself,
> And—were tears misplaced in that revel of drunken noonday?
>   I whistled a tune to myself.

When I first met her in London she seemed to me to be living in the midst of rather difficult surroundings, which she always confessed when she was in one of her violent tempers. She was fascinating, nervous, passionate. She showed no surprise, only laughed mockingly, when I told her how her verses had come into my possession. She was explicit enough in her stories of d'Annunzio's various adventures. Naturally, neither of us then had the faintest idea that soon after the atrocious and destructive war began he would set on fire with his fiery eloquence the hearts of the Italians, and that he would, being himself as typical an egoist as the egoist of Meredith, defy the entire world. A modern Prometheus, the modern Zeus has overcome him.[7] * * *

[Mental Collapse in Italy]¹

I

To trace, to retrace, to attempt to define or to divine the way in which one's madness begins, the exact fashion in which it seizes on one, is as impossible as to divine why one is sane. That I inherited madness from certain ancestors of mine—one never knows how many generations back —is unquestionable. That I ever imagined it in myself is perhaps just as unquestionable. Yet, when the thunderbolt from hell fell on me, which for a time destroyed my reason, I was utterly and absolutely unprepared for so unimaginable a crisis as that which befell me in Italy at the end of 1908. Was I not really in the situation of my Christian Trevalga? "He had never known what it was to feel the earth solid under his feet. And now, when he waited for the doctor who was to decide whether he might still keep his place in the world, and make what he could of all that remained to him of his life, the past began to come back to him, blurred a little in his memory, and with whole spaces blotted out of it, but in a steady return upon himself, as the past, it is said, comes back to a drowning man at the instant before death."² * * *

In my own youth when I had nightmares, I awoke, stifling a scream, my hair damp with sweat, out of impossible tasks in which time shrank and swelled in some deadly game with life; something had to be done in a second, and all eternity passed, lingering, while the second poised over me like a drop of water always about to drip: it fell, and I was annihilated into depth under depth of darkness. In those dreams of abstract horror there began to come a disturbing element of Sex. To me it was something remote, implacable; and there was an infinite curiosity, which I hardly even dared dream of satisfying, a curiosity which was like a fever. Above all, I was uneasy about myself, because I saw that others were uneasy about me, and my voracious appetite for life was partly a kind of haste to eat and drink my fill at a feast from which I might at any time be called away. And then I was still more uneasy about hell. I felt the eternal flames seizing me, and some foretaste of their endlessness seemed to enter into my being.

I have no intention of giving many details of the month I spent in

Venice in September 1908, nor of the adventures that happened to me either in the Palazzo that gave on the Grand Canal or at the Lido or in the streets of Venice. I was over-excitable and overstrained; several misadventures had occurred in the previous year which had greatly and deeply upset me. I had become irritable and extravagant. Even then my eyes were hurting me. I was troubled by one crisis after another, over which I had no control. My nerves reacted on my imagination: reacted, almost recoiled, on my body. Too many burdens had been imposed upon me by I know not how many task-masters. I was hallucinated, obsessed. Even the heat enervated me: much more so in Venice with closed windows and mosquito nets around the beds; often enough sleep forsook me and I got out of bed and began to write and write and write. * * *

II

The first time I stayed in Bologna I had a room in the ancient hotel where Byron spent some time before he went to his heroic death in Missolonghi; one of those old-fashioned hotels that one fancies, not for their luxury, but for their comfort; with the open court and the wooden balconies outside all the rooms, where I heard the rain fall insidiously. * * *

This sad and learned town revealed itself to me with a certain severe charm, a little fantastic also, fascinating rather the mind than the senses. Coming from Naples I suddenly felt the north. In the bedroom of my hotel, when I heard the rain fall, outside my door, on the little open balcony over the central court, I remembered that for a month I had been sleeping where I could look from my bed and see nothing but sky and sea. Wherever I went in Bologna I came upon something medieval: a bewildering church, a pillar, the Podestà dwindling away under the portico of Vignola into cafés and shops; the two leaning towers which, like most of the caprices of the Middle Ages, are a lasting wonder, a riddle without an answer, a sort of gigantic joke, stupefying as the jokes of Rabelais. My most profound impression was the one I received from the Museo Civico—where the weight of so much, so ancient and so forgotten death began to weigh on me. In the delicate work of Cellini and John of Bologna I could see only that they were the portrait of dead men and women, and that the pride of life which had perpetuated them was after all only another glory which had gone down into the dust, ridiculously despoiled by death. Never had I felt so acutely the pathos of transitory things not suffered to die; many separate houses which had each been a home, turned into a public show; never had I felt such an odour of death, not even in Pompeii. * * *

The second time when I was in Bologna I stayed at the Hôtel Brun, in the Palazzo Malvasia, Via Ugo Bassi; there was a fine view of the town from the loggia. There was something ominous in the effect of this huge edifice which jarred my nerves; there was an enormous courtyard on which many of the windows looked, where one had coffee; but, as for the huge door, that moved on iron hinges, that also jarred on my nerves; most of all on that night when I returned and beat in vain on that closed door: and this—this awful kind of connivance with the Evil Powers—was a thing unheard of in all my travels. * * *

It was noticed by the people who kept the hotel and by the woman who was with me[3] that I was in a state of intense exasperation; which is the inevitable penalty of the sins one has and has not committed. One night I went out and took a ticket for some theatre where I spent the evening; it was the Teatro Brunelli, in a wide street between the Via Castiglione and the Via Santo Stefano. I was very uneasy; the people who thronged the theatre disturbed me in the extreme; they irritated me. The next night I went to a circus—such shows always amused me—where I talked with some of the performers: one was a queer little girl, a clever horse-rider, who sat on my knees and wickedly caressed me. When I left the circus I forgot my way back to the hotel. I went to some miserable little hotel—such as those Baudelaire was too often obliged to frequent when the exasperation of the nerves of Jeanne Duval reacted on his and hurled him like a whirlwind on to the pavements of Paris—where in my miserable room I tried in vain to sleep. I locked the door and examined my smoking candle; horrible imaginations racked my brain, I seemed on fire; so, next morning, I paid what had to be paid to the surly manager, and returned to the Hôtel Brun, where my sudden reappearance created a certain amount of surprise and astonishment. * * *

Next morning I found myself in Ferrara, where I took a room in a most forbidding hotel—the Hôtel Europa, opposite the post office, near the Castello Vecchio. I wandered along the streets and saw the most horrible shapes and shadows. I may have said to myself, then, for all I know, with Gérard de Nerval: "I attribute to myself an influence over the course of the moon, and I believe that this star had been struck by the thunderbolt of the Most High, which had traced on its face the imprint of the mask which I had observed."

On the second night after my arrival in Ferrara I wandered along the streets and came—under the moonlight—on a horrible apparition that loomed hideously against the horizon—the Castello Vecchio, which had been the Ducal Palace; it was built in 1383 by Niccolò il Zoppo after the revolt. This is certainly one of the most imposing examples of medieval military architecture in Italy. The huge edifice rises out of the midst of a dark basin of water, its four corners guarded by four towers, which dominate the low roofs of the sunken city stretching far on all

sides. Seen from the outside where the grass is swampy, one sees the
Porta degli Angeli, which keeps its ancient form and presents a long
vista of crumbling bastions which are overgrown with tangled thickets.
One sees no signs of habitation above the walls; the shrunken city is
far withdrawn within. In 1579 a horrible accident happened in the
tournament, when four of the knights of the noblest houses were upset
into the moat; upon which the crude Duke insisted that the tournament
should continue to the end, under his inflexible eyes. Therefore the dense
and dire horror of Death's intrusion still hangs about the place, like
some form of the Black Plague; for upon it has fallen the curse which
attended the ancient brood of Este. As for the Castle itself, the sight of
the massive foundations, and the heavy arches beneath which the waters
of the moat look so sinister and so secret, raised in me a sensation of
terror. Yet, on that night, the effect of the building was extraordinarily
impressive, so many of the hideous details were lost to one's sight; yet
one had to be insidiously aware that the immense mass of the Castle that
towered up, with its stone balustrades and its frowning machicolations,
was itself as evil as the dungeons themselves had always been and still
were. At the north-east angle rises the Torre de' Leoni, the largest of the
four towers, which had and has dungeons beneath it, inside whose grim
and gaunt walls criminals used to be exposed in iron cages—as in the
time of the Asiatic Bajazet.

III

The next afternoon I began to walk across the city, and found myself
outside one of the gates; then, not knowing my way, so bewildered I was
with nerves and with the intense heat and with an exasperation of all
the senses, I walked and walked and walked—always in the wrong
direction, always under the hot sun that hurt me, always imagining I
was on my way back to Ferrara. It is literally impossible for me to say
how often I stopped on my way, and how often I continued walking
interminably—always in the wrong direction. As night came on, night
with all its oppression, I felt an enormous fatigue creep over me. I sat by
the wayside for hours, then, being observed by certain curious people, I
got up wearily and resumed my endless wanderings. I climbed several
haystacks and rested on them. I remember vividly that wonderful poem
of Morris, "The Haystack in the Floods." * * *
    Being chased away from one haystack, I began to run. Following on
my heels were three country folk, and, so as to escape their pursuit, I fell
headlong into deep ditches, into ponds and pools; came out wet through,

besmeared with mud. I hid myself behind a hedge. I heard their loud voices far off; there I fell asleep for I know not how many hours. At any rate, I woke at dawn, and began again my endless and, as it seemed to me, my hopeless wanderings. I see myself sometimes in the depths of a dream walking on a high plateau to which I had somehow climbed. The scenery on both sides was curious and unfamiliar to me; there was far below me the railway and the train I would have given anything in the world to have been in.

Finally, worn out with fatigue, after many a rest on this painful pilgrimage, foot-sore and hungry and thirsty—as a matter of fact I had been given both food and drink by several kind women on both days, for they had pitied me—I came on an immense farm-house. The door was open. I went in. There were several women in that room; some were at work, some seated at a table, and the sunshine entered into the room. One strange old woman seated near the hearth reminded me of a witch, so warily she stared at me, but with no suspicion. I spoke to them quietly in the best Italian I was capable of; they made me sit down at the table and they gave me red wine and bread and meat. Then I asked if there was any place where I could sleep that night. They looked at me curiously. One said: "Just you wait here, till the Padrone returns." I sat there, idly watching the sunbeams and these women's faces. The Padrone finally entered. He asked me to step outside with him. We walked up and down the courtyard. I told him some of my story and of how I had lost my way. He was one of the kindliest men I have ever met. He patted me in his familiar way on the shoulder and said: "Come with me; you shall have a nice bed to-night." We walked a long way. I could hardly walk, so he took my arm. Then we came to where he kept his cattle. He took me up to an enormous cattle-shed. The cattle were in the sheds; over them was quite a comfortable loft. I went into it. He wished me good-night. He left me and went on his way. I slept soundly that night, and when I woke before noon I heard all around me the pleasant sounds and noises of the cattle underneath me.

Next morning I found my way to the farm-house. They gave me a good breakfast, then the Padrone walked some miles with me along the road, explaining the nearest way back to the town. Then he stopped, shook my hand warmly, and said Good-bye! I walked on, refreshed by the sleep I had and by his kindness; tried on my way to find more directions; tried in vain to get any help from those who were driving their carts: all refused. Finally I came on a man whom I hailed. He stopped; he was driving a cart on the top of which was a huge barrel of wine—the biggest I ever saw. He said to me: "Get on to the top of that barrel— mind you hold on tight as the thing always jostles—and I'll drop you at the tavern where I have to turn off on a different road."

I got on top of the barrel, and was jostled to and fro in a most uncomfortable fashion. I certainly held on tight, and when we came to the tavern he helped me down, took me inside, gave me some wine and food, then went his way. I wandered onward for I know not how many hours; never in my life was I so utterly fatigued, in spite of resting every half-hour near some hedge. Dark came on, and I went to a café, sat down there and ordered coffee. I drank it with some relief.

Then the unforeseen happened. Two Bersaglieri were strolling along. They saw me; in an instant they seated themselves beside me. I was questioned and cross-questioned. Then they promised to take me back to the Hôtel Europa. I walked between them. At a certain tavern we stopped. We went in: I imagined they were going to give me a drink. On the contrary, to my horror I was thrust into a dark room without one ray of light. I stumbled about, in vain. Then they let me out, and I walked between them—an endless journey, it seemed to me. They took me to the hotel, where, or course, I asked for my room. There was no answer. Then ensued a long conversation between these two men and the hall-porter, who brought some under-manager who was made to sign some documents—I was unaware of their contents.

Then, escorted between those two terrifying beings, I found myself face to face with the Ducal Castle. They knocked. I was thrust in, and, with no examination whatsoever, I was seized by two gaolers—something about me having been said to them—pushed down interminable stairs to a dark corridor. The iron-barred door of a dungeon was flung open. They fastened and locked manacles on my wrists and ankles; they flung me on to the stone floor, which stunned me. When I woke I saw what I had never imagined possible: myself supposed to be a Criminal and a Lunatic or a Vagrant, unjustly hurled into hell. There was a small grated window high up on one of the walls; there was the "Judas" (so ironical and so cruel a name used for so cruel a purpose!)—the slit-hole of hell through which the horrible goalers are obliged to look—in the middle of the door; there was a narrow wooden bed—a bed of torture in a torture-house. With an effort which was incalculable I got on to the bed; there was a wooden block behind my head instead of a pillow. Otherwise the cell was utterly naked.

Fettered on both ankles and on both wrists, after the whole horror of this nefarious attack on my liberty had begun to exasperate me beyond any imaginable exasperation, I dragged myself with painful steps round and round the stone walls of my cell, gazing hopelessly at the barred window that let in but a little light, and at the Judas, which was continually opened and shut, showing me the grimacing faces of those inhuman beasts. The desire of escape, which has, more than anything else, always kept me alive, was certainly awake then—then, when the chances were a thousand to one that I should never leave that cell alive. Utterly worn out with the intolerable fatigue of those days and nights on which I had wandered, I crawled back to my bed of torture—and, mercifully, slept till dawn. Dawn glared on me like those unendurable dawns that the damned alive in hell must experience, if they are alive there. I dragged myself helplessly to and fro: still the grimacing faces stared at me. I had been given nothing to drink, nothing to eat. I imagined their intention was to keep me in that cell deprived of all that is necessary to us in our human needs, and to let me die there in convulsions after those agonies caused by thirst and hunger had exhausted me; and then to bury me in some deep hole in the earth. At noon these men entered my cell, unlocked my manacles, and took me to that place in the corridor which one calls the cabinet. I noticed the long corridor and the sharp flights of stairs that went up and down. After they had let me breathe some air, that abnormal nervous strength which I have always possessed in an extraordinary degree, raised all the madness that was burning me like hell's fire; and I fought with these three huge gaolers—in the wild idea of escape—with a ferocity which at least equalled theirs. I know not how long that struggle went on. I caught one of them by the throat and nearly strangled him; I hit another in the pit of his stomach so furiously that he fell backward on the floor. Then—in Balzac's phrase—began my Gehenna. My feet were of course naked; these gaolers had iron-shod boots, and two of them attacked my naked feet with such venomous violence, with such inhuman ferocity, that the blood was drained out of them by reiterated kicks, so that the blood which covered my feet and which covered that part of the floor on which I lay is beyond any calculation. In an instant I was manacled and flung back into my den. I probably took an hour to crawl back to my bed, after which I certainly swooned. I cannot imagine how I was able to sleep that night: probably from sheer exhaustion.

The same hideous dawn glared at me. I could neither stir nor breathe. Every vein in my body ached as if I had been on the rack. Then came the miraculous release I was much too worn out to expect. It was indeed a heaven-sent miracle: a miracle for which I have not only to thank the God who created me, but also the Italian Ambassador, the Marchese di San Giuliano, for, no sooner had he been informed of my disappearance in Ferrara, than, with that insight which never failed him, he sent a wire in cypher to the Italian government requiring them to have search made for me immediately in every direction. They searched everywhere, until they found me in my intolerable misery, which might have been my last agony. Indeed, I have not only to thank that Ambassador, but also, two women whose devotion was more than angelical.[4] Suddenly the door of my cell was flung open; there entered several men who were unknown to me, together with the gaolers who had nearly killed me. They had to obey the wired message of the Italian Ambassador, who had been informed of my disappearance by the two women of whom I have already spoken. These men unlocked my manacles; they carried me most carefully up those steep flights of stairs I was so well aware of; I was gently placed inside a *carrozza;* the other men I had seen seated themselves beside me, and, after I know not how prolonged a journey, the *carrozza* stopped in the midst of some wonderful scenery. I was lifted out with infinite tenderness. As a matter of fact I was in a *Stabilimento di Bagni,* not far from Ferrara. There I literally swooned, after having been bathed and my wounds carefully dressed. I can but imagine that during the time I remained there I was in a state of coma, in a state of stupor; which, with the rest I had there and the marvellous care those Italians had for me, most certainly saved my life.

I have a vague remembrance of a priest who was very kind to me. He would sometimes read aloud his Latin breviary beside my bed, which always had a lulling effect upon me. I was finally taken out into a kind of open court, where I sat with some of the others; their conversation had for me no meaning. I was so unutterably exhausted, the pains in the whole of my body were so intolerable, that often enough I fell sound asleep. Apart from this I have no distinct recollection of exactly what the place was like. It was certainly *une maison de santé.* I believe that on the day when I left the priest gave me his Latin breviary.

Finally I was taken from this place to an asylum not far from Bologna, where I was perfectly looked after. It was a mad-house; all of us were supposed to be mad. I was certainly aware that I was by no means mad, as I took in the whole situation from an almost ironical point of view. I had a very comfortable bed, where I always had good nights, in spite of the fact that there were more men who had beds in the same room as mine. Some were noisy; none of these ever disturbed me, in spite of the way they had of shrieking, screaming, yelling, cursing. There were no doors to these rooms; there were long corridors. A night watchman was always there; he never, so far as I remember, entered our rooms, but sometimes when I was wide awake—there were lights in these rooms— I got out of bed and glanced this way and that way; the man was generally half asleep on a bench covered with his cloak.

There was a big, open court; we were let out every morning and afternoon; the air was dry and hot; there were many seats for us to sit on, a few meagre trees, and an awful lot of dust. I enjoyed all my meals, in spite of my terrible state of weakness. The men there bandaged my wounds as only Italians can. We all sat together in a large room with wooden tables. I, being the honoured guest, always had a seat kept for me at the head of the table. I was the best served—with coarse red wine and good bread; in fact, they gave me all I wanted, even an extra glass of wine when I was parched with thirst.

As I could only walk a few steps and with an extreme difficulty, I was always helped in and helped back. They generally gave me a bench with a back to it where there was some shade from the sun's heat. There I sat, dazed, and imagined many wonderful things. One of these men, who was good looking, went to and fro in the yard, one hand stuck in his waistcoat; with the other he made gestures. He was always talking vividly of some girl, some mistress of his, he had lost. He invented imaginary dialogues with her—she seemed, though absent, to be always there with him. Many of the others crowded against the walls and hardly ever moved.

There was a beautiful young Italian who took an immense fancy to me; he was continually near me; he helped me in every way; he helped me to dress and to undress; he had a curious way of saying in his deep voice: "Io son molto ricco, molto ricco!" So, when I was finally taken away, certainly as much to my delight as to his regret, he expressed to me with his Italian fervour how much he would miss me.

The details of my return from Bologna to London are not worth relating. There were two men with me, one an Italian, whom I liked; one an Englishman, whom I disliked, in spite of the fact that he did all in his power to please me and that he carried out his duty minutely. When I saw the white and impregnable cliffs of Dover loom up before me—yet with I knew not what menace—my heart leapt with joy: that gate of England is always open, and there are always wardens awake at the gate. So, when I came back to that house which had been mine for a few years, which was no more to be mine, I ran up the steps and fell, helpless enough, into the arms of my wife, who stood inside the open door. Still, I must always feel that, had the authorities of that hideous prison kept me there for even a week longer in the state I was then in, my name would not have been obliterated out of men's and women's memories: only, I can but imagine that no human being would have known where I had been assassinated, nor in what obscure corner of that obscure hole in the earth I should have been interred.

IV

I was more dead than alive when I returned to England at the end of November 1908. Yet, when I came face to face with a house which had been mine for several years, which I knew not then I was fated never to again inhabit, I was so nervously excited that, seeing the door wide open,

I ran up the steps and embraced my wife with passionate emotion. The house itself was said to have been haunted; many years afterwards this ominous sentence of Pater in "The Child in the House" returned to me: "Afterwards he came to think of those poor, home-returning ghosts, which all men have fancied to themselves—the *revenants*—pathetically, as crying or beating with vain hands at the doors, as the wind came, their cries distinguishable in it as a wilder inner note."[5]

Finally I was put to bed. No sooner was I there than I became filled with fears and terrors, with delirious hallucinations. The sudden return, the emotion of the moment having passed, acted on my tortured nerves. I was quite conscious all the time that I was there, but a feeling of fearful isolation crept over me, insidiously. I believe that my excitement became so intense that I got out of bed one night and escaped into the street. I was taken back. I have never forgotten the hatred I conceived for the man who had brought me back from Italy, and who was supposed never to leave me alone. I noticed that he stole the keys from the doors, which added to my exasperation. A physician [Dr. J.S. Risien Russell] had been hastily summoned. He came; behaved as such doctors invariably do, by minutely examining me, asking me the inevitable questions; and then, in the next room, informed my wife in the usual professional manner: "I am afraid Mr. Symons cannot live for more than three months; he is in so critical, he is in so perilous a state. In any case, I know where to send him in the meantime, to Crowborough, where I have sent many of my patients: Charles Conder, for instance, you must remember, who is of course incurable."

A friend took me there in his motor. I was placed in charge of a doctor, whose name, curiously enough, was Griffin: he was the very image of one; but I must say he was most kind to me. I was looked after by two men; one who was Irish I liked, the other, who was not, I disliked. I had a nice bedroom with a window wide open, where the man I liked spent every night; but, as I was rather sleepless, I noticed that he often got out of bed and lay down somewhere near the window. I had a bath every morning, breakfast in bed, meals in a small drawing-room, and every day they took me for a long walk, at least twice, if not more. All this I enjoyed immensely, in spite of the fact that I found it almost impossible to walk; we stopped often on the way and sat on gates; and they talked with me, they amused me. If only I had been left there for another year, things would have been very different from what they actually were. The Fates were against me.

I could neither read nor write. I understood nothing of what was going on in the literary world, which was my world, nor the world in general. Yet I was content. The air was invigorating, the scenery was new to me. I often walked alone in the grounds. I noticed with some curiosity that before night none of the doors was locked and that my bedroom door was never locked.

Then—as always—there came over me the desire of escape. I was of course penniless and in a hopeless state, in all conscience. What do these things matter when one has an inventive brain? I wondered if by some means I could escape out of one of the windows; or, what seemed much more likely, when I was left alone in the grounds at the approach of night. Finally, I really succeeded. It was late in the afternoon; I walked quickly up the side path into the main road, whence I directed my steps in the direction of a well-known hotel I had seen every day. I went in, I sat down at a table, I ordered dinner: I ordered—as if that might have been the best and the last dinner I was ever to have—the best food there was to be had and a bottle of champagne. When he presented the bill to me, unfortunately I said: "Dr Griffin will pay." At the same time I asked one of the waiters if there was a motor that could take me back to London. He said: "Yes, sir, you shall have one." Instead of the motor, what do you suppose came? Not the motor. The two men. Ignominiously, I was taken back to the house; the Irishman, who was full of strange humour and warm-hearted, could hardly restrain his laughter. That was my last escapade.

Once only, I think, my wife and a woman friend came to visit me. They were very emotional and fearfully sorry for me. I had only a few vague ideas in my head. I said to our friend: "You and I will people the world with men children." I said to the other: "I am planning a map of the world; I shall divide it into small divisions; each shall have a King and Queen; I have not yet decided as to what these shall be." I said to one: "I am the Pope in Rome," and I made a sweeping gesture; and I described, not so much the Papal vestments, as those of Cardinal Rampolla, who said High Mass at St. Peter's on Christmas Day 1896. The large, rigid figure in the red robes and the gold mitre, who sat there under his golden vestments, lifting a white-gloved hand on whose third finger shone the emerald ring set with diamonds, performed the sacred functions with a dignity which was a little weary, and in the priest's expressionless way, with that air of fixed meditation (as of a continual commerce with heaven) which is the Church's manner of expressing disapproval of the world.

I was very disappointed after a few weeks to be made to leave a place I had come to like so much; where so much that had always been familiar returned to me; where I felt the appeal of Nature. I was taken back to London in another car; I was again examined by the specialist. I was sent on that same day in that same car to a private asylum.[6] A huge door grated on its heavy hinges as it was unlocked: I was taken inside this hideous den of thieves, for so I imagined it to be; I was left there alone in the midst of such fiends with faces of men that I can only compare them with the fiends in Dante's *Inferno*. * * *

There, in that prison of mine where I was confined for a year and a half, were what were called "Keepers"; one of these, the most hideous of the lot, was appointed to be my gaoler. He had to lock me up every night in a room with barred windows and closed shutters through which not one ray of light, at least in the winter, ever penetrated; in fact, I was in pitch darkness—the worst torture that could ever have been inflicted upon me. Never have I forgotten the horrible grating sound of that key in my bedroom door—which I heard every night and morning. I have always been highly strung, over-nervous, over-excitable, over-sensitive; and the least jar on my nerves always upsets me. I hate total darkness as much as men who are on the point of being hanged hate hell. The moment after that infernal door had clanged behind me and I was alone and yet never alone, I knew exactly what was bound to happen: madness, and for a time, absolute madness.

Two men, one only really, ran, as they say, "the house": one heard nothing but "the house," "the rules of the house," "the rules that must never be infringed," "the rules that were the laws of the house." There was also that damned routine, which is one of the most hopeless and one of the most useless of all such institutions. These people were inflexible. The doctors never gave me—as they ought to have done—any treatment of any kind; they gave me, as far as I know, no medicine. They never gave me, by any chance, in spite of the piteous way in which I implored them to give me, one sleeping draught. They were aware of my insomnia. What did that mean to them? Less than nothing. They were utterly heartless. A prison it was, it was nothing but a prison; they were the keepers of the prison: they knew it and I knew it.

As for the sanitary conditions of this establishment, they were unspeakable. * * *

V

* * * I look back upon those terrible years, when I was in utmost peril of my life, when my actual existence was menaced over and over again, with a sense equal to Shelley's, of the horrible injustice of the oppressors of mankind, of their lack of the moral sense, of their lack of such judgement as only the wise possess: that men who are born free ought always to remain free. Capture a lion, a tiger, any beast, and confine him inside a barred cage for the rest of his existence: can any device be more cruel than that? They have found an enemy craftier than they; they have been

conquered and carried away captive, and they are full of smouldering rage. Exactly the same kind of torture is inflicted on men and women; these resent their torture and their confinement as much as the wilder beasts resent the useless and cruel theft of their liberty. We too, in our narrow cages, in which we move to and fro, restlessly, all on fire with a life that tingles in every vein and dilates the nostrils, are consumed with smouldering rage. Years ago when I passed through the Saturday crowd on the Edgware Road, between two opposing currents of evil smells, I heard a man who was lurching along the pavement say in contemptuous comment: "Twelve o'clock! We may all be dead by twelve o'clock!" That is what our torturers no doubt say to themselves: "What does it matter if that patient or this other patient dies at midnight, as long as we, the torturers, survive?" * * *

I am impelled to say, with absolute certainty, not only that my case, my case of survival and of recovery, is unique in the judgement of the wisest doctors and in the judgement of others, and that I am perfectly aware of the fact, but that, so far as my knowledge extends, no man, such as I am, a poet, a writer of prose, a dramatist, a traveller, who has lived with the certainty of being always free, has been so cruelly and so unjustly confined in a prison whose name I shall never mention—where I should never have been sent—the scars and stigmata of which, the scars of persecution and the stabs that my flesh has received, will remain, part and parcel of this suffering self of mine, until the last wind extinguishes the last flickering candle.

It is not for me to say how far and to what extent I was conscious or unconscious of the place where I was confined and of my physical condition. When the veils of the Temple are shattered, or when some Isis one has worshipped suddenly unveils her face and the vision of her incarnate beauty is beyond one's endurance, then the earth may be no longer solid under one's feet and women's treachery might be made more manifest than ever. * * *

What amazes me now is the break that occurred then between my reason and my sense of reality; it was not then evident to me but it was absolute. After a certain length of time I had half forgotten my own existence; I had forgotten what I had written, the name of Byron and of Coleridge, of Wagner and of Rodin, the memory of things past, the memory of things present—which went by like the flowing of some dream river—and in fact I had lost tangible hold of everything; of all I had done, of my visions, of my friends, of the cities I had loved, of the music I had adored, of those women who had meant more to me than the whole world. I was not altogether oblivious. I had lucid moments, when something of my former self returned to me—only in flashes. Obliged to have all my meals at one long table where an odious

lot of hideous patients were assembled, with one doctor at one end
of the table, another at the other end, where for I know not how long
I hardly uttered a word or understood one word that was spoken, I
returned to my wretched room in exactly the state I was in when I left
it. There were books I could not read: there was paper I could not write
on; there was my bed of torture, which I never regarded without that
creeping sense one has when one is about to tread on a reptile.

One of the most ignominious things that they did to me was, that
every night when I had to go to bed, and I had put on my pyjamas,
that keeper of mine picked up all my dry clothes, and carried them out,
then he returned and after some casual word went out and double-locked
the door. Never shall I forget the horrible scraping noise the key made
in the key-hole, which sent a shock to my very bones. All the lights were
turned out something after ten o'clock. I was left there from that hour
in total darkness, without one glimmer of light, till the hour when the
same man unlocked that infernal door. It was out of some sheer, some
obstinate necessity that I was almost entirely deprived of sleep for the
whole winter: I doubt if I ever had more than one or two hours of even
slumber. With all my nerves on edge, with insomnia like some unclean
fiend always at one side of me, inside of me, inside my bed, on the
floor, on the pillow:

> Thin are the night-skirts left behind,
> By daybreak hours that onward creep,
> And thin, alas! the shred of sleep
> That wavers with the spirit's wind:

with a thousand devils raging in my brain, with something horrible
gnawing at the pit of my stomach, utterly unable to remain in bed, I
crawled out of it in my naked feet—remember that this was one of the
coldest winters I have ever known, that I was half naked and shivering
from head to foot—I paced round that accursed room with tireless
rapidity, with the tireless rapidity of madness, hitting myself on every
object I stumbled on in that pitch darkness, counting—of course in vain—
a million steps, then another million; that is what I did every night
without exception. Insane to a certain extent I was; but can anyone
who is sane imagine for one moment that any torture so abominable as
this which was inflicted upon me can be conceived as a bare possibility?
The Spanish Inquisition was an affair of the Middle Ages: an insane
idea which germinated in the mad imagination of Torquemada. What
I wish more than ever in this narrative of mine to accentuate is, the
glaring, the uncontrovertible fact, that only a form of insanity which

was not mine could have conceived and executed what those tyrants did. What they did, mind you, was done in cold blood; and yet with a terrible fixity of will which causes such people as these to be cruel and inflexible and implacable. These deliberately put in practice malignant arts so as to injure others, they exhibit no remorse, they have an abnormal self-confidence, and no moral sensibility; they ignore with impunity the distinctions between the common notions of wrong and right in the ordinary relations of life, and that vice and virtue, when exhibited by themselves, are to be found singularly balanced in "the whirligig of time."

VI

How I contrived even to exist under that curse of insomnia, during that intolerable winter, I shall never fathom. There was for our recreation a huge garden enclosed between high walls where we could walk whenever we liked. That exercise, for one thing, helped to keep me alive. I began to be interested in the sounds I heard from the roads near by, in the storms and sunsets, in the changes of weather; which, finally, made me feel that I was not altogether out of the world I had loved so much: apart from the fact that soon dawned upon me that where I was confined was an asylum for mad people.

Gradually these excited my curiosity, which was always insatiable; I began to study their characters, their manias, their aberrations. In a kind of annexe, divided from the other house by a small wall, the worst of the patients were kept. There was one who seemed raving mad, who always walked and cursed and laughed like a hyena; there were many others I hardly noticed. One man, who was famed for his learning, who was a great Greek scholar, had been kept there for I know not how long a period; he was far and away the most dangerous of those patients; he was confined in a padded room which contained not much more than his bed, where he used to exhaust himself with wild leaps in the air, stamping his feet in a regular rhythm (he always said it was the rhythm of the angels) with rushing to and fro like a bull, so as to dash his head against those walls that were noiseless. He fairly often dined with the others at the long table; he was always proud and insolent; he used strong language; he made himself hated, yet they feared him for his immense strength. When I had recovered enough to be on terms of conversation with anyone he often absorbed my attention; I did his; he always called me "The Sensitive Plant."[7] Sometimes he talked lucidly; then, relapsing to his self-absorption, he went on stamping his feet; he had forgotten everything, even himself. * * *

In this prison of mine, in which I sighed for liberty, after a series of months, I began to write verses, prose essays, stories, satires, sonnets, songs. I did volumes of translations from Balzac, Baudelaire, Gautier, Gérard de Nerval. Far and away the best thing I did—I think it was done half a year before I was set free—was a one-act play in blank verse on *The Death of Marlowe*. I wrote, I imagined, I created, the whole thing in a Spanish *quaderno* with bright, yellow paper and yellow covers: it seemed to me, and to a painter to whom I read most of it, tragic and dramatic; it had in it something imaginative and lyrical; there was a wide sweep in it; it was full of passion and of mystery and of pure lust; it took place in the tavern where Marlowe was killed; I brought in Shakespeare, Drayton, and Marlowe's last mistress—in whose arms he died. There was in it something flame-like and furious; and, in the midst of its horror, in the midst of this perilous situation, there was much beauty and tenderness and pity: it ended on a tragic note. * * *

I also wrote an extraordinary bit of prose, *The Crucifix in the Desert*, which was done after *La Tentation de Saint-Antoine* of Flaubert; a poem, *Salomé*,[8] which was quite impossible, yet it had some lyrical quality; then my absurd Odes, my sonnets in French, my parodies, my amazing experiments in all directions. All this shows the feverish activity, the tension of my nerves, the obscure workings of my imagination, the indefatigable energy with which I devoured time: and all this and much more than this to kill time as rapidly as I could before the event of my deliverance. I read a certain amount of books: these meant less to me than my passion for writing, which was almost volcanic.

Gradually these friends who were keepers and the mad people they watched over became somewhat more human. I always loathed being there; I loathed, without one exception, all the inhabitants. This loathing, this disdain, this insolence, this haughtiness, this aloofness, this sense of pride and of one's position in the world of letters, helped to keep me alive, even when my chance of escape seemed less than ever probable. I knew for certain that I myself had no means of escape, in spite of my intense desire to attain my freedom. Yet, had I not been certain of my own self, and of the fact that deliverance was near at hand, I might have withered away. With strength of will, with an infinitely more nervous strength than most people suppose me to possess, endowed with an obstinate nature, with an almost inflexible belief in myself which has made me for the most part disregard the opinions of others; because I have been called an aristocrat of Letters, because I have never "prostituted myself" for any lying or servile tasks; because I have a devouring and flaming temperament which must prey on something if it is not to prey mortally on myself; because I have always known that whatever is not absolute truth, truth to conviction, is a wilful lie;

because I have declared that I am ungrateful and yet have always been capable of gratitude: it is because I possess these good and bad qualities that I have survived what no living man has ever survived; and perhaps because, as I wrote on Léon Bloy, the Thankless Beggar: "If, in addition to that mere human right—the right to assistance—one is convinced one is a man of genius, the right becomes more plainly evident, and, if in addition, one has a divine message for the world, what further need be said?"[9]

VII

It was in the spring of 1909 that I had a terrible attack of pneumonia, which all but killed me; in fact, the doctors said that either I should die of this disease or that I should survive and that my reason would gradually return to me. I must have been several weeks in bed; all that time I could only gibber and grimace; I was an absolute lunatic; I became a skeleton, I became emaciated, all skin and bones. The doctors, who were afraid I might die in the night, did me a fearful wrong which I have never forgotten, which I shall never forgive: they had a bed placed in my room near one of the walls; on that bed keeper after keeper snored: and this, which is the most horrible of all noises, kept me awake in a state of fever—that is, when my reason had begun to come back to me—so much so, that with that force of madness which nothing can check I not only cursed them incessantly, but as I writhed on my bed of torture I contrived with much kicking of my heels and a heave of my body to make this hideous machine knock against the other wall with all the exertion my emaciated body was capable of, to make that accursed bed move under me as far as I could make it move. Finally, these fiends made their departure, and for the rest of the time I was unmolested. * * *

X

* * * All this time I had been mixed up with madmen and their keepers; but, just then, I was supposed to be by no means stark staring mad. Never was I assured by any of the doctors as to when I should have my release. I was taken out with one of them in his car to be examined by a number of outside doctors, some of whom were most encouraging, some of whom were not. Always the same, to my mind, absurd but inevitable examination: how one's knees dance, how one's

pulse beats, one's temperature, sometimes one's blood-pressure; mostly one's eyes, in the depths of which are centred one's nerves, with flashlights. Then the questions: one's memory, one's former occupations, one's sense of oneself and of others: and all this, of course, and every examination, had one meaning only—the testing of one's nerves; then the chance of one's recovery. All tried to detect my errors, which varied a good deal: errors, naturally enough in the state I was in just then, which are always supposed to be the proof of an unstable mind. I have never forgotten how, when I was driven across London in that car, I envied every man, girl, woman, whore, priest, criminal, rake; who were all as free as air, who laughed and joked and hurried past one; who were those among the millions who inhabit London that I most envied. There was I, a man of letters, who had travelled half over Europe, who had known the most wonderful artists of his time, who had made what seemed a solid position for himself, with the dint of much labour and much more so with his insight and his imagination, who adored wandering, the music-halls, those foreign folk who alone are amusing, and besides these the most wicked and wanton quarters of the cities he had lived in and their depraved and perverted inhabitants; I, that is, who write these words, to have been horribly aware that he was a prisoner and that he had only been taken out of prison to be taken back to prison.

XII

* * * [Rhoda] gave up, as it were, the whole world, to use a Bible phrase, that world which had been ours also, which was never to be the same world to us again: she gave up, besides that, almost her life for my sake. How far she believed in my final recovery—that is my deliverance from that madhouse—I cannot say: all I can say is, that if anyone did, she did. She took a room close to the asylum; day by day for the whole interminable length of my imprisonment, she came to my one room there, sat with me, read to me; every day, at certain hours. What was *Inferno* to me—not quite from the beginning—must have been worse to her even, during those horrible and hopeless winter months when I was almost unconscious of where I was, or of who I was, or for what reason I was there. No one else was allowed to see me. The stories she has told me, during these last years, of the tortures she endured, of her despair, her hopelessness, her intense misery, of my impossible conduct to her, of my ignorance for some months of who she was, of the way I would rush out of the room and disappear up some corridor, of my absolute insanity, of the oblivion into which this disaster had hurled me—a mist or a mirage, an illusion or a delusion, of some unspeakable calamity, which was like one who is on the deck of a steamer and who is washed clean over by the whirling waves of some prodigious storm and who in the very heart of this whirlwind or whirlpool loses heart as he loses hope until suddenly some unexpected rescue saves him—and, besides these things, things unspeakable and awful and abominable, which even I dare not write, so branded are they on my memory like some hot iron applied to a convict's arm by which he must always be recognized; things of the fruitless imagination, of the senseless senses, of the absent instinct, of the deadened impulses, of the checked desires, things emptied out of one by some unheard-of calamity—the vision of an empty world, a world of darkness, a world of torture, a world of annihilation.

And there was I, in that infernal madhouse, confined in that infernal room, in a state of absolute destitution, of absolute poverty, penniless, in fact, without even a knife in my pocket to sharpen a pencil with—as if I were considered to be in so dangerous a condition that, were I to have had a knife, I might have knifed myself or tried to stab one of those gaolers. I was not so dangerous as they supposed. Still, I often assured my wife that I meant to become a millionaire; that, meanwhile, as soon as I had contrived my escape, I would buy a Darracq and drive it myself: that I had carefully planned and cunningly plotted these contrivances of mine; that I only waited for the exact moment of escape; that she would go with me, and that we would vanish into Spain.

Such wild imaginings as these kept me warily awake and intensely alive: I lived a kind of double life, inward and outward, both jumbled together in an inextricable confusion. And yet in all this there was a reflex and a reduplication of things and of images. My natural inventiveness did not by any means always waste itself upon the empty air. All power of creation had of course vanished: I mean not my own peculiar creative power. I put some of my best inventions into stories and one-act prose plays. One, called *The Land,* which took place in Galway, was cruelly conceived; it was the question of the quarrelsome nature of two Irish peasants who squabbled about the extent of land each of them had; there were, of course, the roughly made stone walls which limited both fields: one or the other would creep out at dead of night and move away some of the stones which divided the field in his direction: and so that went on and there was no end of litigation. * * *

I wrote many corrupt things which were valueless: there was always in my mind the Priapus of Catullus and his Lesbia standing at the crossroads of Rome.[10] It is not only in the Bible that we read of "the seeds of corruption": they exist in our perishable bodies, but their action or reaction on one's body varies infinitely. It is inevitable for one who is in confinement, who hates it more than he hates hell, to be obsessed with ideas of sex and of the perversities of sex. Even when the body has lost most of its vitality, as in my case, then, one's brain and one's imagination are in a state of continual ferment. So, one's sex, when it does not function naturally, functions unnaturally.

It was also inevitable that, the more lucid I became, the more anxiously and feverishly I longed for my wife's presence; in fact I counted the hours of her absence. Just then I had nothing much more to live for. She was my only support, my only encourager—my only possible plank of escape from moral and physical shipwreck. * * *

I had wandered half over the world, and it had come to that. All the roads of the earth lead to six feet of earth, and all the way there has been a losing of the way. * * *

Notes

Abbreviations of Periodicals Cited

CR   *Contemporary Review*
FR   *Fortnightly Review*
MR   *Monthly Review*
NAR   *North American Review* (New York)
VF   *Vanity Fair* (New York)
WR   *Westminster Review*

Introduction

1. Unpublished letter from Yeats to Rhoda Symons, 13 October 1908, in Arthur Symons Papers held by Mrs. Hope Rutherford, Cheltenh..m, England.

2. T.S. Eliot recorded his debt to Symons in *The Sacred Wood* (London, 1920), p. 5; Yeats recorded his in "Four Years: 1887–1891," sec. 23, and in "The Tragic Generation," sec. 11, *The Autobiography of William Butler Yeats* (New York, 1965), pp. 131, 214; see also *The Letters of Ezra Pound,* ed. D.D. Paige (New York, 1950), pp. 216–18, and Pound's letter to Floyd Dell in G. Thomas Tanselle's "Two Early Letters of Ezra Pound," *American Literature* 34 (1962): 118; and finally David Hayman's *Joyce et Mallarmé* (Paris, 1956), 1: 27–34, and James S. Atherton's *The Books at the Wake* (New York, 1960), pp. 48–52.

3. *Men and Memories: Recollections of William Rothenstein, 1900–1922* (New York, 1932), p. 47.

4. "The Tragic Generation," sec. 11, *Autobiography,* p. 213. For an account of the personal and artistic relationship between Symons and Yeats, see John M. Munro, *Arthur Symons* (New York, 1969), pp. 56–71, 78–79.

5. Roger Lhombreaud's *Arthur Symons: A Critical Biography* (London, 1963) establishes the foundation for such an interpretation.

6. Sylvia Beach Papers, Princeton University Library.

7. Symons-Pinker Correspondence, Berg Collection, New York Public Library.

8. Ibid. Quotations from other Symons letters to Pinker are from this collection.

9. In the same letter, Symons says of Welby: "In 1925 he published a small volume on me which I disliked intensely. I gave a copy to Augustus John, and one night when we were dining at the Café Royal, he said to me, 'That book should never have been written, it's damned bad.'"

10. Letter to Lady Gregory, 25 April 1898, in *The Letters of W.B. Yeats,* ed. Allan Wade (London, 1954), p. 298.

Prelude to Life

1. From *Spiritual Adventures* (London, 1905).
2. Symons was born in Milford Haven, Wales, on 21 February 1865, the son of Mark Symons (1824–98), a Wesleyan preacher, and Lydia Symons (1828–96), both of Cornwall.
3. Michel Ney (1769–1815), one of Napoleon's marshals, who was executed for resistence to the restoration of Bourbon rule.
4. Richard D. Blackmore (1825–1900), novelist, best known for *Lorna Doone* (1869); Charles Kingsley (1819–75), clergyman, poet, and novelist, best known for *Westward Ho!* (1855).
5. Charles Churchill Osborne (1859–1944), who, from 1884, was editor of *The Salisbury and Winchester Journal,* in which Symons published some early reviews.
6. *Lavengro* (1851) by George Borrow (1803–81), who recorded his wanderings over Europe in his novels.
7. The harlot of Jericho, who hid Israelite spies in her house and thereby found mercy for her family when the city was destroyed (Josh. 2 : 1–21).
8. Probably in 1885, when Symons was writing introductions for several volumes in the Shakespeare Quarto Facsimiles, whose general editor was Frederick James Furnivall (1825–1910), founder of the Browning Society.
9. In July 1886, when Symons was editing the plays of Massinger for the Mermaid Series of Elizabethan dramatists, under the general editorship of Havelock Ellis (1859–1939), later an eminent authority on human sexuality.
10. Symons actually lived in Fountain Court, The Temple, for ten years and periodically maintained residences in London after his marriage in 1901.

Robert Browning

1. "Some Browning Reminiscences," *NAR* 204 (1916): 602–9.
2. Two passages from Browning's "Introductory Essay" to the spurious *Letters of Percy Bysshe Shelley* (London, 1852).
3. That is, in 1888.
4. *Poetical Works of Samuel Taylor Coleridge,* ed. J. Dykes Campbell (London, 1893); Campbell, *Coleridge: A Narrative of the Events of His Life* (London, 1894).
5. Included in Symons' *Days and Nights* (London, 1889).
6. Thomas Buchanan Read (1822–72), American poet and painter.
7. See Joanna Richardson, *The Pre-Eminent Victorian: A Study of Tennyson* (London, 1962), p. 240. Tennyson had sent the letter on Browning's birthday.

Coventry Patmore

1. "Coventry Patmore," *MR* 23 (1906): 75–83; rpt. in Symons' *Figures of Several Centuries* (London, 1916).
2. Edmund Gosse, *Coventry Patmore* (London, 1905), p. 171.
3. Frederick Greenwood (1830–1909), man of letters and editor of *Cornhill Magazine,* 1862–68, and the *Pall Mall Gazette,* 1868–80.

4. Symons errs in the title of Champneys' work, which is *Memoirs and Correspondence of Coventry Patmore,* 2 vols. (London, 1900–1901).

5. Dr. Richard Garnett (1835–1906), poet, biographer, anthologist, and Keeper of Printed Books, British Museum, 1890–99. He became a close friend of Symons.

6. Dr. William Alexander Greenhill (1814–94), physician and author, published his obituary on Newman in *The Academy* 38 (1890): 130–31.

7. William Barnes (1801–86), clergyman, published three series of *Poems of Rural Life in the Dorset Dialect* (London, 1854, 1859, 1862).

8. See Symons' "Religio Poetae," *The Athenaeum,* 30 December 1893, pp. 902–3.

9. Alice Meynell (1847–1922), poet and essayist.

10. Champneys, *Memoirs,* I: 103.

11. William Drummond (1585–1649), first important Scots poet to write in English.

12. Cowley's *Davideis* (1656), a heroic poem dealing with the troubles of the Israelite King David.

13. Gosse, *Patmore,* p. 109.

14. William Ernest Henley (1849–1903), poet, critic, and editor of the *Scots Observer,* later titled *National Observer,* 1888–94.

Edmund Gosse

1. "Edmund Gosse," MS and TS, Princeton.

2. Leigh Hunt (1784–1859), poet and critic.

3. James Kenneth Stephen (1859–92), poet and author of a book on international law.

4. Theo. Marzials (1850–1920), poet, musician, and songwriter. For an account of Marzials' relationship with Gosse, see John M. Munro's "Introduction" to *Selected Poems of Theo. Marzials* (Beirut, 1974).

5. See John M. Munro, *The Royal Aquarium: Failure of a Victorian Compromise* (Beirut, 1971).

6. After Flaubert's heroine in his novel *Salammbô* (Paris, 1852).

7. At this point, Symons includes a previously published review of Gosse's *Questions at Issue* (London, 1893) from *The Athenaeum,* 12 August 1893, pp. 215–16.

8. Zola's cycle of novels published between 1871 and 1893.

Walter Pater

1. "Walter Pater," *MR* 24 (September 1906): 14–24; rpt., slightly revised, in Symons' *Figures of Several Centuries* (London, 1916).

2. From "A Fragment on Sandro Botticelli," *FR* 14 (1870): 155–60; rpt. as "Sandro Botticelli," in *Studies in the History of the Renaissance* (London, 1873), in later editions titled *The Renaissance.*

3. "Diaphaneité," written in July 1864, was read by Pater at the Old Mortality Club, Oxford; published posthumously in Pater's *Miscellaneous Studies* (London, 1895).

4. Passages from Pater's famous "Conclusion" to *The Renaissance.*

5. That is, in 1886.

6. Pater had urged the publisher George Macmillan to publish Symons' *Days and*

Nights (London, 1889), which was dedicated to Pater. See Letter 135 in *The Letters of Walter Pater,* ed. Lawrence Evans (Oxford, 1970).

7. Symons is mistaken. Pater did not edit a selection of Coleridge's poems; he contributed an introduction to Coleridge's poems in *The English Poets,* ed. Thomas Humphry Ward, 4 vols. (1880), 4: 102–14. Pater combined the introduction with a revised version of "Coleridge's Writings," *WR* 85 (January 1866): 106–32, and published "Coleridge" in his *Appreciations* (London, 1889).

8. "A Revenge" and "Bell in Camp," both included in *Days and Nights.*

9. Lawrence Evans states that Symons' transcription contains a "few minor errors." See Letter 121 in Pater's *Letters.*

10. Paul Bourget (1852–1935), French poet and novelist. *Essais* appeared in 1883.

11. Giovanni Battista Moroni (c. 1525–78), Italian painter.

George Moore

1. "Confessions and Comments," *Dramatis Personae* (Indianapolis, 1923).

2. Typographical errors in the dates of Pater's essays: "Coleridge's Writings," *WR* 85 (1866): 106–32, revised, enlarged as "Coleridge" in Pater's *Appreciations* (London, 1889); "Winckelmann," *WR* 87 (1867): 80–110, rpt. in *The Renaissance.*

3. From Blake's "Infant Sorrow," *Songs of Experience* (London, 1794).

4. Another typographical error: the date should be 1891.

5. Moore later wrote in his memoirs: "When Symons came to live in The Temple I looked forward to finding a boon companion in him. He is intelligent and well versed in literature, French and English; a man of somewhat yellowish temperament, whom a wicked fairy had cast for a parson." *Ave,* Vol. I of *Hail and Farewell* (London, 1911), p. 62.

6. Probably Tomás Luis de Victoria (1548–1611), Spanish composer of church music.

7. From Tennyson's "To the Queen," appended as the epilogue to the Imperial Library Edition of *Idylls of the King* (London, 1873).

8. "Sandro Botticelli" and the famous description of *La Gioconda* (*Mona Lisa*) in the essay "Leonardo da Vinci" are in Pater's *The Renaissance.*

Paul Verlaine

1. "Paul Verlaine," *NAR* 201 (1915): 743–48.

2. Charles Morice (1861–1919), French literary critic and author of *Paul Verlaine* (Paris, 1888).

3. See *Les Hommes d'Aujourd'hui* 5 (1882?), no. 244.

4. Verlaine visited England in November 1893, to give a series of lectures in London, Oxford, and Manchester. While in London, he stayed with Symons in Fountain Court. See Verlaine's "My Visit to London," *The Savoy,* No. 2 (April 1896): 119–35.

5. Eugène Carrière (1849–1906), French painter and lithographer, whose portrait of Verlaine appears in *Choix de poésies* (Paris, 1891).

6. The first line of the quotation, from Morice's *Eugène Carrière* (Paris, 1906), is from p. 197; the remainder from pp. 194–95.

7. Paul Moréas, pseudonym of Lannis Papadia-Mantopoulous (1856–1910), Greek-born French poet and leading figure in the Symbolist Movement.

Remy de Gourmont and Joris-Karl Huysmans

1. "Confessions: A Few Thoughts, Portraits and Memoirs," *VF* 5 (March 1916): 39, 130.
2. In 1915.
3. Pierre Louÿs, pseudonym of Pierre Louis (1870–1925), French poet and novelist. For his tribute to Gourmont, see "Revue du mois," *Mercure de France* 112 (1915): 523.
4. Rachilde, pseudonym of Marguerite Vallette (1860–1953), French literary critic and founder-editor of *Mercure de France*. For her tribute to Gourmont, see ibid., p. 700.
5. Probably Havelock Ellis.

Bohemian Years in London

1. "The Confessions of Arthur Symons: Part One," *Two Worlds* (New York) 2 (September 1926): 27–34, not included in Symons' *Confessions: A Study in Pathology* (New York, 1930).
2. *The Loom of Dreams* (London, 1901), a volume of verse.
3. Probably an error for "Leves Amores" (Latin: "light loves"), the title of a poem in Symons' *London Nights* (London, 1895).
4. Minnie Cunningham inspired Symons' poem in *London Nights,* "The Primrose Dance: Tivoli," which he dedicated to her. See Sickert's painting, *Minnie Cunningham at the Old Bedford,* in Wendy Baron's *Sickert* (London, 1973), p. 31 and Fig. 37.
5. Poem in Symons' *Silhouettes* (London, 1892).
6. This and succeeding poems alluded to by Symons all appeared in *Silhouettes.*
7. George du Maurier (1834–96), illustrator and novelist, best known for *Trilby* (London, 1894).
8. Sarojini Naidu (1879–1949), Indian poet and later political activist, for whose first volume of verse, *The Golden Threshold* (London, 1905), Symons contributed an introduction. See John M. Munro, "The Poet and the Nightingale: Some Unpublished Letters from Sarojini Naidu to Arthur Symons," *Calcutta Review* 1 n.s. (1970): 135–46.

An Actress in Whitechapel

1. "Impressions: III," TS, Princeton.
2. Symons combines passages from the lengthy account given by Dorian in Chapter 4. See *The Picture of Dorian Gray,* ed. Isobel Murray (London, 1974), pp. 48–50.
3. The central character of the Sanskrit drama *Sakuntala* (sometimes titled *The Recovered Ring*) by Kalidasa (373?–415?), Indian poet and dramatist.
4. In Symons' story "Esther Kahn," in *Spiritual Adventures,* the central character

is also a young Jewish actress, most likely a fictionalized account of his relationship with Rachel Kahn.

5. A phrase from Symons' poem "Stella Maris," which created a stir (because of its depiction of a prostitute with a title recalling the Virgin Mary) when it appeared in the first issue of *The Yellow Book* in 1894; as used here, the phrase quite obviously carries a different meaning.

East and West End Silhouettes

1. "East and West End Silhouettes," TS, Princeton.
2. Compare the opening with that of "Esther Kahn" in *Spiritual Adventures*.
3. Charles Méryon (1821–68), French artist, whose etching *La Rue des Mauvais Garçons* is his best-known work.
4. *Thérèse Raquin* (1873), Zola's play adapted from his novel (1867) of the same title.
5. Ada Rehan (1860–1916), Irish-born American actress, a member of Augustin Daly's company, 1879–99.
6. A slightly different version of this section, titled "A Conversation at the Café Royal," appeared in *VF* 8 (July 1917): 49; rpt. as "The Café Royal" in *The Café Royal and Other Essays* (London, 1923).
7. John Davidson (1857–1909), Scots poet and dramatist, named here after the stock character Scaramouche, the servant famed for his intrigue in the Italian *commedia dell'arte;* John Barlas (1860–1914), Scots poet and Socialist, who published several volumes of verse as "Evelyn Douglas," is named here after Louis de Saint-Just (1767–94), ideologue of the French Revolution and leading figure in the Reign of Terror, 1793–94. Barlas once fired a pistol at the home of the Speaker of the House of Commons.

Ernest Dowson

1. "Ernest Dowson," *FR* 73 (1900): 947–57; rpt. in Symons' *Studies in Prose and Verse* (London, 1904). A portion of this article has previously appeared as "A Literary Causerie: On a Book of Verse," *The Savoy*, No. 4 (August 1896): 91–93, though Dowson's name is not mentioned.
2. Symons first met Dowson in May 1891. See *The Letters of Ernest Dowson,* ed. Desmond Flower and Henry Maas (London, 1967), p. 201.
3. The Rhymers' Club, founded by W.B. Yeats, Ernest Rhys, and other poets, in early 1890, continued to meet regularly until late 1894, sporadically as late as 1896. See Karl Beckson, "Yeats and the Rhymers' Club," *Yeats Studies,* No. 1 (1971): 20–41.
4. *The Book of the Rhymers' Club* and *The Second Book of the Rhymers' Club* (London, 1892, 1894).
5. The Crown, situated between the Alhambra, demolished in 1936 (the Odeon Cinema now occupies the site), and the Empire Theatre (the "Home of the Ballet"), which closed in 1927.
6. Adelaide Foltinowicz ("Missie"), daughter of the Polish owner of a restaurant in Soho. Dowson dedicated *Verses* (London, 1896) to her.

7. For Dowson's amused response to this and other passages in Symons' article in *The Savoy* (see note 1 above), see *Letters of Ernest Dowson,* pp. 371–72.
8. From Verlaine's "Colloque sentimental," *Fêtes galantes* (Paris, 1869).
9. Frederick Wedmore (1844–1921), short story writer and art critic.
10. First published in *The Savoy,* No. 4 (August 1896): 66–74; rpt. in *The Stories of Ernest Dowson,* ed. Mark Longaker (Philadelphia, 1947).

Henri Toulouse-Lautrec

1. "Exasperations," TS, Princeton. Symons first met Toulouse-Lautrec in Paris in June 1890, at the Moulin Rouge.

Auguste Rodin

1. From *From Toulouse-Lautrec to Rodin* (London, 1929).
2. Gustave Moreau (1826–98), French artist best known for his elaborate biblical and mythological paintings.
3. Pierre Puvis de Chavannes (1824–98), French painter who achieved fame for his symbolic and allegorical decorations on such public buildings as the Panthéon and the Hôtel de Ville in Paris and the Boston Public Library.
4. Symons quotes inaccurately: see the opening of Pater's "The Poetry of Michelangelo" in *The Renaissance.*
5. See Rodin's *Cathedrals of France,* trans. Elizabeth Chase Geissbuhler (Boston, 1965), pp. 3–4.
6. *The Hand of God,* now in the Rodin Museum, Paris.
7. *The Age of Bronze* is now in the Tate Gallery, London.
8. Symons errs. The title is *La Belle Heaulmière,* based on Villon's poem of the same title.
9. Domingo Faustino Sarmiento (1811–88), Argentine statesman, educator, author, and President of Argentina, 1868–74.
10. Hieronymus Bosch (c. 1450–1516), Flemish painter of the macabre; Félicien Rops (1833–98), Belgian painter, etcher, and lithographer, best known for his interest in erotic subjects.

Music Halls and Ballet Girls

1. Untitled TS, Princeton.
2. Les Ambassadeurs, the Parisian music hall, is the subject of Symons' poem "At the Ambassadeurs" in *London Nights.*
3. In *Poems* (London, 1881), Rossetti prefaced "The House of Life" sequence with a poem beginning "A Sonnet is a moment's monument."
4. Symons had published "In Sligo: Rosses Point and Glencar," *The Savoy,* No. 7 (November 1896): 55–61, the result of his visit to Ireland with Yeats in the summer of 1896.
5. See Symons' "At the Alhambra: Impressions and Sensations," *The Savoy,* No. 5 (September 1896): 75–83.
6. "Tragic Generation" (sec. 14) of *The Autobiography of William Butler Yeats* (New York, 1965).

7. In the first edition of *London Nights,* the "Lilian" section consists of twelve poems; in Symons' *Poems* (London, 1901), Vol. I, "Lilian" is changed to "Violet" and the number of poems reduced to ten.
8. In "At the Alhambra," Symons spells the name "Forde."

John Addington Symonds

1. "A Study of John Addington Symonds," *FR* 121 (1924): 228–39.
2. *The Romantic Movement in Poetry* (London, 1909), p. 301.
3. The final letter quoted in Brown's *Letters and Papers of John Addington Symonds* (London, 1923) is to Robert Louis Stevenson, dated 24 February 1893, but it is not the last letter that Symonds wrote. See *The Letters of John Addington Symonds,* ed. Herbert M. Schueller and Robert L. Peters (Detroit, 1969), Vol. III, 1885–93.
4. The actual title is *John Addington Symonds: A Biography* (London, 1903).
5. The "Autobiography" remains unpublished; the manuscript is in the London Library.
6. This passage combines parts of three letters to Horatio Brown: 3 March, 3 April, and 10 April 1889. See Symonds' *Letters,* 3: 356, 367, 370.
7. Brown, *John Addington Symonds: A Biography,* p. 152.

Arthur Henry Bullen

1. "An Elizabethan Shadow," TS, Princeton. Bullen (1857–1920), literary scholar, author, and publisher, founded the Shakespeare Head Press in 1904.
2. Charles Whibley (1859–1930), man of letters, who published literary criticism, biographies, political essays, and edited or introduced some thirty English, French, and Latin classics.
3. Island Cottage, which Symons purchased in 1906, in Wittersham, Kent, where Symons lived for almost forty years.
4. *The Works of Dr. Thomas Campion,* ed. A.H. Bullen (London, 1889).
5. *The Works of William Shakespeare* (Stratford Town Edition), 10 vols. (Stratford-on-Avon, 1910).

A Study in Morbidity: Herbert Horne

1. "A Study in Morbidity," TS, Princeton.
2. Selwyn Image (1849–1930), poet, engraver, designer of stained glass, and member of the Century Guild of Artists in Fitzroy Street, London. From 1910 to 1916, he was Slade Professor of Fine Art, Oxford University.
3. In the early 1920s, Symons was writing what he called *Confessions* (see note 1 to "Bohemian Years in London"), but it was apparently abandoned. *Confessions: A Study in Pathology* (1930) may have grown out of Symons' earlier intentions.
4. Herbert Horne (1864–1916), architect, poet, biographer, and member of the Century Guild of Artists, which published *The Century Guild Hobby Horse,* edited by Horne, 1886–92, and its successor, *The Hobby Horse,* which he edited in 1893–94.
5. Horace Horne, an architect.

6. Randall Davies (1866–1946), art historian and literary critic.

7. According to Ian Fletcher, Horne's passport reveals that he was five feet ten inches in height. See Fletcher, "Herbert Horne: The Earlier Phase," *English Miscellany* (Rome) 21 (1970): 127.

8. Symons wrote two stories based on Muriel Broadbent's life: "Pages from the Life of Lucy Newcome," *The Savoy,* No. 2 (April 1896): 147–60; "The Childhood of Lucy Newcome," *The Savoy,* No. 8 (December 1896): 51–61, rpt. in *Spiritual Adventures.*

9. In 1899, she married W. Llewellyn Hacon, publisher, who, with Charles Ricketts, directed the Vale Press from 1896 to 1903. According to Fletcher, Horne seems to have assisted Hacon in his courtship of Muriel Broadbent. ("Herbert Horne," *English Miscellany,* p. 128, note 14.)

10. For Pater's review, see *Oscar Wilde: The Critical Heritage,* ed. Karl Beckson (London, 1970), pp. 83–86.

Paul Verlaine in London

1. "Paul Verlaine in London," *VF* 5 (June 1916): 61.

2. Verlaine's arrival for his lecture tour.

3. William Heinemann (1863–1920), the publisher, who founded his firm in 1890.

4. See "Men and Letters: Verlaine in London," *The Star,* 22 November 1893, p. 1.

5. The Bodley Head was founded and directed by Elkin Mathews (1851–1921) and John Lane (1854–1925); in 1894, the partnership dissolved, John Lane retaining the firm's name. See James G. Nelson, *The Early Nineties: A View from the Bodley Head* (Cambridge, Mass., 1971).

6. Hubert Crackanthorpe (1870–96), short story writer and co-editor of *The Albemarle Review,* 1892, who was found dead in the Seine. Whether the result of suicide or foul play has never been established.

7. Arnold Dolmetsch (1858–1940), French-born musician who moved to London in 1883 and who was primarily responsible for the revival of interest in medieval and Renaissance music and instruments. Symons, a close friend, attended his concerts in the late 1890s. See Margaret Campbell, *Dolmetsch: The Man and His Work* (London, 1975), pp. 75, 122.

Lillie Langtry and Oscar Wilde

1. "Judge's Walk," TS, Princeton, which erroneously spells Mrs. Langtry's first name as "Lily."

2. In The Temple.

3. Edwin J. Ellis (1848–1916), painter and poet, who was a member of the Rhymers' Club.

4. George Frederick Watts (1817–1904), painter; Joseph Joachim (1831–1907), Hungarian composer, violinist, and founder of the Joachim Quartet in 1869.

5. Jane Morris (*née* Burden), who married William Morris in 1859, was the model for several paintings by Rossetti, who was in love with her.

6. Symons had contributed a preface to the Henry Irving edition of Shakespeare (London, 1889); he reprinted it in *Studies in Elizabethan Drama* (London, 1920).

7. Symons errs: *Antony and Cleopatra* was revived on 18 November 1890, at the Princess's Theatre.

8. See, however, Mrs. Langtry's generally favorable account of Wilde in her memoir, *The Days I Knew* (New York, 1925), pp. 83–95.

Frank Harris and Oscar Wilde

1. "Frank Harris," TS, Princeton.

2. "Three Problem Plays," *Plays, Acting, and Music* (London, 1903), p. 152.

3. Quoted in A.I. Tobin and Elmer Gertz, *Frank Harris: A Study in Black and White* (Chicago, 1931), p. 188. See, however, Shaw's generally favorable "Postscript" to Harris' *Bernard Shaw: An Unauthorised Biography* (New York, 1931).

4. Harris was editor of the *Fortnightly Review,* 1887–94, and the *Saturday Review,* 1894–98.

5. Beardsley's dislike of Wilde was gradual; Wilde, however, always seemed to be cordial to Beardsley and appreciative of his genius. See *Letters of Oscar Wilde,* ed. Rupert Hart-Davis (London, 1962), pp. 348, 627, 719.

6. Harris, *Oscar Wilde* (East Lansing, Mich., 1956), p. 75. Harris' biography first appeared in 1916.

7. Symons first met Wilde in 1890. See Wilde's *Letters,* ed. Rupert Hart-Davis, p. 276; Edgar Fawcett (1847–1904), American novelist; Edgar Saltus (1855–1921), American author, first met Wilde on the latter's American lecture tour in 1882 and later published *Oscar Wilde: An Idler's Impression* (Chicago, 1917).

8. Symons' memory errs. Wilde, as editor of *Woman's World,* had initially corresponded with Symons in 1888 to solicit an article. Symons' "Villiers de l'Isle-Adam" appeared in *Woman's World* 2 (October 1889): 657–60, after Wilde had left his editorial position.

9. John Gray (1866–1934), poet and dandy, who later became a Roman Catholic priest. Wilde met Gray *after* publication of *The Picture of Dorian Gray* (1890). See *Letters,* ed. Hart-Davis, p. 311; Brocard Sewell, *Footnote to the Nineties: A Memoir of John Gray and André Raffalovitch* (London, 1968), pp. 9–10.

Sex and Aversion

1. "Sex and Aversion," TS, Princeton.

2. The Piombi ("The Leads") were prisons under the roof of the Doge's palace in Venice. Casanova, denounced as a magician in 1755, escaped to Paris in 1756.

3. Sir Richard Burton (1821–90), author and explorer, best known for his translation of *The Arabian Nights.*

4. Vladimir de Pachmann (1848–1933), Russian pianist, who was the inspiration for Symons' story "Christian Trevalga" in *Spiritual Adventures.*

My Planets

1. "My Planets," TS, Princeton.

2. According to Symons' biographer, Roger Lhombreaud, the date of birth is 21 February 1865. See *Arthur Symons: A Critical Biography* (London, 1963), p. 5.

3. In the poem, Symons alludes to the planet Uranus as "Herschel," after Sir William Herschel (1738–1822), German-born English astronomer, who discovered the planet in 1781.

4. Two volumes of poems: *Lesbia and Other Poems* (New York, 1920) and *Love's Cruelty* (London, 1924).

5. Leonard Smithers (1861–1907), bookseller and publisher with a taste for the arcane and avant-garde. He published Symons' *London Nights* and *The Savoy* (1896). The date of this adventure with Smithers is unlikely, since Dowson and Symons did not meet him until 1895.

6. See Huysmans' *Against Nature,* trans. Robert Baldick (Baltimore, Md., 1959), p. 66.

7. Keats' idea of "Negative Capability," as outlined in a letter to George and Thomas Keats, 27 December 1817. See *The Letters of John Keats, 1814–1821,* ed. Hyder Edward Rollins (Cambridge, Mass., 1958), 1: 193.

Marcelle and Other Parisian Diversions

1. "Paris," TS, Princeton.

2. "La Mélinite" was Jeanne Richepin (1868–1943), whose stage name was "Jane Avril." Symons first saw her in May 1892, dancing at Le Jardin de Paris, "the more provocative because she played as a prude with an assumed modesty; *décolletée* nearly to the waist, in the Oriental fashion. She had long black curls around her face; and had about her a depraved virginity. And she caused in me, even then, a curious sense of depravity that perhaps comes into the verses I wrote on her. There, certainly, on the night of May 22nd, danced in her feverish, her perverse, her enigmatical beauty, La Mélinite, to her own image in the mirror." See "Dancers and Dancing," *Colour Studies in Paris* (London, 1918), p. 107–8; see also Symons' poem "La Mélinite: Moulin Rouge," *Silhouettes* (London, 1892).

Hugues Rebell

1. "Hugues Rebell," TS, Princeton. "Hugues Rebell" was the pseudonym of George Grassal (1867–1905), French playwright and novelist.

2. See Rebell's *Trois artistes étrangers* (Paris, 1901) and Huysmans' *Certains* (Paris, 1889).

3. Maurice Barrès (1862–1923), French novelist, philosopher, and politician, was a member of the Chamber of Deputies, 1889–93, 1906–23; Jean Ernest-Charles (1875–1925), French literary and social historian.

4. Louise Faure-Favier, French poet and novelist.

Jean Lorrain

1. "Jean Lorrain," TS, Princeton. "Jean Lorrain" was the pseudonym of Paul Duval (1856–1906).

2. Adolphe Retté (1863–1930), French literary critic.

3. Louis Octave Uzanne (1852–1931), French man of letters.

4. Unidentified.

5. La Goulue ("The Glutton") was a dancer of Alsatian birth at the Moulin Rouge, whom Toulouse-Lautrec depicted in some of his posters.

Édouard Dubus

1. "Édouard Dubus," MS, Yale; TS, Princeton. Symons' corrected typescript, which differs in various respects from the manuscript, is followed here.

2. According to Arthur Hobson Quinn's *Edgar Allan Poe: A Critical Biography* (New York, 1941), p. 639, Poe was found lying outside a polling place, located in a public house. Whether he had been drugged has never been established.

3. Symons errs: Dubus died in 1895. See Adolphe Retté's *Le Symbolisme: anecdotes et souvenirs* (Paris, 1903).

4. Marquis Stanislas de Guaita (1871–98), French author and occultist, died from an overdose of drugs.

5. "A First Sight of Verlaine," *The Savoy,* No. 2 (April 1896): 113–16.

Lydia

1. "Lydia," MS and TS, Princeton. Attached to the manuscript is a slip of paper with the date "December 20, 1920" in Symons' hand, presumably the date of its completion. For a different version of his relationship with Lydia, a dancer at the Empire Theatre, whom he met around 1894, see Symons' privately printed *Amoris Victima* (London, 1940). When the relationship ended in 1896 (she married a businessman), Symons wrote a series of poems, also titled *Amoris Victima* (London, 1897), which traces the affair. In *London Nights,* he refers to Lydia as "Bianca."

2. From Symons' translation, *From Catullus, Chiefly Concerning Lesbia* (London, 1924), p. 55.

3. Daniel Nicols (né Thevenon) (1833–97), formerly a wine merchant in Paris, founder (in 1865) of the Café Royal in Regent Street. For a sympathetic account, see Guy Deghy and Keith Waterhouse, *Café Royal: Ninety Years of Bohemia* (London, 1955).

4. *Greek Studies* (New York, 1895), p. 53.

5. Included in *Amoris Victima* (1897).

6. Katherine Willard (1866–1932), the niece of Frances Willard, founder of the W.C.T.U.; Symons dedicated *Silhouettes* to her.

7. Frank Willard (1869–1907), novelist and vagabond, who wrote under the name of "Josiah Flynt." Symons contributed a preface to Willard's autobiography *My Life* (London, 1908). The "tragic incident" occurred in August 1891, when Symons was returning, with Katherine and Frank, from a visit to the Willards in Berlin, where Katherine's mother conducted a school for American girls.

8. *The Bells,* by Leopold Lewis (1828–90), first produced in 1871 and revived periodically, was one of Irving's greatest successes.

9. See "Mundi Victima, X," *Amoris Victima* (1897).

10. The typescript reads "Bianca," with Symons' inked-in change.

Aubrey Beardsley

1. The original version of this essay appeared as "Aubrey Beardsley," *FR* 63 n.s. (1898): 752–61. For a volume of Beardsley's prints published later in 1898, Symons expanded the essay by four additional paragraphs (at the beginning), which are included here.

2. Symons had forgotten his meeting with Beardsley in 1893; he apparently had little contact with Beardsley until the summer of 1895, when they were planning the first issue of *The Savoy*. See Ian Fletcher, "Symons and Beardsley," *Times Literary Supplement* (London), 18 August 1966, p. 743.

3. At the time of Wilde's arrest and trial in April-May 1895, Beardsley was fired from *The Yellow Book* as the result of pressure brought to bear on John Lane because of Beardsley's association with Wilde. See Stanley Weintraub, *Beardsley: A Biography* (New York, 1967); rev. ed., *Aubrey Beardsley: Imp of the Perverse* (University Park, Pa., 1976), chapters 6 and 7.

4. The "Editorial Note" reads in part: "We hope to appeal to the tastes of the intelligent, by not being original for originality's sake, or audacious for the sake of advertisement, or timid for the convenience of the elderly-minded." *The Savoy*, No. 1 (January 1896). The "café": Café des Arcades or Café Suisse. See Wendy Baron, *Sickert* (London, 1973), pp. 364–65.

5. Jacques-Émile Blanche (1862–1942), French portrait painter and author. Blanche's portrait of Beardsley is now in the National Portrait Gallery, London.

6. Yet to the first number of *The Savoy*, Beardsley contributed an illustration, *The Bathers*, for Symons' prose piece "Dieppe: 1895," *The Savoy*, No. 1 (January 1896): 84–102.

7. Three chapters of Beardsley's *Under the Hill* appeared in *The Savoy*, No. 1 (January 1896): 151–70; a fourth chapter in No. 2 (April 1896): 187–96. An unexpurgated version, titled *Venus and Tannhäuser*, was privately printed by Smithers in 1907.

8. *Les Liaisons dangereuses* (1782), an epistolary novel by Pierre Choderlos de Laclos (1741–1803), later one of Napoleon's generals.

9. Beardsley's poetry appeared in the following issues of *The Savoy* in 1896: "The Three Musicians," No. 1 (January): 65–66; "The Ballad of a Barber," No. 3 (July): 91–93; "Catullus: Carmen CI" (a translation), No. 7 (November): 52.

10. Yvette Guilbert (1867–1944), French *chanteuse* about whom Symons wrote frequently; Cléo de Mérode (1875–1966), French ballet dancer, the "divine De Mérode, with her slim, natural, and yet artificial elegance . . . who, more than anyone else, sums up Dieppe for me." See Symons' "Dieppe: 1895," *The Savoy*, p. 102.

11. Adolphe Léon Willette (1857–1926), French painter and author.

12. Eugène-Samuel Grasset (1841–1917), Swiss-born French painter, illustrator, and architect.

13. Jules Chéret (1836–1932), French illustrator who raised poster design to a high art.

14. Charles Eisen (1720–78), French book illustrator and engraver; Gabriel Jacques Saint-Aubin (1724–80), French painter and engraver.

15. Charles Ricketts (1866–1931), artist, author, book illustrator and designer; editor of *The Dial*, 1889–97.

16. Thomas Rowlandson (1756–1827), painter, best known for his humorous drawings of the lower classes.

17. William Bouguereau (1825–1905), French painter.

Charles Conder

1. "Charles Conder," TS, Princeton.

2. Louis Anguetin (1861–1932), French painter.

3. Meredith's *Emilia in England* (1864) was published in 1886 as *Sandra Belloni*.

4. See the Hippogriff, Meredith's invention, in Chapters 44 and 45 in *Sandra Belloni*.

5. According to John Rothenstein's *The Life and Death of Conder* (London, 1938), the Conder family was "purely English in blood" (p. 3).

6. *Honoré de Balzac* (Paris, 1859), p. 149.

7. An allusion to Symons' Lydia and to Louise Kinsella, the American girl whom Conder painted in *The Green Apple,* now in the Tate Gallery (see Rothenstein, *Conder,* pp. 82–84). Whistler painted her in *Rose et Vert, L'Iris: Miss Kinsella,* begun in 1893 and exhibited in Paris in 1904.

8. Ricketts, "Charles Conder," *Pages on Art* (London, 1913), p. 12.

9. Verlaine's "Mandoline" appeared in *Fêtes galantes* (Paris, 1869); Symons' version appeared in *Poems* (London, 1901), I, "Translations."

10. Stella Conder (d. 1912) married Charles Conder in 1900.

11. Dr. J.S. Risien Russell (1864–1939), neurologist and author.

12. Constance Collier (1878–1955), actress, who was a leading member of Herbert Beerbohm Tree's company by the age of twenty-three.

13. *Thaïs* (1890), a novel by Anatole France.

Sarah Bernhardt

1. "Impressions of Sarah Bernhardt," *London Mercury* 8 (1923): 595–99.

2. Benoît-Constant Coquelin (1841–1909), French actor and author, appeared at the Comédie Française, 1860–86. He created the role of Rostand's Cyrano de Bergerac in Paris in 1897.

3. *L'Aiglon* by Rostand was first performed at the Théâtre Sarah Bernhardt in Paris in 1900.

4. *Daniel* was produced in Paris in 1920. Louis Verneuil, Sarah Bernhardt's grandson-in-law, lived in the United States from 1939 to 1950, staging many of his plays on Broadway, including the highly successful *Affairs of State*. He died, in Paris, a suicide.

5. "Rachel," the stage name of Elisa Félix (1821–58), Swiss-born French actress, who made her debut at the Comédie Française in 1838; Anne-Françoise-Hippolyte Mars (1779–1847) made her debut at the Comédie Française in 1795; Pauline-Virginie Déjazet (1798–1875), actress and founder of the Théâtre Déjazet in 1859.

6. Charles Lamb's failure, *Mr. H.,* was produced on 10 December 1806. See Lamb's letter to Thomas Manning, 26 February 1808, in *Letters of Charles Lamb,* ed. George Woodcock (London, 1950).

Edouard de Max

1. "A Note on the Genius of de Max," *Life and Letters* 2 (July 1924): 163–69.
2. Marcel Schwob (1867–1905), French poet and novelist; Aurélien François Lugné-Poe (1869–1940), French actor, producer, and director of the *avant-garde* Théâtre de l'Oeuvre in Paris, 1892–1929.
3. A play by Casimir Delavigne, first produced in Paris in 1832, translated by Dion Boucicault, Irish playwright. Sir Henry Irving appeared in it first in March 1878.
4. A play by the English novelist Francis Marion Crawford, translated into French by Marcel Schwob. It was produced in 1902 at the Théâtre Sarah Bernhardt in Paris. De Max was Bernhardt's leading man in some twenty productions.
5. Marguerite Moreno (1871–1948), French actress, whom Schwob married in 1900.
6. "Réjane" was the stage name of the French actress Gabrielle Réju (1857–1920). *Sappho,* by Paul Silvestre, was first produced in Paris in November 1881; *Zaza,* by Pierre Berton and Charles Simon, was first produced in Paris in May 1898.
7. These lines, from "muscles and nerves," are taken from Symons' "Réjane and Jane Hading," *Plays, Acting, and Music* (London, 1903), p. 44.
8. Ibid. Symons does not, however, quote himself accurately.

Alfred Jarry

1. "Notes on Alfred Jarry," TS, Princeton.
2. Alfred Vallette (1858–1935), French author and founder-editor of *Mercure de France;* "Rachilde" was his wife (see above, Remy de Gourmont and Joris-Karl Huysmans, note 4).
3. See Jean Saltas, "Souvenirs sur Alfred Jarry," *Les Marges: Revue de littérature et d'art* 23 (1922): 22–23.
4. See Guillaume Apollinaire, "Feu Alfred Jarry," ibid., pp. 28–32.
5. Previously published, in a slightly different version, in *Saturday Review* (London), 82 (1896): 643–46; rpt. in Symons' *Studies in Two Literatures* (London, 1897) and *Studies in Seven Arts* (London, 1906).
6. Firmin Gémier (1865–1933), French actor, producer, and teacher.
7. Catulle Mendès (1843–1909), French novelist, poet, and playwright; founder, in 1861, of *La Revue fantaisiste,* an anti-Romantic journal.
8. Published in *Mercure de France* 19 (September 1896): 467–73.
9. The central character of Huysmans' *À Rebours* (Paris, 1884), who cultivates a morbid interest in artifice.
10. "Sansculotte": an extreme republican during the French Revolution (from *sans culotte:* "without breeches"); "unspeakable word of the gutter": in Jarry's play, Père Ubu's first word is "Merdre!"

André Gide

1. "André Gide," MS, Yale; TS, Princeton.
2. Following this sentence, the manuscript contains a deleted passage: "He can be brilliant or taciturn; in his green eyes one sees the excess of his nerves; also in his abrupt gestures."
3. Following this sentence, the manuscript contains the following passage (reveal-

ing the date of composition as the period of World War I): "So now, as this interminable war goes on, much of such temperaments as ours are forced against our will, he to remain in France and I to remain in England. Still, even now, at least in imagination, we move, insatiably curious, amid the phenomena of our world."

Algernon Charles Swinburne

1. "Algernon Charles Swinburne," *FR* 107 (1917): 795–804.
2. Martin Tupper (1810-89), popular poet, whose *Proverbial Philosophy* (1st series, 1838) went through fifty editions.
3. Theodore Watts-Dunton (1832-1914), poet, critic, and novelist, who took care of Swinburne for many years at The Pines, Putney. See Mollie Panter-Downes, *At the Pines: Swinburne and Watts-Dunton* (London, 1971).
4. "Morris's 'Life and Death of Jason,'" *FR* 2 n.s. (1867): 19–28; rpt. in Swinburne's *Essays and Studies* (London, 1875).
5. The line, inaccurately quoted (it should read "all mankind" instead of "all the world"), is from the pornographic play *Sodom; or the Quintessence of Debauchery* (Antwerp, 1684), long attributed to John Wilmot, 2nd Earl of Rochester (1647-80) but probably the work of the poet Christopher Fishbourne. See Rodney M. Baine, "Rochester or Fishbourne: A Question of Authorship," *Review of English Studies* 22 (1946): 201–6.
6. See Swinburne's letter to his sister, Alice, dated 10 August 1869, in *The Swinburne Letters,* ed. Cecil Y. Lang (New Haven, Conn., 1959), 2: 23.
7. Sir Frederick Pollock (1845-1937), author and Corpus Professor of Jurisprudence, Oxford University, 1883–1903.
8. "Dirae: Twenty Sonnets," *Songs of Two Nations* (London, 1875).
9. See "L'Année Terrible," *A Study of Victor Hugo,* in *The Complete Works of Algernon Charles Swinburne,* ed. Sir Edmund Gosse and Thomas James Wise (Bonchurch Edition), (London, 1925; rpt. New York, 1968), 13: 242, 245–46.
10. Ibid., pp. 247–48.
11. *The Duke of Grandia* appeared in 1908.

Whistler

1. From *Studies in Seven Arts* (London, 1906). Portions of this essay were previously published as "Whistler," *Weekly Critical Review* 2 (30 July, 6 August, and 13 August 1903): 36–37, 59–60, 81–82; "A Second View of Whistler," *The Outlook* 15 (1905): 289–90; "Whistler at the Carfax Gallery," *The Outlook* 16 (1905): 626–27.
2. According to Roy McMullen, Symons met Whistler at dinner held in London in April 1900. See *Victorian Outsider: A Biography of J.A.M. Whistler* (New York, 1973), p. 269.
3. An allusion to the celebrated suit brought by Whistler against Ruskin, who, in 1877, had written of the price asked by Whistler for his painting *The Falling Rocket* (then on show at the Grosvenor Gallery): "I have seen and heard much of Cockney impudence before now, but never expected to hear a coxcomb ask two hundred guineas for flinging a pot of paint in the public's face." Whistler was awarded one farthing in damages (his legal expenses were 500 pounds).

See Ruskin, Letter LXXIX, in his *Fors Clavigera: Letters to the Workmen and Labourers of England* (New York, 1886); Stanley Weintraub, *Whistler: A Biography* (New York, 1974), pp. 194–216.

4. Frederick R. Leyland (1831–98), a wealthy Liverpool shipping magnate and art collector, who became Whistler's patron.

5. In Whistler's collection of writings, *The Gentle Art of Making Enemies* (London, 1892; rpt. New York, 1967).

6. A reference to Botticelli's depiction of the Madonna and Child, now in the Gardner Museum, Boston.

7. The dining room which Leyland had commissioned Whistler to design for his new house in Kensington. Difficulties arose between Leyland and Whistler, who went beyond his patron's original intent. The room, completed in 1877, is now in the Freer Gallery of Art, Washington, D.C. See Weintraub, *Whistler*, pp. 169–81.

8. The most famous of Whistler's portraits, first exhibited in 1872, titled *Arrangement in Grey and Black, No. 1,* now in the Louvre.

9. Gautier's poem "Symphonie en Blanc Majeur," *Émaux et camées* (Paris, 1858).

10. Eugène Ysaÿe (1858–1931), Belgian violinist, later conductor of the Cincinnati Symphony Orchestra, 1918–20; Pablo de Sarasate (1844–1908), Spanish violinist and composer.

11. Whistler's letter to *The World*, 22 May 1878; rpt. in *The Gentle Art*, pp. 126–28.

12. Whistler's "Ten O'Clock" lecture, so called because of the unusual time of its delivery, was given in London on 20 February 1885, at Cambridge on 24 March, and at Oxford on 30 April; included in *The Gentle Art*, pp. 131–59.

13. "Propositions—No. 2," *The Gentle Art*, p. 115.

14. "Peintres et Aqua-Fortistes," *Oeuvres* (Pléiade edition), ed. Y.-G. Le Dantec (Paris, 1954), p. 847.

15. "Notes nouvelles sur Edgar Poe," the introduction to Baudelaire's translation, *Nouvelles histoires extraordinaires* (Paris, 1857), p. xxiii.

16. "A Further Proposition," *The Gentle Art*, pp. 177–78.

17. Giovanni Boldini (1845–1931), Italian portrait painter who settled in Paris in 1872. Boldini's *Whistler* is in the Brooklyn Museum, New York.

18. Comte Robert de Montesquiou (1855–1921), dandy and *littérateur*, whose portrait by Whistler, titled *Arrangement in Black and Gold: Comte Robert de Montesquiou,* is in the Frick Collection, New York.

19. In 1884, Whistler completed *Arrangement in Black: Pablo de Sarasate,* now in the Carnegie Institute, Pittsburgh.

20. A section of *The Gentle Art*, pp. 297–331.

Eleonora Duse

1. "Eleonora Duse," *CR* 72 (August 1900): 196–202; rpt. in *Studies in Seven Arts* (London, 1906) and in *Eleonora Duse* (London, 1926).

2. In 1860, Rossetti married Elizabeth Siddal, his model for some of his greatest paintings. When she died of tuberculosis in 1862, Rossetti placed the manuscripts of his poems in her coffin. In 1869, he was urged by friends to disinter

and publish them. The publication of *Poems* (1870) established Rossetti's reputation as a poet.

3. *Fedora* (1882), by Victorien Sardou; *The Second Mrs. Tanqueray* (1893) by Arthur Wing Pinero.

4. Magda, central character in *Magda* (trans. 1896) by Hermann Sudermann; Gioconda in *La Gioconda* (1898) by D'Annunzio, translated by Symons in 1901; Marguerite Gautier, heroine of *La Dame aux Camélias* (novel 1848; play 1852) by Alexandre Dumas fils.

Duse and D'Annunzio

1. From *Eleonora Duse* (London, 1926). A portion of this section previously published as "A Reading at Count Primoli's," *Today* 3 (May 1918): 104–7.

2. Duse played the role of Thérèse Raquin in Naples in 1879.

3. The novel *Il Fuoco* (1900) traces D'Annunzio's relationship with Duse.

4. Count Guiseppe Primoli (1851–1925), Italian author, at whose home Symons first met D'Annunzio. In an unpublished typescript (Symons Papers, Princeton), titled "Duse and D'Annunzio," Symons writes: "When [D'Annunzio] entered Primoli's study, I admit that I was startled by his appearance: something sinister in his aspect, a certain cruelty in his perverse eyes, and then there was the intense animality of the mouth. I saw in him then as afterwards an abnormality which was of the flesh and of the blood, as it were of a wild beast."

5. "Villa Chigi," *Elegie romane* (Bologna, 1892).

6. *Novissima and Other Poems* (Rome, 1896), by Magda Sindici, who translated, under the pseudonym of "Kassandra Vivaria," D'Annunzio's *Il Fuoco* as *The Flame of Life* (New York, 1900).

7. An allusion, apparently, to D'Annunzio's seizure, in 1919, with a small group of followers, of the port city of Fiume, which D'Annunzio claimed rightly belonged to Italy. After ruling the city for almost two years, he surrendered when Mussolini, leader of the newly formed Fascist Party, refused to support him.

Mental Collapse in Italy

1. From *Confessions: A Study in Pathology* (New York, 1930).

2. From the opening of Symons' "Christian Trevalga," *Spiritual Adventures*.

3. Rhoda, Symons' wife, left Italy for London at the end of September, when quarrels between her and Symons became intense.

4. Rhoda Symons and Agnes Tobin (1864–1939), American poet and translator.

5. "The Child in the House," *Macmillan's Magazine* 38 (August 1878); rpt. in Pater's *Miscellaneous Studies* (London, 1895).

6. On 2 November 1908, Symons was sent to the less expensive Brooke House, Upper Clapton Road, London, where he was officially certified as insane. His mental state, from that point on, deteriorated.

7. From the title of Shelley's poem.

8. None of these works was ever published.

9. See Symons' "Léon Bloy: The Thankless Beggar," *Colour Studies in Paris*.

10. See Symons' translation, *From Catullus, Chiefly Concerning Lesbia* (London, 1924), p. 31.

Index

Numbers in boldface indicate each selection by Symons.